Industrial Location

D1500840

Industrial Location

Principles and Policies

2nd Edition

Keith Chapman and David F. Walker

Basil Blackwell

Copyright © Keith Chapman and David F. Walker 1987, 1990

First published 1987
Second Edition 1991

Basil Blackwell Ltd
108 Cowley Road, Oxford, OX4 1JF, UK

Basil Blackwell, Inc.
3 Cambridge Center
Cambridge, Massachusetts 02142, USA

All rights reserved. Except for the quotation of short passages for the purposes of criticism and review, no part of this publication may be reproduced, stored in a retrieval system, or transmitted, in any form or by any means, electronic, mechanical, photocopying, recording or otherwise, without the prior permission of the publisher.

Except in the United States of America, this book is sold subject to the condition that it shall not, by way of trade or otherwise, be lent, re-sold, hired out, or otherwise circulated without the publisher's prior consent in any form of binding or cover other than that in which it is published and without a similar condition including this condition being imposed on the subsequent purchaser.

British Library Cataloguing in Publication Data

A CIP catalogue record for this book is available from the British Library.

Library of Congress Cataloging in Publication Data

Chapman, Keith.
    Industrial location: principles and policies/Keith Chapman and David F. Walker.
        p. cm.
    Includes bibliographical references.
    ISBN 0–631–16789–7
    1. Industry—Location. I. Walker, David F. II. Title.
    HD58.C37 1991
    338.6′042—dc20   90–419
                                                                         CIP

Typeset in 10 on 12 pt Sabon
by Photo·graphics, Honiton, Devon
Printed in Great Britain by
T. J. Press Ltd, Padstow, Cornwall

Contents

Figures

Tables

Preface and Acknowledgements

The second edition of this book has provided the opportunity to make what we hope are significant improvements whilst, at the same time, retaining the basic structure of the first version. As before, we recognize two sets of principles, applying to developments in business (chapters 2–8) and to the development of places (chapters 9–12). More than half of the chapters have been completely re-written, taking account of the criticisms and suggestions of others and also incorporating our own second-thoughts. Nevertheless, the book retains its essential concern not only with identifying the principles of industrial location, but also with demonstrating the welfare implications of changing spatial patterns of manufacturing with reference to the public policies designed to modify these implications.

The maps and diagrams were all produced in the cartographic section of the Department of Geography at the University of Aberdeen by Kay Leiper, Alison Sandison and Jenny Johnson. The manuscript was also typed in Aberdeen by several different people although special thanks are due to Christina Anderson who made a major contribution in dealing with a last-minute crisis!

Keith Chapman
David Walker

Illustration Acknowledgements

Every effort has been made to trace all copyright holders, but if any has been inadvertently overlooked the publishers will be pleased to make the necessary arrangement at the first opportunity.

The author and publishers gratefully acknowledge permission to reproduce or modify material from copyright works from:

A.R. Pred and Department of Geography, The Royal University of Lund (2.1)[1]; D.M. Smith and John Wiley and Sons, Inc. (3.1, 3.4); A. Lösch and Gustav Fischer Verlag (3.3); Hillier-Parker Ltd. (3.6); A. Weber and University of Chicago Press (4.1); W.H. Miernyk and McGraw-Hill Book Co. (4.2); F. Peck (4.3); S.J. Prais and Cambridge University Press (5.1); M.B. Green, R.G. Cromley, Cambridge University Press and Routledge (6.2); M.J. Taylor and Cambridge University Press (6.3); L. Håkanson and David Fulton Publishers (6.4); P. Gough and Canadian Association of Geographers (7.1); Shell UK Ltd (7.3); G. Bloomfield, Ford Motor Co. and David Fulton Publishers (7.9); ICI plc (8.5); OECD (8.6); D.E. Keeble and Methuen and Co. (9.1); A.R. Pred and Unwin Hyman (9.2); UNIDO (10.1, 10.2); J.O.C. Onyemelukwe and Heinemann Inc. (10.4); Industrial Activity Study Group, A.R. Townsend and Longman Group Ltd. (11.2); F. Meyer-Krahmer and Cambridge University Press (11.3), R.L. Fales and L. Moses and Regional Science Association International (12.2); P.E. Lloyd and C.M. Mason and Institute of British Geographers (12.3).

[1] Numbers refer to figures in this book.

Part I
Perspectives on Industrial Location

Manufacturing has played an important role in the emergence of contemporary society in many countries of the world. This role is reviewed in chapter 1, especially the significance of questions of location as reflected in, for example, the complex reciprocal relation between the rise of industry and the development of towns and cities. Chapter 2 turns from this consideration of general issues to an appraisal of the evolution of ideas relating to the significance and study of industrial location. Taken together, these opening chapters are an essential introduction to the rest of the book.

1
Manufacturing and Manufacturers

Students of industrial location have always concentrated on manufacturing industry. Even though other 'industries' are sometimes considered, the main focus is not in dispute. The topic has traditionally been explored from two main angles: that of firms and that of places. In the first approach, interest centres on locational choices by the firm – why it locates at a particular site, where it might best locate and how it uses its sites. In the second, attention is given to the nature of industries in an area (country, region or city) – how they relate to each other, and whether or not they are appropriate to the policy objectives of government. In both cases, analyses can be historical, descriptive, predictive and/or normative.

In this way we have tried to define the core of our chosen field. However, it must be admitted that it has been undergoing considerable peripheral expansion, related partly to the changing interests of scholars and partly to the changing nature of business itself. Firms now are increasingly multisectoral as well as multinational, so it is difficult to understand their locational choices without considering the non-manufacturing elements of the firm (administration, research, business services, distribution). Moreover industry is so bound up with national, regional and community development policy that a broad view of the overall working of an economy is essential for astute planning. In fact, in many parts of the world, governments own manufacturing industry and themselves make locational choices according to broader criteria than those employed by the private sector. Add to this a further complication: industrial location can be studied from the point of view not only of firms but also of workers. This aspect of the field is assuming greater attention after years of neglect. So while this book is to some extent necessarily narrow, let us not forget the wider context as we delve into the complexities associated with the location of manufacturing itself.

Manufacturing and the evolution of economies

Change in the role and significance of manufacturing within a national economy may be measured in various ways, including the value of industrial output or its share of total Gross Domestic Product (GDP). An alternative, indirect, approach, which is often easier from the point of view of data availability, is to analyse trends in employment relative to other sectors. Figures 1.1 and 1.2 indicate the importance of employment in manufacturing within the United Kingdom since the Second World War expressed in absolute numbers and in proportions of total employment respectively. An historical peak of 8.7 millions was reached in 1966, but manufacturing employment has since fallen to 5.0 millions by 1987. This absolute decline was preceded by a relative decline which started in 1955, when manufacturing accounted for its highest proportion of total employment (i.e. approximately 38 per cent). Direct comparisons through time are difficult because of changing statistical definitions, but the corresponding figure for 1988 was around 23 per cent. By contrast, service employment has increased steadily in both absolute and relative terms. The United Kingdom's poor economic and industrial performance as compared with its principal competitors over the past-war period is well known and it may be argued that it is not a good example to make a general point. The decline of manufacturing certainly started earlier in the United Kingdom and the rate of change has been more rapid, but there is abundant evidence of similar shifts within the employment structures of virtually all the developed economies. Thus manufacturing reached its greatest share of total employment in the United States in 1968, in Italy in 1969, in West Germany in 1970 and in Japan in 1971 (Kellerman, 1985). This secular trend has prompted considerable academic and policy interest in the phenomenon of 'de-industrialization' and in the nature of 'post-industrial societies' (Bell, 1973; Blackaby, 1979; Martin and Rowthorn, 1986). Such terms clearly imply a diminished role for manufacturing and, by inference, less concern with the problem of industrial location. There are, however, good reasons for believing that the subject matter of this book will continue to be of fundamental importance.

First it is necessary to recognize that a significant proportion of service-employment growth is inextricably linked to manufacturing. Various analyses have suggested that approximately one-fifth of total employment within developed economies is engaged in the provision of

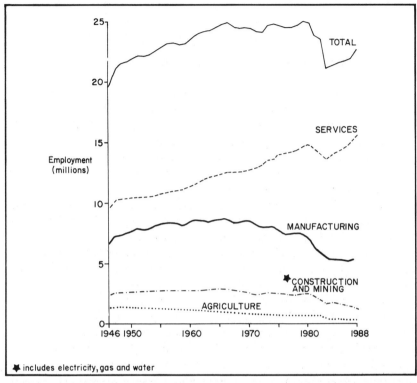

Figure 1.1 United Kingdom employment trends by sector, 1946–1988 (absolute)
Source: Ministry of Labour and Dept of Employment

producer services (Wood, 1987). Unlike occupations in retailing, hotels and catering, for example, these activities are mainly geared to meeting intermediate rather than final (i.e. consumer) demand. They include financial, business and professional services such as accountancy, advertising, insurance and so on. Their importance is reflected in the high and growing proportion of office-based employees within large industrial corporations required to support the activities of production workers. Indeed, Gershuny and Miles (1983) demonstrate that the expansion of producer services since 1950 has typically been the most dynamic element of overall service employment growth within developed economies. Not all of this growth is attributable to manufacturing since retailing, for example, utilizes producer services, but there is no doubt that the traditional distinction between manufacturing and service employment tends to under-represent the true importance of the former.

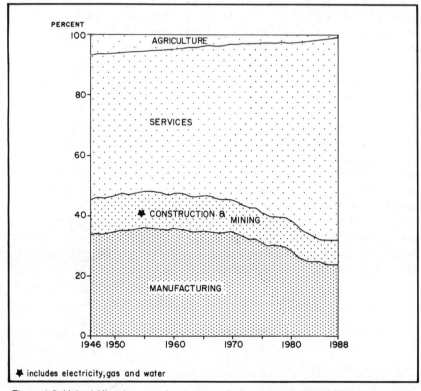

Figure 1.2 United Kingdom employment trends by sector, 1946–1988 (relative)
Source: Ministry of Labour and Dept of Employment

It is easy, especially in the United Kingdom with its sharp fall of manufacturing employment during the early 1980s, to gain the impression that industry is wasting away, to be replaced by a service-dominated economy. It is important, however, to appreciate that manufacturing remains a major component of all developed economies, and it has been argued, for example, that the erosion of its manufacturing base is at the root of the economic difficulties of the United Kingdom (Bacon and Eltis, 1976). Despite its erosion, this base accounted in 1982 for more than one-fifth of the GDP, provided more than one quarter of all jobs and contributed more than two-thirds of the total value of the country's exports (NEDC, 1985).

A preoccupation with the developed economies provides a misleading impression of trends in manufacturing employment and production at the global scale. Figure 1.3 focuses upon production rather than employment, emphasizing the contrast between selected developed economies and two of the more rapidly industrializing countries. Rapid growth is, of course, easier to achieve from a much smaller manufacturing base in a country such as the Philippines, but the contrast may, to some extent, be related to the general model of economic development and structural change indicated in figure 1.4. This suggests that development is accompanied by a continuous rise in the share of services in total employment. Initially this is achieved at the expense of agriculture. The relative decline in agriculture is reinforced by the simultaneous growth of industrial employment. Eventually, an intermediate or mature stage of development is reached at which the share of industry stabilizes, whilst services continue to increase and agriculture to contract. Eventually, when agriculture has reached an irreducible minimum, further growth in services is inevitably at the expense of industry.

Figure 1.4 is a simple empirical model and offers no explanations for the changes it describes. Nevertheless, there is ample evidence to support its validity and it has been suggested that the typical 'market' economy (as opposed to the 'planned' economies which until very recently have

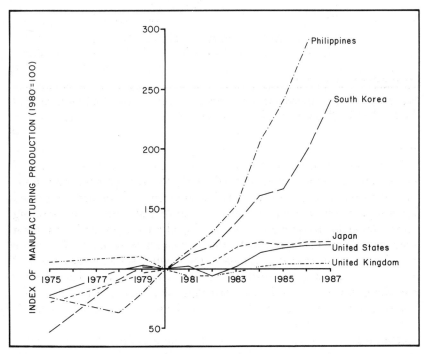

Figure 1.3 Indices of manufacturing production for selected countries, 1975–1987
Source: VN Statistical Yearbook, 1988

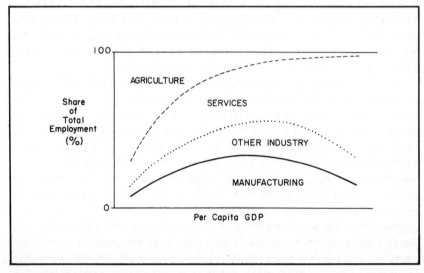

Figure 1.4 Employment structure and economic development

been characteristic of the socialist bloc) reaches maturity when per capita GDP is approximately $4000 (at 1975 prices) (Rowthorn and Wells, 1987). The majority of the world's countries fall below this threshold. It therefore follows that, whatever the prospects within the developed economies, the manufacturing sector is likely to grow in importance in most nations. Furthermore, few would argue that the absolute level of industrial production will decline within developed economies which have generally maintained a steady increase in the output of manufactured goods apart from a few historical 'blips' in the upward trend, such as the recession of the early 1980s.

Overall, it is clear that the role of manufacturing changes significantly as economies develop and yet it is also clear that this role is always central to the process of economic growth. Using the analogy of a motor car, manufacturing seems to function as an engine of varying efficiency and size relative to the economic vehicle which it drives, but there is no sign of any revolutionary change which will lead to a new form of propulsion. We will now turn to consider three key variables affecting the changing performance and design of the engine.

Technology

The method of production is of fundamental importance because it governs the nature of inputs, the quantity of inputs in relation to output, the energy requirements, the balance between labour and machinery, the nature of jobs and the potential scale of production. It sets the ground rules for factors of production and, in doing so, controls also the factors of location. Major changes in manufacturing location have been associated, therefore, with technological evolution.

This relationship is not perfect, partly because location is affected not only by costs of production but also by demand and the location of the market. Furthermore, not all production factors manifest themselves as significant location factors. They only do so when they are immobile or at least difficult and expensive to move. Mobility is critical. A few key managerial employees can usually be attracted to most locations if they are paid enough, and the total costs are rarely very large. Similarly construction of the plant itself and the supply of machines may be more expensive in some locations, but these costs form 'one-shot' or occasional capital expenditures. Markets, however, cannot be moved, nor can the location of the suppliers of inputs required by the production process itself, so transport costs linking the plant to both will be a regular, continuous expense. Similarly, if a relatively large labour force is required, it is not possible to transport employees far on a daily commuting basis, and resistance to permanent relocation could be high. The more specialized the labour requirements, the greater the locational restrictions on the plant. Many aspects of infrastructure and business service taken for granted in the industrialized countries are not available in large parts of the world, and to build road and rail networks, provide utilities and serviced sites is time consuming and costly. It takes even longer to establish varied banking and financial institutions, and firms specializing in management, computer servicing and the repair of industrial machinery.

To some extent, it is possible to overcome problems by substitution. If labour is in short supply, a more capital-intensive method may be used. A very large plant may be forced to provide its own rail connections or an electricity generating station if the infrastructure is poor, while a textile manufacturer can switch to artificial fibres if natural ones become difficult to obtain or expensive. Nevertheless, the limitations are real and alternatives are usually either less satisfactory or more expensive.

Technology has been evolving over the last two centuries in such a way that restrictions on location have gradually weakened. Before the Industrial Revolution, the typical craft operation could certainly locate more or less anywhere there was a market, but the changes ushered in at the end of the eighteenth century tightened things up considerably. The first factories operated from water power, an energy source that had already been used for centuries. Water power sites implied a regular flow of water and enough of a drop in height to provide an easy fall to drive the machinery. The production had to take place at the power source, because this form of energy could not be transferred at all. The earliest stage of the Industrial Revolution, bringing increased factory size and requiring more energy, meant that even fewer sites were appropriate than before. Many factories were built on quiet streamsides in hilly areas away from the main settlements. Villages and towns often grew around them, and for some activities (flour mills, sawmills, textiles) this energy source proved adequate until the late nineteenth century when it was sometimes possible to convert to hydroelectricity.

In comparison, the other energy source of the Industrial Revolution allowed much more flexibility, yet had a far-reaching effect on settlement patterns. Coal was important for heat, for power, and as a raw material in iron- and steel-making and some chemical processes. It was also required in sizeable quantities by many other industries as well as, in smaller amounts, by households. Coal was transportable and therefore did not fix a location in the way that water power did. Nevertheless, it was required in such large amounts that iron and steel industries moved to its source to save transport costs. Such was the importance of these processes in providing materials for a wide range of metal-using activities that the latter gravitated to the iron and steel complexes, and the major new areas of heavy industry such as Birmingham and the Black Country, the Ruhr and Pittsburgh were built up. These major new concentrations of industry had such an associated population growth that they attracted many other businesses as well. But even industries requiring coal just as an energy source moved to, or were encouraged to further develop on, coalfields. The British textile industries of Lancashire and Yorkshire both settled in coalfield regions.

As the nineteenth century progressed, the necessity to locate in coalfield regions declined from the technical perspective of production and distribution costs. The efficiency of coal use improved dramatically and dense rail networks cheapened movement. By the end of the century, however, population had concentrated in the coalfields of the industrialized countries, so the market factor encouraged locational stability. Potential flexibility was increased with the development of electricity. Its production was often from coal (thermal), but it could also be produced from a fall of water (hydro). Hydroelectricity gave useful power sources to areas other than coalfields. Also around the turn of the twentieth century it became possible to transport electricity, and grid systems were soon built in developed areas. Industry no longer had a necessary association with smoke and grime, and some new sectors grew up that required large amounts of cheap electricity in their manufacturing process (eg. aluminium, carborundum, electrolytic processes).

Another element in breaking the restrictions imposed by coal was the use of petroleum and natural gas. Although first extracted in the late

1860s, petroleum came into its own early in the twentieth century with the internal combustion engine. Motor transport has freed most plants from railside locations, which were characteristic of nineteenth-century industry, and since the Second World War has increasingly dominated goods movements in most market economies. Petroleum and/or natural gas have replaced coal in many industrial and domestic uses, although electric power has perhaps been even more important as a power source. Even more than electricity, petroleum has generated its own industries. As well as fuel products, there are now an enormous number of petrochemicals ranging from industrial chemicals and fertilizers to synthetic fibres. New petroleum-based industrial complexes are found in many locations, but they have not had such an impact upon population as coal-based activities because the processes are very capital intensive. Whilst great fortunes have been created, relatively few people have made them. Indirectly, however, the link between the internal combustion engine and petroleum has been one of the most powerful of the twentieth century. The automobile industry grew to be one of the major sectors by mid century, and the impact of the truck on industrial location has been considerable.

Currently another major revolution is taking place, based not on an energy source but on communication and computing. This is revolutionizing methods of production in almost every sector, affecting not only the shop floor, but offices as well. It threatens jobs in many sectors, but could also improve the quality of working life as robots are used to perform dangerous and boring tasks. In established industrial regions, jobs are being lost as new methods reduce the necessary workforce, often leading to greater and/or more efficient production. This requires at least short-run adjustment, which could turn out to be permanent for some workers. Nevertheless, the new methods are also creating jobs in the manufacture of all manner of computers and data processing devices, in software and service firms, and in the production of robots and computer-aided machinery. None of these require much in the way of physical inputs relative to the value of output, so that the choice of location is showing some new patterns related to the life styles of the well-educated and well-paid engaged in these activities. The availability of high-quality educational facilities, diverse cultural opportunities and good amenities all seem to be very important. As these new industries mature and their labour requirements shift to semi- and unskilled workers, some branch plants will be attracted to locations with cheaper land and labour costs. Indeed the trend can be seen already for electronics and computer firms.

This latest technological revolution is contributing to locational flexibility and will significantly reduce the technical constraints on the decentralization of business activities. Worldwide communication, visual as well as oral, is possible, while data can be quickly transferred from one plant to another. A large firm may now follow locational factors to the far corners of the earth without losing its internal cohesion.

Organization

Technical change has prompted and necessitates organizational change. Craft workers and small manufacturers operated, and still often operate, more or less as an extension of family life; business and family finances are not separated. Sometimes two or more partners get together to expand the financial base. However, the development of limited liability was essential to the expansion of manufacturing. As long as individuals were liable for more money than originally invested in their firm, many people could see no point in running the risk of losing everything they had. Although joint stock arrangements allowed companies to expand, most have in fact remained private, often run as a family business at one site. Nevertheless, the way was open for rapid and considerable growth, especially if the entrepreneur went public to raise funds. Those companies which took this route soon built plants at new sites or, alternatively, bought up existing companies and acquired additional sites with the purchase.

From the point of view of locational studies, this difference is quite important. First, location is often an explicit consideration in the expansion of public companies, but usually has no bearing upon the decision to establish a small firm, the location of which is determined by the entrepreneur's domestic circumstances and existing business contacts, without any real evaluation of alternative sites beyond the local scale. When a branch plant is to be located, however, a real locational choice is unavoidable, even if it is not carefully carried out. Second, the choice of another location may partly depend on the structure of the organization itself – especially the relationships between existing and new plants. Third, the company necessarily becomes involved in spatial planning and management. It must decide what to do at which plant, or perhaps even to close a plant somewhere. The company's own planning strategy then becomes relevant as an independent element in the fortunes of particular places, and one company's evaluation of a site is not necessarily the same as that of another.

Around the end of the nineteenth century a surge of merger and acquisition activity created corporate giants such as had never been seen before; the process began in the United States, but was quickly evident elsewhere. The twentieth century has seen other intensive merger periods.

The resulting expansion of a few corporations has led to their increasing domination of the developed market economies and gradually, with international expansion, those of the developing world as well. With corporate growth has come increasing specialization at each site. The larger the corporation, the easier it is to capitalize on scale economies and to use to the full the different locational advantages of specific places. Routine manufacturing operations may well be carried out in a developing country or a rural part of a developed one, while regional offices generally seek major cities with as full a range of financial and business services as possible. The separation of high- and low-paying jobs within companies has become a more important element in today's spatial structure than a simple employment total. The tendency until recently was for ever greater power to become concentrated at head office, even when the company operated multinationally.

Since mid century, the character of large corporations has begun to change. The earlier ones were usually confined to one sector or at least to an interrelated set of activities, but continuous expansion has more recently led to corporations with a wide variety of interests, called conglomerates. The top executives leave day-to-day matters to sectoral specialists, so that the critical decisions in conglomerates may be quite decentralized. In fact many large corporations now seem to recognize that, from an organizational point of view, greater decentralization is beneficial (Toffler, 1985). This trend could have important social and economic consequences because it may encourage a return to a situation in which those responsible for key management decisions identify more closely with particular places than with a geographically rootless corporation.

Work and the workers

The technological and organizational changes in manufacturing have had a major impact on both the amount and nature of jobs, and therefore the living and working conditions of ordinary people. Before the Industrial Revolution most manufacturers worked for themselves, whereas today there are relatively few who can be described as anything other than cogs in a machine over which they have little control.

There are a number of dimensions to the changes which have taken place in the last two hundred years. First, there is a loss of control over one's life when self-employment is replaced by employment for another. Increasing plant size brought with it a few owners and many workers. With time and joint stock companies, the number of owners (shareholders) increased but control remained in a few hands. It has gradually moved to management. As Galbraith (1967) has emphasized, the major decisions are now made by a 'technostructure' of professional executives from which the actual owners of the company are frequently excluded. Generally speaking, the 'technostructure' works well without any one particular person: it is self-perpetuating. Second, very few people now produce a final product from beginning to end. Division of labour has become extreme, not only in the manufacturing process itself, but also in the separation of such functions as invention, research, development, marketing, advertising, distribution, purchasing, etc. into different jobs. Each requires particular skills, and often there are specialized units within a company or indeed separate businesses concentrating on one function and employing people with similar backgrounds. Such specialization of task encourages locational specialization as well, so that the research laboratories of a company, for example, might be considerable distances away from either head office or production facilities.

Management has become increasingly unlike the entrepreneurs who start companies and know the business and its technology inside out. What is more, the flair and risk-taking of entrepreneurs is rarely passed on to succeeding generations, which tend to take on the tastes and attitudes of the management class. High incomes and advanced education tend to perpetuate this class as a very different group from the shop-floor workers, but they may also have little common ground with those involved in research and development. To maintain a creative atmosphere, then, is not easy in larger companies. In fact the whole business environment of mature industrial areas may have been lulled into a traditional routine which is quite inappropriate for changing times.

The blue-collar workers have generally been paid poorly in comparison with management, and in the early phases of industrialization in most countries there has been or is tremendous exploitation of the poor, including children. A long history of worker conflicts and union activity has helped to bring dignity and better working conditions as well as improved wages. The increased internationalization of industry and the spread of manufacturing to developing countries, however, pose a threat to those parts of the world where a satisfactory situation has been achieved. So far workers have not been able to stand firm internationally: in fact there are frequently interregional differences within a country.

It has been a dream of many to remove these class conflicts and to encourage a situation where all work for the common good. On the large scale a communist or socialist state is supposed to do this, but has often failed. State-run or nationalized industry is one method of bringing the economy under the people's control, but it is debatable whether it has been very successful in either socialist countries or mixed economies. Generally, it has not been very innovative or particularly responsive to either its employees or its markets. At a smaller and often community scale, cooperatives are a way of drawing in the public at large to business ventures. However, the cooperative movement, which has done so well in some other sectors, has not made much impact in manufacturing. In any case, these ownership forms deal with only one element of hierarchy – that some own, others don't, and the owners can take the created surplus. There still has to be a hierarchy of management. Two critical questions are the relationship between employee rewards and management rewards, and the determination of this relationship. Even in co-operatives, it is often management which decides and its action is governed by circumstances in comparative private firms.

Not surprisingly there has been a revival of interests in the possibilities for small businesses to overcome these problems of worker alienation. They could, in theory, provide a more satisfying work experience by narrowing the gap between employer and employee. Given the dominance of large corporations in manufacturing, however, it is not easy for small firms to avoid a dependent (peripheral) role in the marketplace, and most successful small business operations are in other sectors. Firms that do well soon face the consequences of their success in resolving the pressures for expansion with a desire to retain the social benefits of the more personalized work place.

Given the structures that are now in place, it is imperative to create a greater sense of the benefits of co-operation between everyone in a firm: owners, management, office staff, researchers, blue-collar workers. Class attitudes are deeply entrenched in some countries, reinforced by a history of bitter conflict and often by unfair contemporary situations. Nevertheless the success of any company depends on all working well together, and a sense of this seems to permeate countries such as Japan and West Germany where strikes are rare and methods have been developed to encourage working together. In difficult economic times, strife within a company will simply mean that the winners retain more of a declining pot but receive less absolutely, while the losers rapidly head towards the poverty line.

Manufacturing, economy and society

Manufacturing is clearly related to all aspects of the economy and it has had a major role to play in shaping the nature of work available today, but its significance extends far beyond narrowly defined economic relationships. Massey (1984, p. 6) holds that one can 'explore the geography of industry and of jobs through an interpretation of the spatial organization of the social relations of capitalist production', or indeed any other form of production. She also notes that 'changes in labour process and technology are both the outcome of social relations and the basis for the creation of new forms of such relations' (p. 6). That this is broader than an economic choice is clear from the role that women and immigrants play in the workforce, as well as traditions about demarcation based on established union practice or professional regulations rather than skill to do the job. Many such practices are enshrined in institutions, laws or government policy and reflect the attitudes of society as a whole.

Galbraith (1967), like many Marxists, argues that the relationship between governments and big business is close, and the two support each other via subsidies, grants, education of workers, infrastructure and reduced economic uncertainty on the one side, and cash, goods and required research on the other. The spatial ramifications of the government side of the bargain can be great, including as they do the location of critical elements of infrastructure (roads, rail lines, ports, industrial parks, electricity, etc.) and the selective granting of funds, which may only be available at specific locations. Nevertheless, government policy does not just reflect the desire of technocracy, and indeed capitalists and management are far from unanimous in their views. Such differences can show up sectorally, where they may or may not have spatial relevance, but also regionally and nationally. In federal countries where some economic power resides in provincial governments, this opens the way for greater decentralization of activity as well as more conflict with the federal government and other managements.

There are, however, broader attitudes and social movements which are not governed by manufacturers or businessmen. The deeply entrenched attitudes towards competition in the United States, for example, has held up merger movements within an industry at a certain point, and even led to the breakup of large corporations. There are those who would argue as well that technological change has a forward movement all of its own, and that business is responding to what the scientists are producing rather than controlling its own direction. Certainly business people decide on commercial exploitation, but as long as discoveries are publicized and they seem to have usefulness public pressure is great for their application. Growing environmental awareness, for example, is placing pressure upon manufacturers to reduce pollution and to discover new ways of production which do less damage. Pressures are also building up to reduce military expenditure in many countries and these could have important consequences for manufacturing, bearing in mind the pervasive influence of the 'defence industry'.

There may also be changes in the extreme spatial segregation of activities that have been a result of capitalist development. These have implied richer and poorer regions in the past, as we have already noted in discussing the spatial organization of firms. More broadly, however, they have encouraged residential segregation within metropolitan areas as well. The wide range of incomes has encouraged distinctly working-, middle- and upper-class areas with associated schooling and cultural activities; this geographical element in class distinction was much less evident before the Industrial Revolution. To change this, however, will require a shift in the direction of income equality that is too great to imagine in the foreseeable future.

Conclusion

Manufacturing has been central to many of the great developments affecting society for over two hundred years. Despite the rise of services and the associated absolute and relative decline of manufacturing in the more developed economies of the world, its impact is unlikely to diminish if we take a global view of current trends. More specifically, changes in the spatial distribution of manufacturing at this scale emphasize the importance of the question of industrial location which is the central focus of this book. Many of the issues raised in this introduction will be explored further in subsequent chapters, but we will first review some of the different approaches which have been adopted to provide explanatory frameworks for the interpretation of historical and contemporary patterns of industrial location.

Further reading

Galbraith, J. K. 1967: *The New Industrial State*. London: Hamish Hamilton.

Landes, D. S. 1969: *The Unbound Prometheus: technological changes and industrial development in Western Europe from 1750 to the present*. Cambridge: Cambridge University Press.

OECD 1983a: *Industry in Transition*. Paris: OECD.

Pollard, S. 1981: *Peaceful Conquest: the Industrialization of Europe 1760–1970*. Oxford: Oxford University Press.

Rosenberg, N. 1976: *Perspectives on Technology*. Cambridge: Cambridge University Press.

2
Approaches to the Study of Industrial Location

There have been significant changes in approaches to the study of industrial location which, to some extent, have reflected changes in the nature of manufacturing itself. Industrial location theory, formulated by economists in the early part of the century, was most appropriate to an analysis of the location of such basic, heavy industries as iron and steel which were in the vanguard of contemporary industrial progress. The emphasis was firmly placed upon the individual factory as the object of study and, more specifically, upon the variables influencing the choice of new sites. A similar emphasis is apparent in behavioural studies which, nevertheless, focus directly upon the way in which the variables identified by normative theory are actually perceived and interpreted by those responsible for making location decisions. Such decisions were for many years assumed to lie with individual entrepreneurs, and the small single-plant firm was the point of departure in attempts to explain the location of industry. This premise has become more difficult to justify in view of the growth of large enterprises controlling many establishments, often in diverse industrial sectors. It has been recognized that the location of individual factories can often only be understood in relation to the wider corporate systems to which they belong. These systems often extend across national frontiers, and interest in the global distribution of manufacturing is just one aspect of a growing awareness, reflected in contributions from differing political perspectives, of the importance of industrial location as a vital influence upon patterns of economic development at various spatial scales.

Normative industrial location theory

Most analytical, as opposed to descriptive, work before 1960 was concerned with interpreting the location of individual plants or industries by reference to the conceptual framework provided by normative location theory. This approach is deductive, in that it proceeds from a set of basic propositions regarding the objectives of those responsible for the industrial location decision, and normative, in that it indicates the optimal outcome for the manufacturer which may be expected under a clearly specified set of conditions defined by a series of simplifying assumptions. The essence of the normative approach is the search for the best or optimal location at a particular time. However, it is possible to distinguish branches of industrial location theory on the basis of both different assumptions and different criteria of optimality.

Least-cost location theory rests upon the work of Weber, originally published in German in 1909 and translated into English 20 years later (Weber, 1929). Weber started from the premise that the best location was the one at which costs are minimized. Considerable emphasis was placed upon the transport costs involved in assembling materials at the manufacturing site and in delivering the finished product to the market, although Weber also recognized the influence of labour costs and the possibility that economies may be achieved as a result of the agglomeration of several plants in close proximity to one another. Despite the latter aspect of Weber's model, he took no account of the potential effect of the location of competitors upon sales. Thus demand was effectively held constant and it was assumed that the manufacturer could sell all he produced regardless of his location and the actions of his competitors. Moreover, the location of demand was also endogenous to Weber's model. Given these conditions, it is not unreasonable to regard the least-cost location as the best location.

In contrast, other writers have allowed demand to vary, but assumed that costs were fixed (Fetter, 1924). Interest then focuses on the way in which markets are shared spatially and on the location which best captures sales (the market area approach). Another group of writers has recognized that decision-makers react to competitors, giving a degree of locational interdependence as the best location changes according to the strategy of others. These writers, starting with Hotelling (1929), have also assumed zero costs so that their work has similarities to the market area workers. Lösch (1954) in fact combines the approaches in his general theory, but they tend to be more appropriate to retailing than manufacturing.

Lösch did in fact recognize that the goal of the rational entrepreneur should be to select the location at which profits are maximized and that, in reality, neither demand nor costs are spatial constants as assumed by the least-cost and locational interdependence schools respectively. However, he maintained that a model which simultaneously relaxed both of these assumptions, to define the optimum location at the place at which total revenues minus total costs is greatest, was impossible to construct. Greenhut (1956, 1963) and Isard (1956), nevertheless, attempted to move in this direction and to derive more ambitious theoretical representations of location which incorporated the variables influencing both cost and revenue sides of the equation (see Stafford, 1972).

The principal features of the various normative models are discussed in chapter 3 with references to the single-plant location problem. However, it is their similarities rather than their differences which are most relevant to an appreciation of their impact upon the development of industrial geography. Central to the normative approach are certain assumptions regarding the characteristics of those responsible for selecting the best plant location. These are embraced within the concept of *economic man*. This notional decision-maker is distinguished by the single-minded pursuit of the goal of profit maximization and by the possession of complete knowledge of all relevant economic information, including the ability to predict the actions of competitors and future events. No individual can, in reality, possess such omniscient powers and, even if all of the other simplifying assumptions of location theory were accepted, the optimal locations of these normative models would remain unattainable objectives. Greenhut (1963) was certainly aware of this problem, but retained the assumption of economic man in his theoretical work. Others, however, attempted to moderate the super-human attributes of economic man whilst retaining the essential normative requirement of seeking an optimal location. Rawstron (1958) originally identified the existence of *spatial margins to profitability* which defined the boundaries of an area, focused upon the best location, within which profitable operation can be achieved. This idea was developed by Smith (1966, 1981) who incorporated it within both least-cost and locational interdependence representations of the industrial location problem. Smith's models replaced the notion of a single best location at which *maximum* profits are achieved with a broader area of economic viability within which *sufficient* profit may be made to allow continued operation. Although critics have argued that the concept of the spatial margin is of no practical value because the boundaries of the area of profitability are just as difficult to identify as the maximum profit location (Bater and Walker, 1970; Taylor, 1970), Smith (1981, p. 115) observed that it 'remains more a formal extension of traditional theory than a guide to location practice'.

However the rapid economic growth of the 1960s which resulted in an exceptional and probably unique volume of investment in new manufacturing establishments in Western Europe, North America and Japan provoked an increasing academic and policy interest in the practice of location decision-making. The abstract models of normative theory appeared to provide little useful guidance to, for example, governments wishing to influence the distribution of new manufacturing investment in accordance with their regional development objectives, and it seemed more relevant to focus on how decisions are actually made as opposed to how they should be made.

Behavioural approach

The concept of spatial margins to profitability recognized the possibility of sub-optimal behaviour in the choice of factory location. This was something that empirical studies of industrial location decisions seemed to confirm, as responses to questionnaire surveys of industrialists frequently stressed the importance of 'personal considerations' over the more obvious and conventional factors such as proximity to raw materials (see Katona and Morgan, 1952; Greenhut and Colberg, 1962; Luttrell, 1962; Mueller and Morgan, 1962; McMillan, 1965; Cameron and Clark, 1966). Such apparent contradictions stimulated the emergence of a so-called *behavioural* approach to the study of industrial location which derived its inspiration from the work of Simon (1957b) and March and Simon (1958) in administration theory. Simon observed that whereas economic man is an *optimizer*, his real-world equivalent is a *satisficer*. In other words, since decision-makers do not, in reality, possess either the level of knowledge or the powers of reason ascribed to economic man, they adopt courses of action which are perceived to be satisfactory. Such behaviour was defined by Simon (1957b) as *bounded rationality*, and it seems to accord with our everyday experience, quite apart from its relevance to more momentous decisions such as the choice of location for a new factory.

Pred (1967, 1969) incorporated these ideas within his concept of the *behavioural matrix*, which he applied to a variety of decision-making situations including the selection of a new factory location. The matrix is a device to identify the position of decision-makers relative to the normative concept of economic man. The axes of the matrix measure the quantity of (relevant) information available to a decision-maker and his ability to use that information. It is clear from figure 2.1 that whereas decision-makers positioned in the top left corner of the matrix may be described as incompetent and ignorant in economic terms, those in the bottom right represent the opposite end of the spectrum of ability and knowledge. Pred argued that individuals in the latter position are more likely to make economically rational decisions, but accepted that they could also benefit from chance factors not related to their own choices. Figure 2.1 links this idea to the notion of spatial margins. It is postulated that there are three areas within which a hypothetical industrial activity may be profitably undertaken. An optimal location is identified within

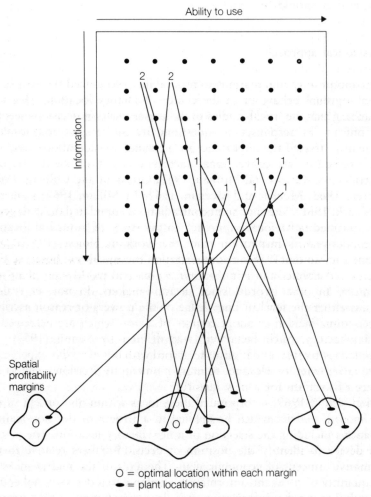

Figure 2.1 The behavioural matrix and industrial location decisions (the numbers indicate the number of firms occupying specific positions in the matrix)
Source: Pred, 1967

each of these areas. The geographical position of a number of imaginary firms is linked to their behavioural position within the matrix. Generally speaking, firms in the bottom right of the matrix have chosen locations near one of the optima, whilst most, but not all, of the firms characterized by positions in the top left have selected unprofitable locations.

Although in many respects naive and virtually impossible to test in practice, Pred's behavioural matrix is an important concept for a number of reasons. As far as the study of industrial location is concerned, it emphasized that decisions are taken by individuals and organizations that diverge, to varying extents, from the theoretical norm of economic man. Notions of probability and uncertainty are introduced, and the acknowledgement that survival is only possible for a limited period outside the spatial margin is an implicit recognition of the dynamic character of manufacturing distributions. Furthermore, the possibility that some firms, which are remote from the norm of economic man in their decision-making capabilities, may be 'lucky' in their choice of location, may be related to certain important ideas concerning the dynamics of industrial location patterns. Following the earlier work of Alchian (1950), Tiebout (1957a) distinguished between businesses that are adopted by the economic environment and those which adapt to prevailing conditions. The former are equivalent to the 'lucky' decision-makers from the top left quadrant of Pred's behavioural matrix: the latter will tend to be drawn from the bottom right. It should be noted here that normative location theory paid no explicit attention to dynamic aspects of plant location. The relevant location factors were considered at one time so that it was not necessary to examine how decisions from one period affected those in the next, whether in the context of a firm's own development, of the impact on and reaction of other firms, or of long-term changes in the cost and availability of necessary factors of production (Walker and Collins, 1975). This neglect of the dynamic context has played a major role in the necessary evolution of new approaches to studies of industrial location.

Although Pred referred to 'deaths' in contributing to the evolution of industrial patterns, most studies of industrial change continued to concentrate primarily on new plant decisions until the 1970s. These studies included attempts to derive conceptualizations of the location decision-making process in general (see Stafford, 1969; Townroe, 1969; Rees, 1972; Walker, 1975; Lloyd and Dicken, 1977) as well as numerous empirical surveys which sought to test these ideas (see Townroe, 1971; Cooper, 1975). The results of some of these surveys are reviewed in chapter 3, but two general conclusions, with implications for the future direction of industrial geography, emerged from this flurry of research activity in the late 1960s and early 1970s. First, there was an increasing realization that the new plant location decision is an exceptional event which is taken with great reluctance. An indirect consequence of this realization was a shift away from the analysis of this particular type of decision and a growing awareness that 'all business decisions have locational implications' (Hamilton, 1974a, p. 14). Second, empirical studies tended to emphasize the significance of firm size as a variable influencing the nature of the location decision-making process, and to provide some evidence in support of the proposition that the kind of rational behaviour upon which normative theory is based is more frequently associated with large organizations than with small businesses (Walker, 1975). Thus, in responding to some of the limitations of normative theory, the behavioural approach itself opened up new lines of enquiry.

Geography of enterprise

The behavioural approach, with its emphasis upon the decision-making process, has been influential in many branches of human geography. Much of this influence has been apparent in studies of the spatial aspects of individual choices such as personal migration decisions. However, the geography of modern society is increasingly determined not by the actions of isolated individuals, but by the strategies of large organizations. These include 'public' agencies such as central and local government bureaucracies as well as 'private' organizations epitomized by the major corporations which dominate many areas of economic activity. McNee (1960) recognized the implications of the rise of the large corporation when he called for the development of 'a geography of enterprise' which explicitly focused upon the role of such corporations as what he termed area- or space-organizing institutions. Krumme (1969b) further defined the nature and scope of the geography of enterprise, and a succession of studies followed which took up the ideas first articulated by McNee (see Krumme, 1970; Chapman, 1974; Le Heron and Warr, 1976).

The upsurge of geographical interest in large firms during the late 1960s and early 1970s was part of a wider concern. For example, many disciplines contributed to the development of ideas on the theory and practice of organizational management (see March and Simon, 1958; Simon, 1960; Cyert and March, 1963). On a more popular level, Galbraith (1967) fluently expressed a growing awareness of and concern with the power of large industrial corporations. This power has both practical and theoretical implications. One element of corporate power is the ability to directly influence the spatial distribution of manufacturing activity at every geographical scale from local to international. A consequence of such power has been to accentuate the divergence between reality and a basic premise of normative location theory – the subservience of the individual entrepreneur to the dictates of the surrounding economic environment. Most observers agree that one of the principal objectives of business organizations is the minimization of uncertainties associated with this environment (Dicken, 1971; Wood, 1978), and central to the geography of enterprise approach is an acknowledgement of the fact 'that, to some extent, firms are able to manipulate or modify their environmental context' (Hayter and Watts, 1983, p. 161).

An important consequence of the emphasis upon large firms has been to extend the boundaries of legitimate geographical enquiry into manufacturing (Tornquist, 1977). Thus although the label 'geography of enterprise' has never been clearly defined, the terminology has, by conventional academic usage, come to denote an explicit concern with the spatial ramifications of decision-making within large firms. These ramifications involve much more than the new plant location decision, which is the focus of interest in location theory. Certainly the location decision, as traditionally conceived, has continued to have a place within the geography of enterprise, but it is no longer regarded as the only or even the most important focus of study. Viewed within the context of large business organizations it is evident that the location decision is secondary to the investment decision. Thus the decision to increase output or to manufacture a new product is the cause and the subsequent location of the necessary facilities is the effect. Although geographers remain primarily interested in the effect, it is obviously unsatisfactory to seek explanation without reference to causal mechanisms. Closely related to this point has been the recognition that many essentially non-spatial decisions have geographical consequences. For example, the introduction of new technology may result in a change in the ratio of skilled to unskilled jobs at the different manufacturing sites of a multiplant company. Alternatively, a firm faced with a contracting market for its product may decide to close one or more of its factories. The age or labour relations record of each of these factories is much more likely to influence such a decision than their location. Nevertheless, the effects upon communities and regions of these types of corporate decision clearly fall within the scope of any definition of geography which includes an appreciation of the spatial consequences of economic change. This kind of argument has meant that the geography of enterprise approach has produced a significant shift in emphasis away from a concern, exemplified by normative location theory, with the influence of the spatial dimension of the economic environment upon industrial location (i.e. proximity to raw materials, markets, etc.) towards an interest in the impact of the activities of industrial enterprises upon the environment.

Manufacturing in regional development theory and planning

This broader perspective is reflected in a substantial body of literature concerned with the influence of manufacturing upon spatial patterns of economic development. There is a basic tendency for the process of economic growth to result in polarized development – an accentuation of the differences between prosperous and less prosperous regions. Manufacturing seems to play an important role in this process, and the attempts to understand and, subsequently, to influence the forces responsible for the characteristically uneven spatial distribution of economic development have necessarily contributed to our knowledge of the location of industry. Unlike the normative, behavioural and geography of enterprise approaches which, in their very different ways, focus directly upon the location of industry, this contribution has been a by-product of an interdisciplinary concern with the wider issue of polarized development. One of the most important consequences of this connection between manufacturing and the study of the development process has been to draw attention to the significance of time. Whereas normative location theory, for example, is essentially static, models of regional economic development encourage the adoption of an evolution-ary perspective as existing patterns are regarded both as derivatives of former conditions and as major influences upon future states of the economic system.

The importance of manufacturing in the process of regional develop-ment is widely acknowledged, although some sectors, variously labelled 'propulsive', 'lead' or 'dynamic', seem to be more important than others. In theory, industries such as chemicals, iron and steel and metal products, which are characterized by extensive backward and forward linkages with other sectors, have the potential to transmit growth impulses widely throughout an economy. Furthermore, these impulses rest not only upon the existence of linkages, but also on the induced income or multiplier effect as both corporate and personal expenditures circulate through the economy. There is a close relationship between the role of linkages and multiplier effects in regional economic growth and their relevance to the phenomenon of agglomeration in industrial location. The distribution of economic activity over space is clustered rather than dispersed and considerable effort has been directed towards the explanation of this characteristic. Although Weber recognized its importance, the analysis of agglomeration is generally regarded as 'one of the most unsatisfactory aspects of traditional location theory' (Wood, 1969, p. 33). The surge of geographical research interest in this problem during the 1960s and 1970s partly reflected an awareness of the limitations of the explanations offered by location theory, but was also stimulated by insights provided by the work of economists concerned with wider issues of development and growth. Thus techniques such as input–output analysis, which were originally designed to demonstrate the interdependent structure of national economies by representing the linkages between their various sectors, were modified and applied to smaller geographical units in attempts to identify the forces responsible for the creation and continuity of industrial agglomerations at various geographical scales (see Isard et al., 1959; Karaska, 1969).

Much of this work on the nature of industrial agglomeration has been inspired by an awareness of the policy implications of polarized development. The location of a manufacturing facility, especially a large one, has numerous economic impacts; through its purchasing pattern of services and materials, its effect on the labour market and incomes, its direct and indirect impact on local wealth, and its demand for infrastructure, it can set in motion a whole sequence of circular and cumulative processes (see chapter 9). The operation of these mechanisms clearly has implications for the spatial distribution of economic development – implications which have prompted governments in most developed countries to formulate policies designed to influence the location of industry as part of wider strategies aimed at reducing regional economic inequalities. The nature and effectiveness of these policies are reviewed in chapter 11. However, it is important to stress the contribution of efforts to understand and influence the process of regional economic development to the study of industrial location. Universal agreement regarding the key role of manufacturing in this process has meant that much of this work has been directly concerned with industrial location. Important insights into the nature of agglomeration have been derived from the collaboration of geographers and economists in regional development problems. Another benefit of this work has been to emphasize the need to study industrial location within the context of the total economic system, including the relationship between the distribution of manufacturing and settlement patterns (see Norcliffe, 1975; Beattie and Watts, 1983). Furthermore, a common concern with the various dimensions of unequal development has prompted closer links with other disciplines such as sociology and political science – links which have had important consequences for the nature of research in industrial geography.

Structural approach

The trend toward the adoption of a broader perspective, far removed from the normative concern with the location of the individual plant, has been reinforced by the emergence of a *structural* approach to the study of industrial location (see Massey, 1977, 1979a; Storper, 1981; Walker and Storper, 1981; Storper and Walker, 1983). Whereas the principal concern during the 1960s was with the management and redirection of economic growth, the consequences of industrial stagnation and decline have been the major preoccupation in most developed countries during the 1980s. It is no coincidence that the structural approach, which is one aspect of a wider academic interest in the application of Marxist ideas in the social sciences, acquired a significant following at a time when the world's market economies were experiencing the worst recession since the 1930s. In these circumstances, major readjustments took place which produced significant changes in the distribution of manufacturing industry. Marxist analyses regard such changes as just one aspect of a process of restructuring which represents a stage in the development of capitalism. Thus is it suggested that each of these stages is associated with characteristic distributions of economic activity. Dunford (1979) develops this argument with reference to the evolution of the French economy, emphasizing the significance of the methods of production associated with the Industrial Revolution in bringing about a fundamental redistribution of population away from the rural areas towards the rapidly growing urban centres. By contrast, the present 'crisis of capitalism' is distinguished by the displacement of manufacturing jobs from the metropolitan core toward the rural periphery and the concentration of service employment in the cities.

As Smith (1981, p. 142) observes, 'the chief merit of the Marxian approach ... is its breadth which permits industrial location to be analysed as an integral part of the totality of economic, social and political processes'. This view has become strongly entrenched in the analysis of international development and underdevelopment (see Frank, 1975; Amin, 1976). Moreover, the recession of the 1980s reinforced the credibility of such an all-embracing perspective in the industrial West, where events perceived to be local or regional in character during periods of economic growth are now regarded as manifestations of more general processes operating at national and international scales. Indeed structural analyses have often been focused at the regional or community scale and yet have, at the same time, attempted to integrate events at these levels within a much broader context.

Economic change, especially where it involves job losses or other negative impacts upon labour such as deterioration in the conditions of work, has stimulated interest in the structural approach. The economic dislocations of the 1980s ensured that the spatial distribution of manufacturing seemed to be more a consequence of differential decline than the various processes of expansion and growth with which students of industrial location had traditionally been concerned. The structural approach has been applied to such circumstances as exemplified by Massey and Meegan's (1979) study of the spatial implications of a government-sponsored reorganization of the British electrical engineering industry towards the end of the 1960s. This reorganization took the form of a series of mergers and was itself precipitated by the prevailing economic situation within the United Kingdom. It was necessary 'to design a framework for explanation which allowed location changes to be understood in relation to the general characteristics of the recession' (Massey, 1979a, p. 70). This framework was a 'top–down' sequence which proceeded from a consideration of the basic forces responsible for the difficulties of the industry to a discussion of the nature of the reorganization as it affected the production process and, finally, to a review of the specifically geographical consequences of this reorganization. This scheme emphasizes the impact of processes operating at the macro-economic level upon the individual firm. It therefore displays a reverse direction of causality to that usually associated with the geography of enterprise approach, which stresses the autonomy of large corporations as expressed by their ability to manipulate the environment in which they operate. Nevertheless it is important to avoid creating false and over-simplified dichotomies, and there remain many similarities between Massey and Meegan's work and numerous studies in the geography of enterprise tradition. The firm is the focus of attention in both cases, and Marxists cannot claim to have been the only, or even the first, to appreciate the relevance of macro-economic processes to an understanding of changing patterns of industrial location (see McNee, 1960; Fleming and Krumme, 1968; Hayter, 1976).

Perhaps the most significant contribution of the structural approach lies not in its mode of explanation, but in its challenge to the ideological basis of industrial geography. In the normative, behavioural and geography of enterprise approaches the question of location is viewed from a managerial perspective. The best location is defined in terms of the presumed goal(s) of the entrepreneur or firm. By contrast, the structural approach 'suggests that studies of industrial location should have a greater awareness of the social implications of shifts in industrial activity and should consider more fully what groups are most disadvantaged by changes in employment opportunities and how inequalities are perpetuated by the functioning of the labour market and managerial hiring practices' (Marshall, 1982, pp. 1675-6). These aims are different from those associated with other industrial research traditions and they account for the emphasis in structural analyses upon the role of labour in the production process. Whereas spatial variations in the cost and quality of labour are regarded as variables affecting the profitability of alternative locations in conventional studies, Marxist perspectives tend to stress the impact upon labour of such corporate practices and policies as the introduction of new technology and the determination of conditions of employment. Although such matters are apparently of greater sociological than geographical concern, there is no doubt that the emphasis upon the conflict of interest between capital and labour, which is central to the structural approach, has provided some very powerful insights into such inherently spatial phenomena as the redistribution, characteristic of most developed economies, of industry away from the traditional industrial heartlands to the rural peripheries (see Massey and Meegan, 1978; Massey, 1979b; Massey, 1984). As it moves into a broader spatial–societal analysis, the structural approach covers much of the same ground as that in regional development studies, finding common elements particularly with such writers as Friedmann (1972; Friedmann and Weaver, 1979) on core–periphery structures.

Conclusion

It is apparent that the problem of industrial location has stimulated a diversity of approaches to explanation. With the benefit of hindsight, it is possible to identify shifts in academic fashion as one mode of explanation is, to some extent, displaced by another. Thus, in the late 1980s very few are actually involved in the development of normative industrial location theory, but many claim to adopt a Marxist or structural perspective in the interpretation of changing spatial patterns of manufacturing activity. Although the advocates of particular approaches are sometimes less than generous in acknowledging the contributions of others, no one mode of explanation has a monopoly of insight. In subsequent chapters, this book will make reference to all branches of the literature in an attempt to provide not only an understanding of the forces which influence the distribution of manufacturing, but also an appreciation of the wider social, economic and political significance of the problem of industrial location. Part II (chapters 3 and 4) draws upon the normative and behavioural traditions to explain the location of individual plants in terms of spatial variations in the cost and availability of their inputs and in the opportunities for selling their outputs. In part III (chapters 5, 6 and 7), the emphasis is placed upon the growth of large companies and the corresponding need to consider industrial location with reference to the strategies of such organizations. Part IV (chapters 8 and 9) shifts the level of resolution once more by considering the variables which operate at the industry scale, where location relative to suppliers, customers and competitors replaces the emphasis in the preceding section upon relationships which are internal to specific enterprises. The first four parts of the book are, in general terms, concerned with the impact of the dimension of space upon industry; this perspective is reversed in part V (chapters 10, 11, 12 and 13) where the spatial effects of changes in the organization and technology of manufacturing are examined with reference to such contemporary problems as unemployment, polarized development and pollution.

Further reading

Hamilton, F. E. I. (ed.) 1974a: *Spatial Perspectives on Industrial Organization and Decision Making*. London: Wiley.

Hayter, R. and Watts, H. D. 1983: The geography of enterprise: a reappraisal. *Progress in Human Geography*, 7, 157–81.

Massey, D. 1984: *Spatial Divisions of Labour*. London: Macmillan.

Smith, D. M. 1981: *Industrial Location: an Economic Geographical Analysis*. 2nd edn, New York: Wiley.

Part II
Factories and Firms

Industrial location theory was first formulated when almost all manufacturing businesses consisted of single-plant firms. We also begin with a simple situation, although most location factors apply whether or not the plant is part of a larger entity. We review earlier approaches to the subject but also consider actual decision-making and the reasons why it has led to more behavioural approaches to industrial location. But even if a plant is independent it cannot ignore other businesses, and chapter 4 explores their impact via both linkages and competition.

3

Location Theory, Location Factors and Location Decisions

An understanding of the variables influencing the choice of location for a new factory has been the traditional focus of concern within industrial geography. It is, therefore, logical to begin with this problem, whilst recognizing that it is only one of many actions of industry, such as factory expansions, contractions and closures, which affect the distribution of economic activities and employment opportunities. Both the costs and revenues of a manufacturing business will vary with location. The costs of assembling inputs and distributing outputs will depend upon location relative to sources of supply and markets respectively. Location relative to the market may also influence the level of sales and, therefore, the revenue side in the firm's balance sheet. It is not only purchasing and marketing activities which are influenced by location, but also the production process itself. The costs of many of the factors which are essential to this process, such as labour, vary from place to place. This chapter considers these influences upon plant location. It begins with a review of theoretical approaches to the problem. Transport costs figure prominently in these approaches and some of the complications raised by differences in the nature of these costs between theory and reality are explored in the next section. This is followed by a discussion of other factors which contribute to variations in production costs between one location and another. Finally, attention is focused upon the way in which these variables are actually incorporated within the decision-making processes of the individuals and organizations responsible for the distribution of manufacturing industry.

Location theory

The work of Weber, which was first published as *Über der Standort der Industrien* in 1909 and subsequently translated into English in 1929 (Weber, 1929), is generally taken as the point of departure in studies of industrial location. This work reflected prevailing economic circumstances and must be evaluated in the light of the very considerable changes that have taken place in the manufacturing sector since the turn of the century (see chapter 1). Weber made a distinction between material- and market-oriented industries. He recognized that the costs of assembling the materials required by a manufacturing plant may encourage its location at the source of these materials. This effect depended upon the nature of the materials, which Weber characterized as either ubiquitous or localized. The former are available at similar cost everywhere whereas the latter are only available at specific locations. Localized materials are further sub-divided into pure and gross materials. In the case of pure materials, the whole weight of each unit of input enters into the finished product, whereas part of the weight of gross materials is 'wasted' in the production process. Gross localized materials have the ability to attract industries to locations at their production point, making an industry *material oriented*. On the other hand, by adding to the product's weight wherever it is produced, ubiquities may encourage *market orientation*.

An attempt to apply these ideas to an analysis of the distribution of industry in the United Kingdom was made by Smith in 1955 and they remain a valid basis for understanding general locational patterns in certain types of industry. Gross localized materials are essentially raw materials produced by the primary sector; many of them still have sufficient weight loss to draw early-stage manufacturing to them, even though technology has often increased the use of what were once 'waste' products and generally reduced weight loss. Pulp and paper mills, ore beneficiation and metal-smelting plants, fish, fruit and vegetable freezing and packing, and abattoirs, for example, are all frequently found near to the material source. The importance of coal both as a raw material and as a source of heat and power for manufacturing during the nineteenth century was emphasized in chapter 1. The weight losses involved in many coal-based industrial activities had the effect of drawing population and economic activity to the coalfields. The contemporary economic problems of these areas in many developed economies may, therefore, be regarded as a legacy of spatial patterns created in response to the basic principle of localized materials identified by Weber. This principle is, however, less relevant to many modern industries because an increasing proportion of plants begin not with raw materials but with semi-finished items or components. On these, there is almost no (if any) weight loss and so little tendency to material orientation. Moreover, such 'materials' are frequently obtained in urban centres which also serve as markets for the finished product. In these circumstances, the same place is both a material and a market location. On the other hand, few items today can be referred to, without qualification, as ubiquities. Water, for example, is in short supply in many areas. In most developed countries it could be regarded as ubiquitous for, say, a bakery or a machine shop, both of which use little, but it certainly is not for a steel mill. Electricity could be similarly viewed as a ubiquity in developed countries, but not in the vast amounts required by an energy-intensive operation such as aluminium smelting. In developing countries, nothing can be regarded as ubiquitous.

Weber's analysis of the transport costs involved in assembling localized raw materials and delivering the resulting product to the market was accompanied by a concern with one particular variable influencing the costs of the manufacturing process itself. He noted that wage levels and the efficiency of the workforce vary from place to place and that these variations are geographically fixed, at least for the short run. He acknowledged the existence of differences in wage rates for regions, but argued that labour cost variations essentially relate to specific towns, and also that availability of labour could only be considered at this scale. In his analysis, labour is punctiform in spatial pattern, and immobile. This led him to deal with advantageous labour locations by comparing the savings made at them with those obtained at the least-cost transport point, found by an analysis of transport rates.

Figure 3.1 represents a simple situation in which a plant uses two materials located at A and B to manufacture a product for a market at C. The concentric circles drawn around each of these points are *isotims*. These represent the transport costs incurred either in assembling materials from A and B or in delivering the product to C. These lines may be used to identify a least-cost transport point X around which isodapanes may be drawn. The *isodapane* is a line through points of equal total transport cost away from the least-cost transport point. In figure 3.2, this point is identified by X and L is assumed to be a cheap labour location with a saving of $25 per unit of production in comparison with labour costs at X. A critical isodapane may be drawn (CI_1) showing extra transport costs of $25 per unit. If L is outside that line, it is cheaper to stay at X. On the other hand, if labour savings were $45 per unit and CI_2 were the critical isodapane, production would be cheaper at L. Other location factors could be analysed in the same way,

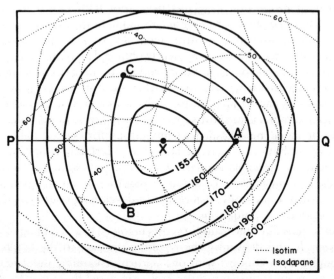

Figure 3.1 The derivation of isodapanes
Source: Smith, 1981

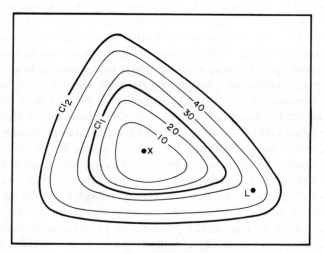

Figure 3.2 Weber's use of critical isodapanes
Source: Weber, 1929

but the analysis clearly depends on the assumption that these costs are locationally fixed at a particular place.

Weber has probably been the most influential of the early contributors to the development of normative location theory, but others have extended the analysis beyond the cost side of the equation, recognizing that demand also varies with location. Lösch (1954) argued that the least-cost point was not necessarily the same as that of maximum profit, which is what a producer is seeking. He noted that every production point has an element of spatial monopoly in that it can best serve itself. The incorporation of transport costs to more distant markets increases the delivered price to customers, so that the quantity demanded gradually declines until it is zero (figure 3.3a). Given a homogeneous plain, evenly settled with homogeneous people, a demand cone may be constructed around a production point, defining the market area and the quantity sold (figure 3.3b). Competition will turn this circle into a hexagon, part of a series serving the region perfectly efficiently, as long as the assumptions of Lösch's model are met. These assumptions, which involve neglecting real-world cost elements and allowing the costs of serving the market to dominate the situation, are most appropriate for service activities and for widely produced consumer goods, such as fresh bread or manufactured ice (see Foust, 1975). Although many firms adopt a policy of uniform spatial pricing within national markets in which customers pay the same regardless of their location relative to the factory (Greenhut, 1981; Norman, 1981), there is abundant evidence of a marked distance decay effect in the shipment of industrial goods and a tendency for firms to have higher market shares within the vicinity of their plants (Dorward, 1979). This evidence emphasizes the validity of Lösch's ideas and the danger of regarding the market as a point and assuming a fixed level of demand regardless of price.

Economists have made the major contributions to the development of industrial location theory, and their focus has often been to attempt an integration of the topic into mainstream economics (Isard, 1956; Beckmann, 1968; Greenhut, 1974). Smith's (1966, 1981) reinterpretation from the viewpoint of an economic geographer developed two important concepts – the space–cost curve and the notion of spatial margins to profitability. These rested upon the premise that, although a single, optimal location may be identified, it is surrounded by other potentially profitable production sites. Figure 3.4 is a space–cost curve derived from the information contained in figure 3.1. It is a cross-section along the line PQ and the lowest point of the curve corresponds to the most profitable location at X. For simplicity, the product is assumed to be sold at a fixed price of $170 regardless of the distance from the point of production and this is represented by the horizontal price (total

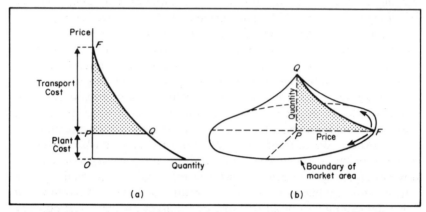

Figure 3.3 Derivation of the demand cone: (a) demand curve; (b) demand cone
(OP = production costs, PF = transport costs, FQ = quantity demanded)
Source: Lösch, 1954

revenue) line in figure 3.4. In these circumstances M_a and M_b define the spatial margins to profitability. Expressed in three-dimensional terms, these margins define an area or zone of profitability. Beyond these margins, the total costs exceed the selling price of \$170 and a loss will be made.

Smith's adaptation of Weber's ideas represents a step nearer reality because it acknowledges that the selection of the least-cost location is not essential for economic survival. Figure 3.4 relates to a very simple situation in which revenues are held constant. The effect of changing

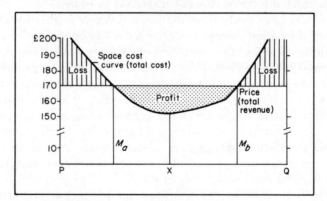

Figure 3.4 Derivation of a space–cost curve
Source: Smith, 1981

various assumptions can be incorporated within such diagrams (see Smith, 1981, pp. 157–221). For example, a more efficient entrepreneur may have a similarly shaped but lower spatial cost curve than a competitor, resulting in wider spatial margins and allowing profits to be made further away from the optimal location at X. Nevertheless, it is important to appreciate the relative simplicity of Smith's situations in comparison with the real world. In particular, many costs are just not spatially smooth enough to plot in this way. There are tremendous discontinuities for most of them, so that Smith's (1981, pp. 263–72) efforts to map surfaces of cost factors are too far from reality to be useful in practice. His work is more helpful as a teaching tool than for solving a practical locational problem, although McDermott (1973) attempted to apply Smith's ideas to various industries in New Zealand.

Employment of such surfaces to depict markets may, however, be more realistic, especially for products geared to final consumer demand or otherwise closely related to population. Market potential models can show the accessibility of a place to given population, measured either as numbers of people or by such data as income or retail sales. The basic formula is simple:

$$MP_i = \sum_{j=1}^{n} \frac{M_j}{t_{ij}}$$

where MP is the market potential at i, M_j, is the population of j (or another mass variable) and t_{ij} is the distance (or transport cost) between i and j, and n_{ij} other points in the system under consideration. Harris (1954) used this formula in an early study of the United States steel industry, but it has often been applied since (Kerr and Spelt, 1960; Ray, 1965). It can be used to anticipate future demand patterns by using estimates for the mass variables at selected future dates, or even employed to examine alternative possibilities by comparing more than one set of estimates. For a discussion of different formulations and the limitations of this statistic, see Houston (1969).

Transport costs

Transport costs and their influence upon the assembly of inputs, the distribution of outputs and levels of demand are the principal concern of industrial location theory. This emphasis was initiated by Weber, but his stress on transportation was not matched by a particularly realistic view of actual transport costs. He worked on the basis of costs being directly proportional to the weight of the product and the distance it was carried, an assumption frequently invalidated in the real world. Hoover (1948, pp. 15–66) provides a useful overview of the complexities of transport pricing, pointing out that costs include more than just freight rates, and are influenced by such aspects of service as insurance and speed. Moreover, the location and orientation of transport networks is a significant factor in the real world. Such infrastructure is expensive to build and confers special benefits on particular locations (Alexander et al., 1958). Industrial areas within cities such as Chicago, which experienced rapid economic growth during the nineteenth and early twentieth centuries, were frequently located adjacent to canals, navigable rivers and railway lines (see Fales and Moses, 1972). Road transport is more important today, and a good road network is frequently taken for granted – almost as a ubiquity – in the modern industrial economy. Nevertheless, expressway junctions are cost-saving locations which often attract industrial development, especially activities associated with distribution (see McKinnon, 1983). In developing countries, where transport links are frequently limited, the relative advantages of the few locations served by a primitive infrastructure may be even more pronounced. Physical features associated with mountainous regions, for example, can also contribute to a rudimentary network by causing high building costs or limiting route choices. Thus transportation makes its mark on location in part by simply *providing opportunities selectively*.

These variations manifest themselves directly into costs. Most firms cannot contemplate building their own road or rail links. What is perhaps less immediately obvious is that, where the infrastructure is dense, competition gives alternatives and keeps costs down. In fact, larger centres usually provide a much wider range of transport services than smaller ones, and at lower costs. This is related to the concept of scale economies, because large centres can generate full car lots or truck loads, whereas smaller places cannot easily do so, and full loads are cheaper for the transporter. While it is not easy to document these variations systematically, the cost differences are often quite considerable (Nelson, 1973; Lowe and Moryadas, 1975, pp. 30–53).

Weberian calculations are also upset by the general tendency for long hauls to cost less per unit weight than shorter ones. This is due to fixed costs, especially terminal charges, which must be spread over the journey and therefore are less per mile or kilometre for longer journeys. For shipping especially, and also for rail, these costs may be considerable. Harbours, storage spaces, rail routes and the like are not cheap to build. Such a freight rate pattern encourages longer journeys and discourages the splitting of journeys into shorter stretches. For example, it is possible as a result of a Weberian analysis to find that the least-cost location is situated at neither a material nor a market point, but an intermediate location. In reality, however, the nature of freight costs makes this unlikely unless there is also an enforced change of transport mode such as at a port. Ports sometimes benefit from their break-of-bulk characteristics, especially in the context of imported material such as grain, sugar cane or petroleum (Hoyle and Pinder, 1981). On the other hand, the expansion of trucking since 1945 has given much greater flexibility in short hauls, because a truck is filled by a much smaller quantity of goods than a boat or train. Thus, the disadvantages of an intermediate location have been reduced.

Two other related tendencies have been important in affecting the relationship between transport cost and industrial location in the twentieth century. The first concerns the way in which freight costs on finished products have risen more rapidly than those on raw materials. An old principle of transport marketing is to charge what the traffic will bear, so that very good deals can be obtained for bulk shipments of cheap raw materials for which owners cannot afford to pay much. They also require less care and special handling, and can benefit from scale economies associated with increasing ship sizes or using unit trains that carry one product directly from point to point. The increasing size of ocean-going bulk carriers for commodities such as iron ore and petroleum has had important effects on the location of the steel plants and refineries which process these materials. The dramatic expansion of oil-refining capacity in Western Europe and Japan during the 1950s and 1960s was, for example, facilitated by the advent of the supertanker, which greatly reduced the real costs of shipping crude oil from the principal raw material sources in the Middle East (see Frankel and Newton, 1968). The cost of moving equivalent quantities of refined products such as fuel oil is significantly higher, thus encouraging the location of oil refineries near to their markets rather than their source of raw material. This example is fairly typical, and the finished products of many industries require special attention, have high insurance rates and are more expensive to ship per unit size or weight than the materials from which they are derived. Thus the tendency is to ship raw materials further, perhaps to the market area, and cut down on shipments of finished products.

A second general trend has been an overall decline in the significance of transport costs as a proportion of total costs in most industries. This has been reinforced by the rise in the relative importance of firms producing finished, higher-value goods better able to bear the costs of transport. Such firms frequently pay little attention to transport costs, not least because these costs are usually absorbed within delivered prices which are inclusive of freight. Nevertheless, there are situations in which the careful evaluation of transport costs is justified. Typically, these are associated with the distribution of consumer goods to widely dispersed markets and they are considered in chapter 7 in the context of the spatial organization of corporate systems.

Location factors

It is generally acknowledged that transport costs are a less significant influence upon contemporary patterns of industrial location than is implied by their central place in normative theory (see Norcliffe, 1975, pp. 21–4). However, in his consideration of labour costs, Weber recognized that other variables affecting the production process itself may also influence the economics of location. Economists traditionally recognize the existence of three *factors of production* – land, labour and capital – although enterprise, defined as the managerial and technical skills involved in their co-ordination, is often recognized as a separate factor of production. The significance of these factors in the production process is reflected in cost structures. The data in table 3.1 are derived by expressing material acquisition costs (including freight charges), gross earnings paid to employees and the costs of purchased fuels and electricity as a percentage of the total value of sales to derive estimates of the significance of material, labour and energy costs respectively for selected industries in the United States. It is apparent that there are significant differences between industries and that these differences tend to become more pronounced moving from the two- to the four-digit level of disaggregation in the US Standard Industrial Classification. Costs at firm and plant level may be expected to broadly reflect these patterns, although significant variations may occur when different processes are used to manufacture the same product. Paper, for example, may be produced from wood pulp and/or recycled material. The cost structure of a plant using the former route may look very different from one using the latter. A further complication arises from the fact that cost structures may change through time. Fluctuations in the international price of oil since 1973 have had a major direct and indirect (through effects on other energy sources) impact upon many industries such as petrochemicals (chapter 8). Despite these difficulties and the very considerable level of generalization associated with table 3.1, an awareness of cost structures is clearly relevant to plant location where their different elements are cheaper in some places than others.

Even if a particular factor represents a significant proportion of total costs, it does not necessarily follow that it will influence location. What

Table 3.1 Cost structures for selected US manufacturing industries, 1986

SIC Code	Industry Group and Industry	Cost elements (as % of total value of sales)		
		Materials	Labour	Energy
20	Food and kindred products	63.7	9.2	1.6
201	Meat products	80.4	7.4	1.0
2011	Meat packing plants	86.5	5.2	0.7
27	Printing and publishing	34.3	25.2	0.9
275	Commercial printing	43.7	28.1	1.4
2753	Engraving and plate printing	28.3	37.1	1.7
29	Petroleum and coal products	83.1	3.4	3.5
291	Petroleum refining	84.7	2.8	3.5
33	Primary metal industries	62.8	17.9	7.4
333	Primary non-ferrous metals	76.3	11.4	16.9
3334	Primary aluminium	71.1	13.4	28.2
36	Electrical and electronic equipment	42.8	25.1	1.3
367	Electronic components and accessories	37.7	29.3	1.9
3674	Semiconductors and related devices	30.3	31.5	2.4
38	Instruments and related products	35.3	23.9	1.0
382	Measuring and controlling devices	35.0	31.7	1.1
3825	Instruments to measure electricity	34.7	33.9	1.1
	All Industries	53.9	19.9	2.4

Source: Calculated from data in 1986 Annual Survey of Manufactures, Statistics for Industry Groups and Industries, US Department of Commerce, Bureau of the Census, Washington DC, 1988

is important is how it varies spatially. Smith (1981, p. 150) makes a distinction between basic cost, the minimum which must be paid anywhere, and locational cost, which varies from place to place. It is the latter which is crucial to the choice of location. Nevertheless, where spatial variations in labour costs, for example, do exist, their potential effect will obviously be very much greater in the manufacture of electrical and electronic equipment than in petroleum refining (table 3.1). Numerous studies have explored such impacts upon the location of individual plants and upon the distribution of industries. Figures 3.5 and 3.6 provide illustrations of locational costs within the United States and the United Kingdom respectively. Figure 3.5 plots variations between the states in the average wages paid to production workers in manufacturing. The data partly reflect differences in the industrial structure of the various states with the average figure for Washington, for example, inflated by the generally high wages paid in the aerospace industry which is important in the state. Nevertheless, these variations provide a crude measure of labour costs to manufacturers and it is apparent that, despite pressures towards convergence associated with the activities of trade unions and with government intervention in labour markets exemplified by minimum wage legislation, significant differences remain. Many of the southern states in particular continue to have labour costs which are lower than the national average and to use this as a positive factor in attracting industry (Cobb, 1982). Figure 3.6 shows how rents for prime quality industrial properties vary between the regions of the United Kingdom. To some extent, such maps conceal more than they reveal because they are scale-specific. For example, significant variations in rents often occur at the local or urban scale and these may be an important influence upon the choice of site for a small business. Measuring spatial variations in costs and assessing their influence upon the location of industry is an important theme which will be pursued in subsequent chapters at a variety of geographical scales from urban to international.

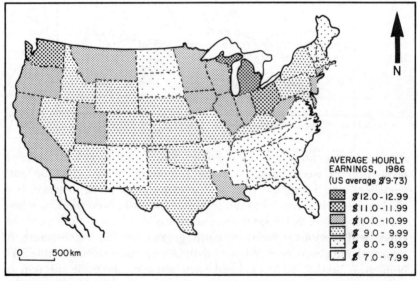

Figure 3.5 Average hourly earnings of production workers in US manufacturing industries, 1986
Source: US Bureau of Labor Statistics

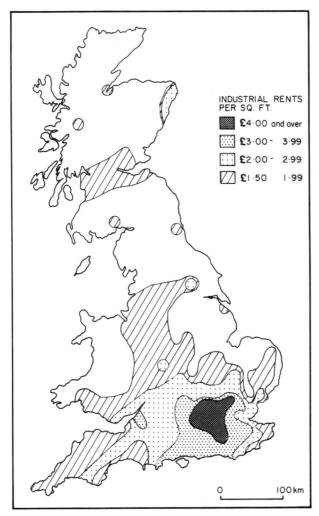

INDUSTRIAL RENTS
PER SQ. FT.

█ £4·00 and over

£3·00 - 3·99

£2·00 - 2·99

£1·50   1·99

0   100 km

Figure 3.6 Industrial rents in the United Kingdom, 1987
Source: Hillier–Parker Ltd

Several attempts have been made to disaggregate the influence of costs and demand upon plant location (see Greenhut, 1956; Townroe, 1976; Schmenner, 1982). These may almost be regarded as checklists for those making location decisions. Table 3.2 is based upon the work of Greenhut (1956). Demand factors include variables which influence the character of demand, such as the location of potential buyers, and the nature of demand, such as the distribution of competitors and the importance of

Table 3.2 Greenhut's location factors

Demand factors

1   The shape of a demand curve for a given product
2   The location of competitors, which in turn partially determines
   (a) the magnitude of the demand
   (b) the cross-elasticity of demand at different places
3   The significance of proximity, type of service, and speed of service; prejudices of consumers
4   The relationship between personal contacts and sales
5   The extent of the market area, which itself is partially determined by cost factors and pricing policies
6   The competitiveness of the industry in location and price; certainty and uncertainty

Cost factors

1   The cost of land which includes
   (a) the rent of land
   (b) the tax on land
   (c) the availability of capital, which partially depends upon
      (i)   the banking facilities and financial resources
      (ii) personal contacts
   (d) the cost of capital, which is also partially dependent upon
      (i)   the banking facilities and financial resources
      (ii) the type of climate
   (e) the insurance rates at different sites, which in turn partially depend upon
      (i)   the banking facilities and financial resources
      (ii) the police and fire protection
      (iii) the type of climate
   (f) the cost of fuel and power, which is partially dependent upon
      (i)   natural resources
      (ii) topography
      (iii) climate
2   The cost of labour and management, which is influenced by
   (a) the health of the community, the park and education facilities, housing facilities, wage differences, etc.
   (b) state laws
3   The cost of materials and equipment, which is partially determined by
   (a) the location of competitors (sellers and buyers)
   (b) the price system in the supply area (f.o.b. mill, equalizing or other forms of discriminatory delivered prices)
   (c) the extent of the supply area, which in turn is partially dependent upon
      (i)   personal contact
      (ii) price policy
4   The cost of transportation, which is partially determined by
   (a) the topography
   (b) the transport facilities
   (c) the characteristics of the product

Table 3.2 Continued

Purely personal factors

1 The importance of psychic income (size of plant)
2 Environmental preferences
3 The security motive

Source: Greenhut, 1956

customer-service. Cost factors can be divided into several different subgroups. The first covers the cost of buying and running the factory itself, including capital costs. The second embraces labour costs, broadly conceived to include all factors affecting the availability, welfare and productivity of the workforce. The last two groups of cost factor are material costs and transport.

In addition to cost and demand factors, Greenhut distinguished a third broad category of what he termed 'personal' factors. This reflected the findings of his empirical research which led him to recognize that many location factors did not fit conveniently into his economic categories (1956, pp. 233–47; Greenhut and Colberg, 1962). In fact, he recognized that manufacturers received rewards other than financial ones, and suggested that one must consider their 'psychic income', or non-monetary satisfaction. Numerous surveys have emphasized the importance of such considerations, and the existence of an attractive environment or climate may be decisive in the choice between two locations with similar economic attributes (see Dean, 1972; Spooner, 1974; Nicholas, 1974; Foster, 1977).

Greenhut's typology of location factors may be refined extended and complicated. It may also be expected to change with time. Nevertheless, the broad categories in table 3.2 are useful and the actual importance of specific factors is an empirical question which many researchers have attempted to answer (see Nishioka and Krumme, 1973; Brown, 1979). Various approaches have been adopted. Most studies involve asking decision-makers within firms to indicate the importance (often by ranking) of individual location factors listed by the investigator (see McMillan Jr, 1965; Logan, 1970; Foltman, 1976; Herron, 1981; Moriarty, 1983), but others use relatively unstructured interviews to obtain information on the circumstances surrounding the choice of location (see Stafford, 1974; Schmenner, 1982). These interviews are then analysed to reveal the most important variables. Table 3.3 summarizes the results of a fairly typical survey of location factors based in this case on interviews carried out with 410 large companies operating manufacturing plants in the United States during the 1970s. Managers of 159 newly established branch plants were asked to identify those factors perceived as 'musts' in the initial choice of region or state and then in the subsequent choice of site. It is evident from table 3.3 that whilst labour- and market-related factors are most important at regional level, access to transport facilities is of primary concern in choosing between sites *within* a region. This distinction emphasizes the importance of scale factors in understanding industrial location. In a study of the location decisions of manufacturers within Atlanta, for example, Wheeler (1981) demonstrates that the variables most important to large companies establishing branch plants to serve the national market were different to those dominating the thinking of smaller firms geared to regional and metropolitan markets. The former are mainly interested in labour supply and cost, whilst the latter are more strongly influenced by the availability of land and/or premises, access to business services and amenities. Nevertheless, once the national firms have actually chosen Atlanta in preference to some other city, their site-selection process at the metropolitan scale is not radically different from that of the smaller businesses.

In theory, location decisions may involve the sequential consideration of factors at successively more limited geographical scales. Multinational corporations frequently evaluate the relative merits of different countries as locations for manufacturing plants. This stage may be followed by a comparison of regions within the chosen country, communities within the chosen region and, finally, sites within the chosen community. In practice, this sequence is rarely followed in such a systematic way. International or even regional considerations may not be relevant to the small firm, whilst the demanding locational requirements of a major factory such as a motor vehicle assembly plant may severely limit the options available at community or site level. There is some evidence of a relationship between the scale or level of resolution and the relative importance of the various location factors. Market size, labour costs, political stability and, for primary manufacturing, raw material availability are especially important at the international level. At regional level, many more factors are relevant, but again market prospects and labour conditions often dominate. At the local scale, numerous attributes affect perceptions of the 'prevailing business climate', including the attitudes of politicians and community leaders, the provision of amenities, housing stock and educational facilities. The connection between location factors and changes in the distribution of industry at these various geographical scales is considered in more detail in subsequent chapters, but we will now turn to consider the way in which location decisions are actually made.

Table 3.3 Location factors for 159 branch plants established by US manufacturers during 1970s

Location Factor	Plant openings citing at least one factor (as per cent of total number of plant openings)
1 *Region/State level*	
Favourable labour climate	76
Near market	55
Attractive place for engineers, managers to live	35
Near supplies and resources	31
Low labour rates	30
Near existing company facilities	25
Environmental permits	17
Others	6
Community attitude	0
2 *Site level*	
Access to rail service	47
Access to expressway	42
Special provision of utilities	34
Rural area	27
Environmental permits	23
Within metropolitan area	21
Access to water transport	16
Available land/building	8
Others	7

Source: Adapted from Schmenner, 1982

Location decisions

It is one thing to identify location factors, quite another to evaluate their significance in the decision making process. Comparing tables 3.2 and 3.3, it is noticeable that relatively few location factors seem to be important in Schmenner's empirical study despite the diversity of potential influences identified by Greenhut. This is significant because it draws attention to the frequent discrepancy between the theory and practice of industrial location decision making. This is not surprising, given the complexity of the problem which involves the simultaneous consideration of many variables as table 3.2 demonstrates. Location theory assumes that manufacturers manipulate all relevant variables to find an optimum location. However, the information required to reach such a judgement is often difficult and expensive to obtain. The analysis of information is also a problem because some variables are binary, others qualitative and only a few easily quantifiable. Table 3.4 is an example of a checklist of factors relevant to the search for a new location. It was devised by Schmenner (1982) as a practical guide for use in the United States and it emphasizes the difficulties involved in quantifying many of the variables. It is also important to remember that decision makers are concerned not only with existing, but also with future conditions. The construction of a new factory is a long-term investment and it is necessary to make predictions of, for example, trends in costs and demand to assess the likely return on this investment.

Industrial location decisions clearly involve considerable *risk* and *uncertainty*. Despite the existence of mathematical procedures to aid decision makers under such conditions (Miller and Starr, 1967, pp. 71–137), individuals and companies may respond in very different ways to the same situation. For location decisions, it has never really been proved that these different evaluations correlate systematically with other objective characteristics of firms. For example, are certain sectors more cautious than others, or are smaller firms less willing to take risks than multinationals? There is a tendency for larger firms to search wider areas and be more narrowly economic in the objectives (Walker, 1975), but that is not the same as saying they will take greater risks. Simon (1959) indicated the widespread tendency of firms to seek well-known solutions first, and some location theorists have suggested that imitation of successful firms may be important (Tiebout, 1957a). This could restrict search areas. Moreover, studies of uncertainty (Webber, 1972, pp. 273–9) indicate an attraction to well-established centres, especially market areas. We will return to this topic in the next chapter and will now briefly review the findings of various empirical studies of location decisions made by entrepreneurs entering business for the first time and by existing firms wanting to establish a branch plant in a new location. This distinction is made because the nature of the problem facing the small firm is often significantly different from that facing the large corporation.

There is abundant evidence that most first-time entrepreneurs set up in business close to their home (see Mueller and Morgan, 1962; Gudgin, 1978; Johnson and Cathcart, 1979; Cross, 1981; Lloyd and Mason, 1984). Indeed, they rarely make an explicit location decision other than the choice of premises at a very local scale. Practical considerations such as the need to avoid the additional costs involved in moving house, the fact that many entrepreneurs begin operating on a part-time basis whilst continuing to work for their existing employer and the advantages

Table 3.4 Major location factors: information quality and availability

Factor	Quality of Information
Access to Markets	
Distribution cost to existing markets	Estimate
Future trends in sales (including additional sales generated by new plant)	'Guesstimate'
Access to Supplies	
Assembly costs	Estimate
Future trends in supplies (including new suppliers)	'Guesstimate'
Competitive Considerations	
Location of competitors	Quantifiable
Reaction of competitors	Non-quantifiable
Transport Facilities	
Availability, quality and cost of services	Estimate
Utilities and Services	
Availability, quality and cost	Estimate
Labour Factors	
Availability, quality and cost	Estimate
Taxes and Financing	
Prevailing tax rates and obligations	Quantifiable
Tax incentives	Quantifiable
Site Factors	
Purchase price and development costs	Quantifiable
Environmental Considerations	
Prevailing regulations	Quantifiable
Ease and speed of compliance	Non-quantifiable
Community Factors	
Cost of living	Quantifiable
Community facilities	Estimate
Community attitudes	Non-quantifiable

Source: Adapted from Schmenner, 1982

involved in exploiting existing business contacts all encourage a conservative strategy (see Eversley, 1965; Gudgin, 1978). Such considerations are concerned with minimizing risk and they emphasize that new entrepreneurs rarely engage in a systematic search for the ideal location, but rather attempt to reduce the problem to manageable proportions. Indeed, the same may be said of large firms despite their more extensive resources for data collection and analysis. Simon (1957a) suggests that such behaviour may be regarded as a rational, but bounded or restricted response to uncertainty. Instead of looking at every possible alternative, the decision-maker is more likely to set limited goals and take the first solution which satisfies them. This 'satisficing' behaviour (Simon, 1959) may well include non-economic as well as economic objectives.

In the case of small firms, it is apparent that the decision-maker rarely makes a clear choice between alternative locations and that the distribution of such firms is largely determined by the circumstances of their formation. This does not mean, however, that the aggregate distribution of new manufacturing firms is random. There has recently been much interest in the geography of new firm formation within developed economies. This has been inspired by a concern with their role in the creation of employment opportunities (see Gudgin, 1978; Birch, 1979), not least because of major manufacturing job losses associated with the actions of many multi-plant firms (see chapter 7). Research has demonstrated clear regional variations in rates of new firm formation. Much of this work has focused on the United Kingdom where South-East England and East Anglia have been shown to have much more rapid rates of new firm formation than most other parts of the country (see Mason and Harrison, 1985; Mason, 1987). The reasons for such differences are complex. They partly reflect existing industrial structures because it is known that many entrepreneurs establish businesses based upon their previous employment experience. In these circumstances, regions associated with more dynamic industries offer greater potential than those associated with declining ones. This is reinforced by the fact that most small firms build up their business by supplying local markets. The propensity to start up in business also seems to be related to a wide range of socio-economic factors such as levels of education, home ownership and the nature of existing employment with communities dominated by large plants and firms apparently less favourable to what might be termed an entrepreneurial culture. Overall, the distribution of small firms is less a consequence of the critical evaluation of location factors by entrepreneurs and much more a result of spatial variations in the economic environments conducive to the decision to set up in business. The nature of these environments is examined in more detail in chapters 9, 11 and 12.

Established firms may be expected to engage in a much more active search for alternative locations than new firms, once the decision to develop a new site has been taken. Following the principle of bounded rationality, however, investment at its existing site is likely to be the preferred strategy of a firm wishing to expand its production capacity and, in the majority of cases there is no consideration of locational alternatives (Schmenner, 1980). Survey evidence suggests that relocations and the establishment of branch plants are considered only when various pressures upon the firm become too great to resist (see Keeble, 1968). Townroe (1969) categorizes these pressures as either internal or external.

Internal pressures, related to growth in output, are the most frequent reason for either a relocation decision or the establishment of a branch plant (see Cameron and Clark, 1966; Keeble, 1968; Townroe, 1972; Schmenner, 1982). A formerly adequate site may prove unacceptable as available space is used up and premises become cramped and unsuitable. Adding capacity by establishing new branch plants is not only a response to the limitations of existing sites, but is also encouraged by the desire to serve new geographical markets (see North, 1974). Such moves obviously modify the frame of reference within which the company operates, as there are changes in not only the location of the market but also the distribution of potential suppliers. External pressures on a site may reflect difficulties in a number of areas. Increases in labour costs or militancy have been prominent in causing locational change (Townroe, 1972; Sant, 1975; Keeble, 1976). In some cases, planning controls from one or more levels of government may be a problem, especially in connection with redevelopment schemes. In large cities, as well, there is frequently pressure on sites because of competition from other land-uses such as offices and retailing (see chapter 12).

Whatever reasons promote the search for a new location, the question of how this search is made is clearly important, bearing in mind the optimizing approach assumed by location theory. Various attempts have been made to develop practical guidelines to assist decision-makers cope with this problem. These may be prepared by external advisers or consultants (Townroe, 1976; Stafford, 1979) or they may be developed internally to assist decision makers within a rapidly growing firm. Such internal guidelines incorporate the accumulated experience of previous location decisions. Schmenner (1982, pp. 60–68) and Moriarty (1980, pp. 121–48) describe the approach adopted by several major US companies and Rees (1974) refers to the case of the Monsanto Chemical Company which established an average of two branch plants per year between 1958 and 1969. Such rapid rates of growth are, however, unusual and the location decision is an infrequent event for most companies. In these circumstances, it is difficult to justify establishing a formal procedure and most case studies of the location decision-making process within firms emphasize that it tends to be pragmatic rather than scientific (see Townroe, 1971; Cooper, 1975; Schmenner, 1982), not least because of the difficulties involved in obtaining information (table 3.4). Typically the process involves a fairly superficial review of possible locations at the regional scale and the effort spent in collecting and analysing data tends to increase as the choice is narrowed down to site level. Even the largest corporations are forced to make judgements on the basis of incomplete information, emphasizing the divergence between the complexities of the real world and the certainties of location theory.

Conclusion

It is important to appreciate the limitations of the approach adopted in this chapter. First, it is concerned exclusively with the establishment of new industrial plants. Recent experience of manufacturing decline in many developed countries (see Bluestone and Harrison, 1982a; Townsend, 1983) emphasizes that any full understanding of changing patterns of industrial location must necessarily take account of factory closures as well as openings. At one level, such closures may be explained in terms similar to those which apply to relocations and the establishment of branch plants. A survey by Schmenner (1982, pp. 235–9), for example, found that site and plant difficulties such as obsolescent equipment and high labour costs were the most frequently quoted reasons for factory closures by multiplant companies. However, such 'explanations' are often immediate justifications for decisions ultimately determined by wider circumstances within the organization, industry or even the national economy. These issues will be considered in later chapters (7, 8 and 9), but it is important at this stage to acknowledge the part which factory closures play in the evolving distribution of industry. Even if attention is focused exclusively upon the location of new plants, the explanations offered in this chapter fail to take account either of the relationships with other businesses – whether competitors, suppliers, customers or unrelated operations – or of the connections between plants within the same large organization. These questions are considered in the next chapter.

Further reading

Greenhut, M. C. 1956: *Plant Location in Theory and Practice*. Chapel Hill, NC: University of North Carolina Press.

Schmenner, R. 1982: *Making Business Location Decisions*. Englewood Cliffs, NJ: Prentice-Hall.

Smith, D. M. 1981: *Industrial Location: an Economic Geographical Analysis*, 2nd edn, Chichester: Wiley.

Townroe, P. M. 1971: *Industrial Location Decisions*. University of Birmingham Centre for Urban and Regional Studies, Occasional Paper 15.

4
The Effect of Other Firms

Although the location decision can often be considered as a problem in which a firm faces an impersonal external environment, this is in fact a simplification. Much of the real environment consists of other firms, and each of these is pursuing a policy of its own. Decisions made by one firm can be critical to the success of another even when taken quite independently and without thought of the other. The choice of town A as a new motor vehicle assembly location over town B could mean the difference between prosperity and struggle to sheet steel producers located in the two towns. In practice, however, some policies are pursued with other firms in mind. Firms try to obtain an increasing market share, and the strategy frequently involves a locational procedure designed to restrict the impact of competitors in new markets. Again, they may choose a site because a major customer or supplier is located nearby or perhaps in anticipation that customers or suppliers will move to the area in the future. In this chapter we examine some of these locational interrelationships.

Scale economies and agglomeration

The distribution of industry is clustered rather than dispersed. This characteristic concentration of economic activity can be seen at a variety of geographical scales. At the urban scale, distinctive quarters associated with such activities as printing and publishing and the clothing trades may still occasionally be found within cities (see Scott, 1984; Steed, 1976a, 1976b, 1976c). In rather different situations, massive agglomerations of industries such as oil refining and petrochemicals have created the distinctive industrial landscapes of places such as the Houston Ship Channel and Rotterdam (Chapman, 1973). These concentrations suggest that the location of one plant or firm is, in some way, influenced by that of another. This possibility was recognized by Weber (1929, pp. 124-72), who made a distinction between what he called regional location factors such as labour and transport costs, influencing the broad patterns of industrial location, and agglomeration factors, which concern the scale of operations in a particular community. Weber argued that economies can be obtained by a plant either internally by growing, or externally by purchasing from other specialized businesses. He also recognized diseconomies of scale (deglomerative factors).

Weber's ideas were developed by Hoover (1937, pp. 89–111) who distinguished three types of agglomeration economies. The first was simply *scale economies* contributing to larger plants. Up to a point, almost all manufacturing operations can benefit from a larger scale of production. This is illustrated with reference to the petrochemical industry in chapter 8 (figure 8.5). Economies of scale at plant level are partly based upon technical and engineering factors. The laws of mathematics, for example, ensure that it does not require twice as much steel to double the capacity of a storage tank. Organizational advantages may also be gained in larger factories by capitalizing upon the possibility for specialization in machinery and personnel. Machines can concentrate on even smaller tasks if production is large enough, and both production and managerial workers can also concentrate on more specific jobs. The general manager of a small company can be replaced, for example, by finance, production, marketing and personnel managers. These scale economies are obtained within the plant as it expands.

Hoover's second category, however, allowed a similar specialization without large-scale plants. *Localization economies* allow independent small businesses to gain by locating near to each other. Thus, for example, a sequence of processes – such as rolling a metal, shaping it into semi-finished items or components, and manufacturing finished metal goods and/or machinery – can be in one plant, but if several plants locate near to each other the production process does not lose much by separation, and independence and flexibility are retained (see Walters and Wheeler, 1984). Various specialized services can be provided by other independent firms as long as the total demand is great enough. Moreover, the chance of building up a pool of local labour is at least as good as for a large-scale plant, and the possibility of spawning new innovation and entrepreneurs probably better. Specialized districts of related businesses were more common a century ago than they are now (Wise, 1949; Hall, 1962; Muller and Groves, 1979), but have remained for some sectors such as clothing. Small units allow enough flexibility to cope with sudden changes in demand, yet benefit from localization both in obtaining suitable labour (in this case female labour needs good public transit) and in marketing. Salesrooms in a concentrated area allow tradespeople to look at a variety of clothing quickly and anyone choosing to locate away from the main group is penalized (Mock, 1976). Moreover, new research-oriented industries show the same tendency to cluster near universities, research establishments and residential areas attractive to their skilled workforce (Dorfman, 1983; Saxenian, 1985). Here, communication linkages rather than the movement of goods are vital.

Hoover's third class of agglomeration economy embraces scale advantages that benefit an even wider group of businesses – indeed, potentially all businesses. These are *urbanization economies*. As manufacturing grows in a particular area, the business services improve in variety and quality, potential suppliers and buyers increase, the size and variety of the workforce expands – in fact, almost all factors required by a firm improve in one way or another. These advantages, however, relate not to only one sector of industry but to all. If general standards of education improve, everybody benefits. If more trucking companies expand the route network serving a city, every business benefits. Thus urbanization economies encourage sectoral diversity to a much greater degree than do localization economies.

Agglomeration is encouraged by responses to uncertainty in the business environment. Webber (1972, pp. 273–9) argues that uncertainty has the effect of limiting plant and firm size by reducing the willingness of capitalists to invest and expose themselves to the risk of large losses. With smaller scales of production, firms cannot so easily internalize services and therefore look to cities with good services (those with strong urbanization and localization economies). In addition, uncertainty increases with distance from suppliers and markets, and firms try to avoid this by moving close by, especially to markets. Large centres in general provide more security in conditions of uncertainty and this is closely related to the important question of new firm formation. The practical considerations influencing the entrepreneur's decision to set up in business were reviewed in chapter 3 and there is no doubt that various aspects of urbanization and localization economies make it easier to take this step in established centres of population and economic activity. Indeed the creation of an environment favourable to new firm formation is part of the wider role of such centres as the focus of innovation. Pred (1977) notes that they have highly developed information links with each other so that knowledge of both new technologies and markets passes between them much more quickly than it diffuses elsewhere. These issues associated with the nature and distribution of economic growth will be explored in more detail in subsequent chapters.

Weber's (1929) graphical approach to the analysis of agglomeration involves the use of critical isodapanes once more. In figure 4.1 three locational triangles are shown, indicating three locations for firms in the same industry. Each could either locate individually at P_1, P_2 and P_3 or they could locate together and gain agglomeration economies. The isodapanes round each point represent a critical isodapane for the increased costs of transport equal to agglomeration savings. In figure 4.1a these cross each other, giving a region in which all plants could locate together and benefit. In figure 4.1b, however, this is not the case, so separate locations would be more advantageous.

The point to notice about Weber's analysis is that everything depends on what other firms do. If, in fact, three firms are considering a site, it is no good if only two of them choose to locate together and the third remains aloof. This will not bring enough savings to make an agglomeration location pay. But how can a firm know in advance? In practice, the management of the first firm to choose an agglomeration site would be taking a chance on the others following. While this problem can be ignored if 'economic men' and perfect competition are assumed, it is highly relevant to sequential development paths. In practice, agglomeration economies are built up over time around existing industrial sites. Most firms look at what is already there as part of their site evaluation procedure rather than anticipating what might happen in the future (Isard, 1977, pp. 161–5).

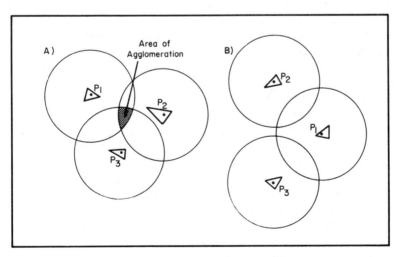

Figure 4.1 Weber's diagram of agglomeration opportunities
Source: Weber, 1929

Agglomeration economies tend to increase through time, but this process does not continue indefinitely. There are limits. At some stage, individual firms may see the advantages of dispersing to serve markets beyond the major urban centres. This demand-led dispersal may be reinforced by supply-side problems increasing the cost of the various factors of production. For example, as pressure upon available space increases, land costs rise, encouraging relocation to sites on the urban fringe (see chapter 12). Similarly, the labour market will reflect growing demand for labour and, often, increases in the cost of living. These problems, which have been termed deglomerative factors or diseconomies of scale, are well documented (see Hoover and Vernon, 1962; Kenyon, 1967; Lever, 1975) and their implications are demonstrated in the models of Hamer (1973). Faced with such difficulties, owners of capital, seeking to maximize the return on their investment, will tend to look to other areas for expansion. This process may be gradual, but it is not difficult to see how it may curtail and even reverse the growth of a previously successful region.

Linkage studies

It is important to make a clear distinction between industrial linkage and agglomeration. Linkages, both within and between firms, may encourage the geographical concentration (i.e. agglomeration) of interdependent activities; more often than not such activities are separated by considerable distances. Thus whilst linkage studies have certainly attempted to evaluate the role of linkages in promoting agglomeration, they have also had the broader objective of illustrating the way a firm or group of firms actually functions. This is a necessary complement to analyses of firm and plant attributes which describe an industrial structure (Bater and Walker, 1970; Hoare, 1985). The most obvious linkages, to material suppliers and to markets, provide a description of the Weberian transport problem. Service linkages, however, can also be very important (Bater and Walker, 1977) in providing ingredients vital to the proper functioning of a firm, whether it be to aid organization and administration, to keep the machinery or plant in good repair, or even to perform some subcontracted improvement to the product itself. Another linkage that has been distinguished is communication or information flows, which reflect contact systems and may be important in analysing both patterns of control and the dissemination of ideas (Wood, 1969; Tornquist, 1973).

Input–output analysis, focusing only on goods, is an important method of highlighting intersectoral relationships. In this technique, devised by

Leontief (1951), the objective is to assess the impact of change in one sector on the development of others. The basic data required come from a transactions table such as figure 4.2. These tables can be assembled most easily for a nation. Essentially, the table shows what happens to the outputs of the various producing sectors (rows) and indicates the inputs required by each sector (columns). The table is really a system of double-entry bookkeeping. Columns 1–6 represent payments for goods and services moving between the country's productive sectors, identified as industries A to F in rows 1–6; columns 7–11 show other purchases, referred to as final demand, including some that contribute to inventories and to private capital formation. Rows 7–11 indicate payments from non-productive sectors, including those in the form of inventory available from an earlier period, and depreciation, which represents a way of distributing capital costs over a longer period than the one year represented here. Although originally developed for a national economy, input–output tables have been produced for regions, and methods of interregional input–output analysis have been developed (Tiebout, 1957b; Isard, 1960, pp. 309–74; Miernyk, 1965).

From the transactions table, it is possible to work out technical coefficients for the processing sectors showing what they require from other sectors to produce a given unit of output. Clearly, the more detailed the industrial breakdown, the more valuable this exercise will be in understanding the intersectoral relationships. The purpose of input–output analysis is to use a transactions table for projection purposes, calculating the impact of a change in demand for the output of any sector upon the rest of the economic system. However input–output tables are only as good as the data contained within them and there is no proof that the coefficients are valid for long periods. At the national level, many developed countries do have regular business censuses which may provide the necessary raw data, but this is not regionally segregated. So, for example, it is not possible to regionally subdivide either the purchases or the sales of the firms in a given sector of a specific region. Thus, a ready-made input–output table of a small region is a rarity. Karaska (1969) was able to use such a table to analyse agglomeration in Philadelphia, but this was an exceptional opportunity.

To perform an effective study of this type, detailed information of inputs and outputs for each plant is required. The collection of data is beset with confidentiality problems as well as being time-consuming and expensive. Nevertheless, several linkage studies have been undertaken, often with the purpose of examining hypotheses concerning the strength of agglomeration. For example, Keeble (1969) showed that local linkage in north-west London was relatively weak. Even amongst smaller firms, over 50 per cent had no local linkage at all, although subcontracting

Industry purchasing

		Processing sector						Final demand					
	Output	(1) A	(2) B	(3) C	(4) D	(5) E	(6) F	(7) Gross inventory accumula- tion (+)	(8) Exports to foreign countries	(9) Government purchases	(10) Gross private capital formation	(11) Households	(12) Total gross output
Inputs													
(1) Industry A		10	15	1	2	5	6	2	5	1	3	14	64
(2) Industry B		5	4	7	1	3	8	1	6	3	4	17	59
(3) Industry C		7	2	8	1	5	3	2	3	1	3	5	40
(4) Industry D		11	1	2	8	6	4	0	0	1	2	4	39
(5) Industry E		4	0	1	14	3	2	1	2	1	3	9	40
(6) Industry F		2	6	7	6	2	6	2	4	2	1	8	46
(7) Gross inventory depletion (−)		1	2	1	0	2	1	0	1	0	0	0	8
(8) Imports		2	1	3	0	3	2	0	0	0	0	2	13
(9) Payments to government		2	3	2	2	1	2	3	2	1	2	12	32
(10) Depreciation allowances		1	2	1	0	1	0	0	0	0	0	0	5
(11) Households		19	23	7	5	9	12	1	0	8	0	1	85
(12) Total gross outlays		64	59	40	39	40	46	12	23	18	18	72	431

Processing sector / *Payments sector* — Industry producing

[a] Sales to industries and sectors along the top of the table from the industry listed in each row at the left of the table.
[b] Purchases from industries and sectors at the top left of the table by the industry listed at the top of each column.

Figure 4.2 Hypothetical transactions table
Source: Miernyk, 1965

arrangements played an important role in providing engineering firms with external economies in the area. In Hamilton, Ontario, the iron and steel mills were attracted by, and have been a significant attraction for, metal-using industries, and numerous service firms have complemented the metal-working complex (Bater and Walker, 1971). Linkage studies have shown significant clustering for other sectors too, especially clothing, printing (Hall, 1959, pp. 37–70; Hoover and Vernon, 1962; Mock, 1976; Steed, 1976a, 1976b, 1976c) and petrochemicals (Chapman, 1973).

Even where local goods linkages are strong, however, more distant ones predominate, suggesting that proximity to suppliers and customers is not a major concern for most firms (see Beyers, 1974; Erickson, 1974; Gilmour, 1974). Some external economies are, in any case, more mobile than others (Britton, 1969; Robinson, 1931, pp. 124–6) and mobility has been aided by the rise of the multiplant firm. Plants which are part of a larger operation are able to draw on head office for many services, and may do so to a greater extent in more distant, peripheral locations than would be the case in an established operating area (see Britton, 1976; Marshall, 1979). Thus they can to some extent overcome the problems associated with inadequate service provision in remote areas, despite the fact that service linkages have been shown to be very much more local than goods linkages (Britton, 1974; Bater and Walker, 1977). The real localizing effects of linkages would appear today to be a result primarily of services, including general community services that encourage a workforce to come to or to stay in an area. The new high-technology agglomerations of Silicon Valley or Boston, Massachusetts, rely on cultural and living environments plus high-quality educational and research institutions which will keep their researchers and executives happy.

It might be expected that goods linkages would reflect a distance bias by gradually falling off away from the plants as the costs of movement increase. Britton (1969) examined this hypothesis by means of a gravity model, but using only very generalized data based on the volume of freight from the Bristol region to other parts of England and Wales. He found reasonable support for the hypothesis that the size of the regional market and the distance to it explained the flow of goods. In a similar analysis based on plant-level data in Hamilton, Ontario, Bater and Walker (1974) also found some evidence for this. In this study, a group of fairly similar metal-fabricating and machinery plants were examined. For every plant, every supply point for each material was regarded as a link, and comparable data were found for each market point. The distance and scale (measured in terms of the volume and value of the annual flow of goods) of each linkage was measured. Explanations for the amount of goods moved were sought and, for the group as a whole, there was virtually no correlation with distance. Plant size was also correlated with linkage size, but the coefficients here were similarly low. Only when the group of plants was divided into foreign and Canadian-owned ones did the correlations become significant. In separate predictions for each subgroup, some good predictions of material linkage were obtained from linkage distance and plant size (floor space or employment). Market linkage predictions, however, were less satisfactory. Interestingly, in these multiple correlations, plant size affected Canadian linkages more than distance, whereas the two factors were of equal importance for foreign plants. The significance of organizational factors as influences upon linkage patterns in this Canadian study has also been demonstrated in other countries such as Israel (Razin, 1988).

Foreign ownership of a plant has many implications for development strategies which are related to the nature of linkages, especially the flow of information. This issue is considered in chapter 10 as it affects Third World countries. It is also relevant in developed economies where the extent and distribution of potential multiplier effects resulting from inward investment by foreign manufacturing firms is often of as much interest to policy-makers as the direct employment created by such projects. Several Japanese car-makers, for example, established assembly plants in North America and Western Europe in the late 1980s. Figure 4.3 indicates the location of input suppliers to Nissan's plant at Washington in north-east England. These suppliers are not only fairly widely distributed at a regional scale, but also include overseas sources. As far as the United Kingdom economy is concerned, it is obviously desirable that such imports are minimized and linkage patterns are often an important element in the negotiations between government agencies and potential foreign investors in major manufacturing facilities. The effect of ownership upon these patterns must be recognized in evaluating the overall impact of a new development such as a car plant. The local or regional effects of a branch from a centralized multinational will probably be less beneficial than from a decentralized one which allows local management to arrange much of its purchasing (see chapter 7).

Policy-makers must recognize that linkages have a temporal as well as a spatial dimension. Input–output methods generally assume that linkages are stable, but Le Heron and Schmidt (1976), following the work of Steed (1970) on the Northern Ireland linen complex, show that linkages are subject to continuous change over short periods. Hirschmann (1977) recognized that change also occurs over the long term, and a study by Weisskoff and Wolff (1977) adopted a historical approach at an aggregate, economy-wide level. Moore (1973) focused attention at the regional scale upon the Pacific north west. He considered the long-

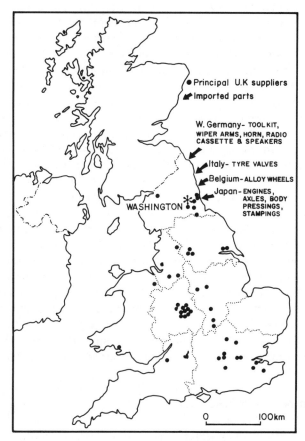

Figure 4.3 Input suppliers to car plant of Nissan UK, Washington, Co Durham, 1985
Source: Peck, 1988

term development paths of two complexes – metals and wood products – and indicated changing linkages of a structural, spatial and organizational character from the late nineteenth century until the 1970s. Unfortunately, few generalized conclusions can be drawn from his study as linkages depended on external economic factors (eg. demand for ships during the two world wars), on the particular location and resource base of the area (more favourable for wood than metal) and on an entrepreneurial corporate policy. If there is one general trend, it is the gradual drawing in of plants into an ever-wider spatial arrangement of production, involving specialization and longer-distance contacts.

Generalizations from linkage studies have been few and far between. This suggests that linkages only reflect other factors and conditions that are the explanatory variables in industrial location. Nevertheless, it is probably true to say that the connection between linkages and agglomeration is strongest for small firms; that is proximity to suppliers and markets is more likely to influence their choice of location or, more accurately, given the frequent absence of an explicit location decision in such firms (see chapter 3), their ability to survive in a particular place. Certainly, localization and urbanization economies (which include linkages) are an important positive element of the external environment of the small firm. At the other end of the spectrum, giant multinational companies create an organizational structure which effectively makes these economies internal to the firm. Linkages are important to such companies, but it is necessary to distinguish between those which are internal and those which are external to the organization. Many of the contemporary flows of materials and components transported by land, sea and air are actually between different parts of the same company (Ettlinger, 1984). These flows may take place over considerable distances and a growing proportion of international trade is accounted for by these intra-corporate transactions which are explained in more detail in chapter 7. The external linkages of such organizations are often equally widespread and, bearing in mind the growing economic importance of large corporations (see chapter 5), the connection between agglomeration and linkage is less direct in the modern economy with improved methods of transport and communication than it was in the past.

Locational interdependence

So far, the discusson has scarcely referred to the fact that every business has competition, that the behaviour of rivals may be an important part of the economic environment in which a firm operates, or that the market type can be influential for locational choice. These issues have admittedly not been central to industrial location theory, and they are not always central to locational choice either, but they are nevertheless important.

The market area approach to industrial location focuses on the division of an area into markets by rival firms, based on the transport costs of reaching the markets. The assumptions of this approach (see chapter 3) ensure that the emphasis is placed on the number of firms involved and their transport costs (Fetter, 1924; Lösch, 1954). The number of firms in a market governs the degree of profitability, because small numbers allow excess profits and excessively large market areas, until new entries come into the market (Lösch, 1954, pp. 109–10). Nevertheless, there is another variable in this situation, and that is the spatial pricing policy of the firms. Its significance is increased as soon as it is recognized that spatial patterns develop sequentially; there is no perfect locational arrangement reached through the simultaneous decisions of co-operating firms.

Take the case of a linear market with customers evenly spread along it and transport costs proportional to distance (figure 4.4a). The first firm A, wishing to serve the whole market, would clearly locate in the centre at O. Assume that the market is large enough for two plants without either making excess profits. What would happen if a rival B followed? If the new firm wished to compete for the whole market, it would be forced to locate with A at the centre of the market. This would not be very good for the customers, who would be better served by having A and B at the quartile location(s) Q_1 and Q_2. Still, if B were to choose an off-centre location, it would not be competitive in the whole market area (figure 4.4b), and would have to settle for a smaller scale of production. This, however, usually means higher costs per unit output, so that firm A would have a competitive edge, as seen by the height of PC_1 compared with PC_2 in figure 4.4b. This advantage, combined with the fact that A would have saved excess profits from its

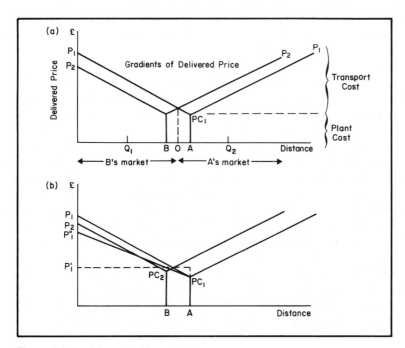

Figure 4.4 Spatial competition with dispersed demand

earlier operations, could lead A to press home its position by discriminatory pricing. This is commonly found and involves the subsidizing of distant customers by those near at hand. For example, the delivery price may be the same everywhere within a very large (P_1') area, or the actual increases per kilometre may be reduced (P_1''). Firm A, by taking some losses at first, could quickly drive B out of business unless B happened to be one plant of a well-capitalized company with the resources to fight unfair competition.

The solution favouring the customer – that is, an even spread of plants – is unlikely to happen because A will not be prepared to relocate and thus waste its invested capital in order to allow a rival into the market. Unfortunately, much of the discussion in the literature (Hotelling, 1929; Lerner and Singer, 1937; Lösch, 1954) fails to recognize this fact, and discusses relocation as though it were costless. In practice, many plants are used for at least a hundred years, and the main reason for continuous adaptation seems to be the reluctance to write off the previous investment. In the case of a rival being determined to share the whole market, then agglomeration will take place. This will be profitable until such time as subsections of the market grow to a sufficient size to allow plants to operate at the same scale as A, implying that the minimum plant size for efficient scale of production has failed to match the growth of demand for the product. Particularly if freight costs are high, this could then encourage production for submarkets, and O would lose its advantage.

The fact that space provides an element of monopoly to any location is an important principle elaborated by Greenhut (1974). Not only does it confer advantages on an initial location (Pred, 1965), but it makes perfect competition, as envisaged in early location theory, impossible. The limited number of good production sites plus the costs of overcoming the friction of distance, and the increasing size of many corporations, make firms in a given market area more and more aware of the behaviour of their rivals (Greenhut, 1974, pp. 32–43). The markets in a space economy are typically oligopolistic, and firms can often influence prices within a given market area. The activities of rivals are also highly relevant to locational choice, and the uncertainty referred to in chapter 3 partly results from not knowing what a key competitor will do in the future.

This has led a number of writers to propose the use of game theory to analyse locational problems. Greenhut (1956, p. 83) argues that the location of rivals is influential whenever firms sell over a wide market area rather than at specific points. Uncertainty is particularly great when production costs also vary significantly. Isard and Smith (1966; 1967; 1968) have used game theory to analyse both Weberian agglomeration and Hotelling's problem of locational interdependence, while Isard (1969) went on to base a very broad general theory on decision-making and game-theoretic formulations. Game theory applies to situations where there is competition between two people (firms, groups) and where the actions of one can have a significant impact on the well-being of the other. One person's strategy depends on his interpretation of what the other may do. A very simple case, analysed by Stevens (1961), is Hotelling's (1929) discussion of the location of two ice cream vendors on a beach.

With realistic transport costs and a fall of demand with increased costs, producers may benefit by selecting separate locations in order to capitalize on centrality to only a part of the market. This tendency to dispersal is offset by the possibility that a central location may benefit from agglomeration economies, as a result, for example, of cheaper wholesale prices. Then, sellers would purchase products at the centre, the reduced cost would help them to increase sales, and it may even be worth while to co-operate to gain agglomeration savings (Isard and Smith, 1967). In today's world, where many sectors in a country are dominated by a few major corporations, it is increasingly likely that the expected behaviour of other companies is a major influence on a firm's locational decision. It must be remembered as well that spatial competition (or the geographical division of a market amongst firms) is not the only or even the most important form of competition. Quite frequently a small number of businesses compete with each other in a given market area on the basis of quality, service and product differentiation as well as price. Thus, market conditions take the form of an oligopoly and reactions to competitors will only occasionally be spatial. Spatial competition does come to the fore in connection with expansion of markets or considerations of developing branch plants to capture new markets (chapter 6).

There is an important relationship between the spatial scale of marketing and the size of businesses. As noted earlier, the element of space gives every firm some degree of spatial monopoly. With the improvements in transport and the increase in business size after the Industrial Revolution, this frequently translated itself into regional oligopolies; by the early twentieth century the national market was oligopolistic in some sectors. Most commonly, these sectors were characterized by large-scale, high-capital costs and high failure rates. With the growth of mass production and even larger companies, it was inevitable that oligopolistic conditions would come to characterize some world markets. So the behaviour has not changed very much over the centuries, but the geographical scale has. Scholars are realizing that some companies are leaders, trying not only new ideas but also new geographical markets, while others react to protect themselves. As Knickerbocker (1973, p. 1) puts it, oligopolistic reaction is 'an interactive kind of corporate behaviour by which rival firms in an industry composed of a few large firms counter one another's moves by making similar moves themselves'.

Several studies have examined the impact of this kind of behaviour upon the spread of the production facilities of multinational companies (see Rees, 1978a; Gwynne, 1979; Laulajainen, 1981). Rees (1978a) described the tendency for the major tyre manufacturing companies such as Goodyear and Firestone to imitate one another in establishing production facilities within specific national markets. Thus whilst the decision to invest in a particular country may be delayed, the first company to do so seems to have been rapidly followed by its rivals, almost regardless of the size of the market. Rees (1978a) refers to the case of Chile in which this type of behaviour resulted in the establishment of several similar plants to serve a relatively small market. Gwynne (1979) further developed some of the ideas explored by Rees and drew attention to the practical difficulties in studying oligopolistic reaction, emphasizing that data limitations may provide misleading impressions of corporate behaviour.

Data problems are even more acute in the case of situations where companies decide that cooperation will serve their respective interests better than competition. Such cooperation finds expression in price-fixing and market-sharing agreements. This kind of behaviour has long been of interest and concern to economists and governments. It is also relevant to geographers to the extent that it may influence the spatial distribution of investments within an industry and may therefore be regarded as a special case of locational interdependence. By allocating markets amongst themselves upon a geographical basis, colluding firms often avoid the kind of uncertainties implicit in figure 4.4 and this is reflected in the distribution of their respective facilities. Watts (1980a) provides examples in industries as diverse as meat-packing, brewing and sugar-beet processing.

Conclusion

The location of an individual plant cannot be considered in isolation, and its success may be closely related to locational decisions primarily concerned with other operations. Both costs and revenues may be affected by these decisions. Interrelationships between a wide range of economic activities, including service as well as manufacturing operations, contribute to the development of agglomerations which seem to offer important cost advantages to individual plants and to firms located within them. On the revenue side, the strategies of competitors can clearly affect the level of sales. While a firm can often reduce the complexities of the locational problem by making assumptions about the spatial behaviour of other businesses, it takes a great risk if it ignores them altogether.

The discussion in this chapter has followed the pattern of traditional location theory in assuming that the question of location relative to other plants is a problem which is part of the external environment of the firm. This is not always the case and the development of multiplant businesses may be regarded as a way of reducing uncertainty in general and competition in particular. Certainly, many mergers and takeovers are motivated by such considerations (see chapter 5). The growth of these companies has ensured that a substantial proportion of industrial plants are themselves individual elements within larger corporate structures composed of many such plants. In these circumstances, the spatial distribution of its existing facilities will exert an important influence upon the company's choice of location for a new plant. Such issues are considered in the next part of the book, which also reviews the nature and contemporary significance of multiplant enterprises.

Further reading

Gough, P. 1984: Location theory and the multiplant firm: a framework for empirical studies. *Canadian Geographer*, 28, 127–41.

Harrison, R. T., Bull, P. J. and Hart, M. 1979: Space and time in industrial linkage studies. *Area*, 11, 333–8.

Hoare, A. G. 1985: Industrial linkage studies. In M. Pacione (ed.), *Progress in Industrial Geography*, London: Croom Helm, 40–81.

Muller, E. K. and Groves, P. A. 1979: The emergence of industrial districts in mid-nineteenth-century Baltimore. *Geographical Review*, 69, 159–78.

Mulligan, G. J. 1984: Agglomeration and central place theory: a review of the literature. *International Regional Science Review*, 9, 1–42.

Part III
Enterprises and Industries

In part II the emphasis was placed upon explaining the location of individual manufacturing establishments with reference to the influence of the various factors of production and the distribution of customers, suppliers and competitors. Implicit in much of the discussion was the assumption that the unit of production (the factory) and the unit of organization (the firm) were combined in the form of the single-plant firm. However, the individual firm may itself be part of a larger organizational structure which constitutes an *enterprise*. Large corporations usually own, or have a controlling interest in, a multiplicity of firms which may themselves have facilities in many locations. The next three chapters outline the growing economic importance of such corporations and the relevance of their rise for the spatial distribution of manufacturing activity.

5

The Rise of the Large Industrial Enterprise

All of the world's giant industrial enterprises started from very small beginnings, as reference to numerous business histories will testify (see Nevins and Hill, 1954, 1957, 1963; Reader, 1970, 1975; Taylor and Sudnik, 1984; Wilson, 1954, 1968). For example, the Anglo-Persian Oil Company was formed in 1909 on the basis of a single major discovery after many years of exploration inspired by the enthusiasm of one man with a belief in the oil prospects of the country now known as Iran (Ferrier, 1982). This venture has since developed into British Petroleum plc which, in 1988, was the world's seventh largest industrial enterprise (in terms of the value of sales), involved not only in the production, processing and distribution of petroleum and petroleum products on a global scale, but also with diverse interests in industries such as chemicals, mining, agricultural products and information technology. It has already been noted in chapter 2 that the growth of such organizations has contributed to the emergence of a distinctive geography of enterprise which acknowledges their enormous significance in shaping the contemporary spatial distribution of economic activities. Before demonstrating this significance, it is desirable to examine some of the background to the rise of the kind of business organization epitomized by British Petroleum. This chapter describes this trend and identifies some of the factors which are responsible for it.

Trends in industrial organization

It is difficult to establish any single universally acceptable measure of corporate size (see Shalit and Sankar, 1977). Various indices have been used, but all have their limitations. Perhaps the most satisfactory single measure of firm or enterprise size involves calculating net output, which is essentially an indication of the value of the work carried out by the organization over a specified period (usually a year). Unfortunately, most international comparisons rely upon data derived from company accounts and annual reports which rarely include estimates of net output. The most readily available measures are indicated in table 5.1 which gives the rank positions in 1988 of 25 of the largest 1000 industrial corporations with reference to the value of annual sales, the value of assets, and the numbers employed. The principal measure in table 5.1 is the value of corporate sales, although this tends to exaggerate the importance of firms, such as the oil companies, which are heavily involved in distribution rather than manufacturing. The value of assets correlates closely with sales, but variations in accounting practices make it unreliable for comparative purposes. Rankings on the basis of numbers employed diverge significantly from the financial indicators, mainly because of differing ratios of capital to labour in the various industries. For example, despite worldwide sales valued at just over one-third of those of Exxon in 1988, the Dutch company Philips employed more than three times as many people. Whatever the technical difficulties involved in making comparisons between companies, however, there can be no question that the enterprises in table 5.1 are large by any absolute standard. All of them have annual sales which exceed the value of the gross national products of many nation states and several of them employ the equivalent, in population terms, of a major city.

Table 5.1 suggests that the largest enterprises are associated with particular sectors such as the oil, motor vehicle and electronics industries, and with particular countries, notably in the core economies of the United States, Western Europe and Japan. However, by providing data for a specific year, the table fails to identify changes in these sectoral associations and geographical origins. Such changes themselves reflect wider circumstances influencing the growth and decline of industries and the development of economies. At the end of the First World War, for example, the largest firms were found in industries such as food, textiles and primary metals and the United Kingdom and Germany were strongly represented in this group (see Chandler, 1986; Dunning, 1988, pp. 71–119). However, the United States was firmly established as the dominant economic power in the aftermath of the Second World War, so that by the 1960s there was growing concern in Western Europe regarding the pervasive influence of US companies (see Servan–Schreiber, 1968). Although the United States retains a powerful leading position in the league table of giant industrial corporations, the extent of its domination has steadily fallen and is reflected in the decline in the share

Table 5.1 The world's largest industrial corporations,[a] 1988

Company	Country	Principal activities	Rank (in top 1000) by		
			Sales (value)	Assets (value)	Employees (number)
General Motors	US	Motor vehicles	1	1	1
Royal Dutch/ Shell Group	Netherlands/ UK	Petroleum	2	2	35
Exxon	US	Petroleum	3	3	66
Ford Motor	US	Motor vehicles	4	6	6
International Business Machines	US	Computers	5	4	4
Mobil	US	Petroleum	6	8	48
British Petroleum	UK	Petroleum	7	5	43
Toyota Motor	Japan	Motor vehicles	8	16	78
IRI[b]	Italy	Metals	9	n.a.	3
General Electric	US	Electronics	10	10	10
Daimler–Benz	W. Germany	Motor vehicles	11	19	8
Texaco	US	Petroleum	12	15	138
American Telephone and Telegraph	US	Electronics	13	11	9
E.I. du Pont de Nemours	US	Chemicals	14	22	33
Volkswagen	W. Germany	Motor vehicles	15	23	13
Hitachi	Japan	Electronics	16	12	24
Fiat	Italy	Motor vehicles	17	9	12
Siemens	W. Germany	Electronics	18	18	5
Matsushita Electric Industrial	Japan	Electronics	19	21	36
Unilever	UK/ Netherlands	Food	20	42	11
Chrysler	US	Motor vehicles	21	32	44
Philips' Gloeilampen fabrieken	Netherlands	Electronics	22	24	7
Chevron	US	Petroleum	23	14	132
Nissan Motor	Japan	Motor vehicles	24	26	61
Renault[b]	France	Motor vehicles	25	39	18

[a] With more than 50 per cent of sales from manufacturing and/or mining.
[b] State-owned.
Source: Compiled from data in *Fortune* 25 April 1988 and 1 August 1988

of American corporations of the total value of worldwide sales by the top 200 from 72.7 per cent in 1960 to 43.4 per cent in 1988 (calculated from *Fortune* listings). This decline has been matched by the entry and increasing significance of companies from other countries into this 'big league'. European multinationals have generally maintained their collective position, but Japanese economies in particular have assumed a more prominent position in the global market during the last quarter century. Samples of the world's largest industrial corporations taken by Dunning and Pearce (1985, p. 50) for successive time periods reveal an increase in the share of Japanese companies from 3.6 to 12.8 per cent of total sales between 1962 and 1982. The same source indicates that companies based in countries outside the core economies of Western Europe, the United States and Japan increased their share from 2.1 to 7.5 per cent over the same period. Indeed there is clearly a link between the emergence of large industrial corporations and the development of their respective national economies. Newly industrializing countries such as South Korea, Mexico and Brazil already have giant corporations of their own and the overall significance of these Third World multinationals seems likely to grow in the future (Lall, 1983).

Whatever changes may have occurred in the positions of individual enterprises at the very top of the corporate league table, the significance of large firms in general is best demonstrated by expressing their absolute size relative to the sectors or economies in which they are involved. Economists have devised various indices to address this problem. The most frequently used is the K-firm concentration ratio, which measures economic importance in terms of market power. K is an arbitrary integer (usually between 3 and 8), and the proportion of the market served by the K-largest firms is expressed as a percentage of total sales in that market. If, for example, the five largest enterprises accounted for 65 per cent of the total value of sales of ball-bearings within the UK in a given year and 80 per cent ten years later, then the difference between the two values provides a direct measure of the increasing collective importance of these enterprises. This importance is expressed relative to a particular market, which is defined in terms of both a specific product and a geographical unit. This hypothetical case is an example of an *industry concentration ratio*. However, most of the largest industrial enterprises manufacture a wide range of products and their activities extend across many sectors of the economy. Thus an enterprise which has a relatively small impact within any single sector may exert a powerful influence upon the economy as a whole. This situation may be represented by the calculation of an *aggregate concentration ratio*, which indicates the percentage share of national manufacturing net output or sales accounted for by the K-largest (usually the top 100) enterprises.

Concentration ratios for selected industries in the UK and US are indicated in table 5.2. The data are broadly comparable despite differences in the national census definitions of the various industries. There is clearly a systematic variation between sectors in the importance of large enterprises. These differences reflect the ease or difficulty with which a new firm may enter a particular industry, which is in turn related to the technology of the industry. The capital requirements involved in motor vehicle manufacture are obviously of a different order of magnitude to those needed to establish a sawmilling operation. Furthermore, there has been a tendency in many industries for the optimal size of the individual production unit to increase as economies of scale have become more important. This has favoured the larger enterprises and made it more difficult for small firms to compete. These technical barriers to entry in many industries are often reinforced by other factors. Advertising, for example, is often regarded as a barrier because of the consumer loyalty which it generates and the expense involved. It is not difficult to appreciate the problems facing a new car manufacturer with limited financial resources in projecting its product in a market dominated by relatively few established firms.

Table 5.2 Concentration in selected industries in United Kingdom (1986) and United States (1982)

Industry	UK (1986) % value of net output[a] (5 largest enterprises)	US (1982) % value of total shipments	
		(4 largest enterprises)	(8 largest enterprises)
Motor vehicles	92	92	97
Iron and steel	86	42	64
Oil refining	71	28	48
Bread, biscuits, cake etc.	54	34	47
Agricultural machinery	52	53	62
Pharmaceuticals	46	26	42
Soft drinks	37	14	23
Printing and publishing	20	7	10
Sawmilling, planing, etc. of wood	19	17	23

[a] Net output is the value of total sales and work done less the cost of purchases, industrial services received and, where applicable, duties etc.

Sources: UK: UK Business Statistics Office. *Report on the Census of Production 1986*. London: HMSO. US: US Bureau of the Census. *Statistical Abstract of the United States: 1987*. Washington DC: US Bureau of the Census.

Although the most obvious pattern in table 5.2 lies in the difference between the rows, there is also a systematic variation between the columns representing the two countries. Direct comparison is made more difficult because the UK data indicate the five-firm concentration ratio whilst K takes values of 4 and 8 in US official statistics. Nevertheless, it is clear that industry concentration ratios tend to be significantly higher in the UK than in the US. It has been suggested that this is partly due to differences in the size of the respective national markets, although the impact of US anti-trust legislation designed to limit the power of large enterprises is probably a more significant explanatory factor. Table 5.2 tells us nothing about changes in industry concentration. Numerous studies have attempted to monitor such changes, especially since the end of the Second World War, not only in the UK and US but also in other Western economies (see George and Ward, 1975; Caves and Porter, 1980; Hart and Clarke, 1980). Despite differences in detail, the trends have been remarkably uniform. Generally speaking, industry concentration increased during the 1950s and 1960s but stabilized in the 1970s and 1980s.

Although trends at the industry level are important, there is ample evidence that the largest enterprises owe their rapid growth and absolute size to strategies of diversification (see Utton, 1979). In these circumstances, aggregate concentration is a more appropriate measure of corporate power than industry concentration. Nevertheless, the technical problems involved in deriving such a measure are formidable, especially when attention is focused on changes through time and upon comparisons between countries. Considerable manipulation of raw census data was carried out by Prais (1976) to assemble the information presented in figure 5.1, which plots the contribution of the 100 largest enterprises to manufacturing net output in the UK and US since 1910. Despite these efforts, the value of the graph as a measure of aggregate concentration is limited by its exclusive concern with manufacturing. Most of the largest business organizations are involved not only in manufacturing but also in other sectors of the economy such as mining and retailing. The truest indication of their influence is, therefore, provided by measuring aggregate concentration relative to the economy as a whole rather than the manufacturing sector alone. Despite this qualification, figure 5.1 remains a useful summary of the changing role of large industrial enterprises in the two countries. As with concentration in individual industries, aggregate concentration in manufacturing displayed a marked increase in the 1950s and 1960s (especially in the UK), but has since levelled off or even declined slightly (see United Kingdom, HMSO, 1978; White, 1981; Clarke and Davies, 1983). The apparent recent reversal of the long-established trend represented in figure 5.1 should not, however, be regarded as a portent of a major change in the scale of economic organization, since it does not take account of the fact that many of the largest manufacturing companies have been rapidly expanding into non-manufacturing activities (Hughes and Kumar, 1984). Although figure 5.1 relates to the UK and US, prevailing levels of aggregate concentration in these countries approximately define the range typical of most developed Western economies; the corresponding values for EEC nations other than the UK lies somewhere between the two (see Locksley and Ward, 1979; Fishwick, 1982), while Australia (Taylor, 1984) and Canada (Canada, Royal Commission on Corporate Concentration, 1978) are closer to the UK.

Industry and aggregate concentration ratios are usually calculated from census data and therefore relate to national economies. However, the ultimate form of the large industrial enterprise is the multinational corporation which, by definition, operates in many countries. Dunning and Pearce (1981) have derived concentration ratios which express the power of these organizations relative to the world economy. For example, the top three enterprises involved in the manufacture of office equipment and computers accounted for over 60 per cent of the worldwide sales (by value) in 1977 of the 20 largest corporations engaged in this industry (Dunning and Pearce, 1981, p. 64). IBM alone had sales more than five times greater than those of the second-ranked corporation in this sector. A measure of aggregate concentration at the global scale has been given as the proportion of all sales of almost 500 of the world's largest

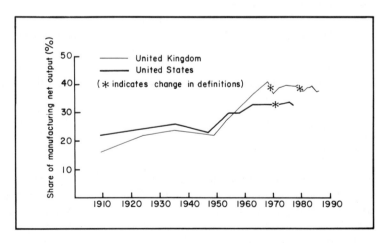

Figure 5.1 Share of the 100 largest enterprises in manufacturing net output in United Kingdom and United States
Source: Prais, 1976

industrial enterprises accounted for by the top 25 members of this group. In 1977, this percentage was just over 30 (Dunning and Pearce, 1981, p. 70). Despite their obvious limitations, such calculations emphasize the global dimension of the activities of large enterprises which is itself an important element of their economic power.

Economic power is, in many ways, even more narrowly based than aggregate statistics indicate. Effective ownership and control of major corporations often lies with complex constellations of interests, including institutional shareholders such as pension funds and banks. Although such arrangements are very different from the personal possession epitomized by family firms, a relatively limited number of wealthy individuals continue to wield considerable power and influence within the capitalist system (see Scott, 1979). What Clement (1975) has described in a Canadian context as 'the corporate elite' represents the faces behind the anonymous exteriors presented by many of the world's major corporations. Whilst these essentially sociological perspectives on the internal structure of corporate capitalism are not universally accepted (see Galbraith, 1967), there can be no doubting the significance of this form of economic organization. Despite the fact that both aggregate and industry concentration ratios have changed little in most economies in recent years, it is clear that giant corporations have a dominating position whatever criterion of importance or size is used and whatever the scale at which the phenomenon is viewed. In the UK, for example, the top 100 (on the basis of net output) of the more than 130,000 enterprises engaged in manufacturing in 1986 accounted for 31.1 per cent of employment, 38.3 per cent of net output and 38.7 per cent of gross value added in this sector (United Kingdom, Business Statistics Office, 1988). The impact of the actions of these corporations upon national economic policy and upon the distribution of industry is obviously out of all proportion to their numerical significance. Before considering the specifically geographical implications of their activities, it is desirable to understand the reasons for their growth.

Dynamics of corporate growth

In accounting for the dominating position of large enterprises within the modern economy, it is important to make a distinction between factors that promote the growth of individual firms and those that promote industrial concentration. The latter process implies that larger firms grow at the expense of others, thereby changing the size distribution of firms within a sectoral or geographical unit. There is no doubt that such a change has taken place within developed economies in which the differentiation between large and small firms has become more pronounced, creating a distinction between what Averitt (1968) has termed core and periphery firms. The *core* firms are the large business organizations which represent the nucleus of the economy and account for a major proportion of its production and profit-making potential. The *periphery* firms include a multitude of small- and medium-sized organizations. Although this dichotomy is an over-simplification and the constellation of peripheral firms is itself subdivided into various 'segments' (see Taylor and Thrift, 1983a), Averitt's concept remains valid, not least because of the contrast between the essentially monopolistic and oligopolistic structure of markets within the core and the fragmented business environment of the periphery. This contrast ensures that whereas the core firm can exercise considerable control over the economic environment in which it operates, the periphery firm is essentially responsive in its behaviour.

In addition to the contrasts between core and periphery which reflect the differing internal characteristics of these segments of the economy, the relationship between them is an equally significant element of Averitt's concept. The relationship is basically one of dominance and dependence, as reflected in franchising and subcontracting arrangements. The terms of such arrangements are dictated by the core firms. For example, IBM purchases various components for its computer manufacturing operations in the US from a wide range of apparently independent small firms. However, IBM is, through its purchasing policies, able to 'make or break' its suppliers and even to dictate their location by insisting that they must lie within a specified distance of IBM's own manufacturing facilities (Susman and Schutz, 1983). This type of situation is not unusual (see Fredriksson and Lindmark, 1979; Johnson and Cathcart, 1979), and it emphasizes the fact that the significance of core enterprises is often much greater than is implied by industry and aggregate concentration ratios, which fail to take account of the 'explicitly unequal power relationships between business organis-ations' (Taylor and Thrift, 1982b, p. 1602).

The notion of a dual economy conflicts with traditional thinking in economics, which visualized an 'optimum' firm size defined with reference to both engineering factors related to the technology of production, and organizational considerations associated with the practice of management (see Devine et al., 1976). The notion of an optimum size suggests that there is an upper limit beyond which further growth is undesirable, but this is contradicted by the continued expansion – albeit in many cases with more decentralized systems of management and control – of relatively few core enterprises and by the fact that the majority of firms remain peripheral in Averitt's terminology. In these circumstances, the concept of 'optimum' size has largely been abandoned, and economists have focused their attention less upon defining absolute limits to growth and more upon identifying constraints to the *rate* of growth.

Downie (1958) equates growth with efficiency, which in turn rests upon technology-based competitive advantages. The possession of superior processes and/or products enables certain firms to establish an initial lead over their competitors which provides the basis for further growth. Research and development (R & D) plays an important part in maintaining such a lead, and individual enterprises go to considerable lengths to protect the results of these activities because such proprietary information is perceived to be crucial to long-term corporate growth (Thomas, 1980, 1981a).

The general relationship between innovative activity and the growth of firms is easy to appreciate on an intuitive level, but difficult to demonstrate. However, the role of technology is easier to see when attention is focused on trends in the size of individual production units. For any manufacturing process, it is possible to define a minimum efficient size of plant. Although the size of this plant has increased in most industries, there are wide variations in the ratio of plant size to market capacity. In the case of certain chemical products, for example, the optimum size of plant from an engineering and cost point of view may have the capacity to meet the needs of markets on a continental scale (Fayad and Motamen, 1986). In these circumstances, the technology of production inevitably results in the domination of particular sectors, especially those associated with the manufacture of capital goods (see Lyons, 1980), by a handful of firms.

What Galbraith (1967) has termed 'the imperative of technology' as reflected in the financial requirements imposed by heavy research and development (R & D) budgets and need to invest in massive production units, explains why large firms are associated with particular industries but not why they have come to dominate the economy as a whole. Whilst the origin of many of the largest enterprises may be traced to certain sectors in which there is a link between technical and organizational scale, such firms frequently maintain high growth rates only by diversifying into other sectors. Such diversification may be regarded as a 'natural' process resulting from attempts to fully utilize the existing managerial resources of the firm. Penrose (1959, p. 85) expresses this view in the following terms: 'Unused productive services are, for the enterprising firm, at the same time a challenge to innovate, an incentive to expand, and a source of competitive advantage. They facilitate the introduction of new combinations of resources – innovation – within the firm.' Thus diversification is the normal approach to corporate growth.

Williamson (1981) argues that the direction of diversification is not random and that the initial stages in the growth of most corporations are associated with strategies of vertical integration as attempts are made to secure control of both suppliers and markets. Essentially, the firm seeks to internalize transactions that were previously regulated by markets, leading to the creation of a managed economic system under the control of a single organization. The motives underlying such a policy of corporate growth are both economic and strategic. *Economies of scope*, for example, are obtained when it is more efficient to carry out two or more activities in conjunction rather than in isolation. These benefits of size are distinct from economies of scale which apply to individual activities at plant level. Williamson (1981) stresses the significance of managerial innovations, notably the development of the multidivisional form of organization, in improving the efficiency of very large enterprises. Such innovations, it is argued, allow the large diversified corporation to act like a mini capital market, channelling funds from low- to high-profit areas more quickly than would occur in an economic system composed of many small firms. From the point of view of the growing enterprise, however, such considerations are probably less important than the opportunity to minimize the uncertainties associated with reliance upon external suppliers and markets. The alternative strategy of corporate growth through horizontal integration, in which the enterprise seeks to increase its share of the market for a particular product at the expense of its competitors, is also frequently motivated by a desire to reduce uncertainty. This is a common thread running through much of the economic literature concerned with the growth of the firm, although it is most explicitly developed in the work of Cyert and March (1963).

Cyert and March regard growth itself as the principal goal motivating the actions of management. Thus corporate growth is perceived as a cumulative and self-perpetuating process, but the proposition that all firms have the potential to develop into global corporations is unconvincing. There are many obstacles to such a growth path (see Taylor and Thrift, 1982c, 1983a). Large corporate size endows power and leverage which is especially significant in the raising of capital to finance further growth. The cost of capital is inversely related to firm size; small firms must rely on bank loans with relatively high interest rates and stringent repayment terms, whereas larger companies have access to a wider range of alternatives which offer 'easier' money (Taylor and Thrift, 1983b). This situation has led to the emergence of 'finance gaps' which face firms seeking to make successive transitions from a small regional base to larger national organizations and then to multinational and ultimately global operations. It has been argued that, when viewed in a historical perspective, these gaps have become wider and that the chances of a small firm developing into a large enterprise are much less today than they were a hundred years ago (Taylor and Thrift, 1982c), although the relatively recent emergence of such organizations as IBM and Hewlett–Packard emphasizes that opportunities for spectacular growth may still arise in new and dynamic sectors. Nevertheless, the possibility of significant changes in the existing structure of the dual economy seems to have diminished through time, not least because successful periphery firms can easily be taken over by those which have already secured their position in the core.

Although much has been written about the conflicting interests and objectives of large industrial enterprises and democratically elected governments (see Vernon, 1978; Watts, 1980b), no review of the factors encouraging the growth of such organizations would be complete without reference to the role of the state in promoting their position within the economy. Galbraith (1967, pp. 300–301) maintains that 'the industrial system is . . . inextricably associated with the state' and that 'the line between public and private authority is indistinct and in large measure imaginary'. His observations are based upon trends in the US, which is usually regarded as the firmest bastion of capitalism, but they are equally appropriate to all Western economies. In many countries, state-owned corporations are frequently amongst the largest industrial enterprises (Anastassopoulos et al., 1987). This is certainly true of France and Italy, for example, where two of the top three are effectively nationalized in both countries. The influence of governments upon industrial structure is not restricted to direct intervention in the form of public ownership. Thus attempts have been made to encourage mergers of smaller firms in particular sectors in the hope of creating larger units capable of serving as national 'flagship' firms in world markets. For example the British government, through its Industrial Reorganization Corporation which operated between 1966 and 1971, played an important role in the creation of International Computers Ltd (ICL) in 1968. This company resulted from the merger of the three existing British manufacturers of computing equipment, and the state acted as midwife at the birth in the hope that ICL would be better able to face the challenge posed by foreign, especially US, firms (Stoneman, 1978). A similar policy was pursued by the Japanese government. The Japanese Electronic Computer Company was created by the state-sponsored merger of several established firms and played an important role in the early development of Japanese technology in this area during the 1960s (Ballance, 1987, p. 274). Governments may also encourage the creation of larger corporate units during periods of economic crisis within mature or declining industries (see chapter 8). In addition to the direct involvement of the state in promoting the growth of large enterprises, governments often reinforce the position of such organizations within national economies in less obvious ways. European governments have, for example, effectively competed against one another by offering subsidies and grants to corporations such as Ford, General Motors and ICI to encourage them to establish manufacturing facilities within their own national territories (see Sinclair and Walker, 1982; Ward, 1982; Hudson, 1983). Equivalent inducements are not available to small firms, and this type of behaviour by governments therefore discriminates in favour of the largest enterprises.

Conclusion

It is evident that many factors have contributed to a steady increase in both the absolute size and, until recently, the relative significance of large business organizations within the manufacturing sector of Western economies. However, these organizations are by no means homogeneous in size or structure. Figure 5.2 provides a framework for classifying them in terms of the diversity and geographical extent of their activities. There is clearly a major difference between multiregional firms which have secured a powerful position within a specific industrial sector in a particular country, and the opposite end of the scale/diversity spectrum represented by such global conglomerates as General Electric and Unilever. Furthermore, the distinction between multinational and global enterprises is more fundamental than figure 5.2 implies. A multinational enterprise does not suddenly become global when it has established manufacturing plants within a threshold number of countries. Multinational operations may be regarded as a series of largely independent activities in which a firm seeks to meet the requirements of national markets by local production. Functional relationships between these operations are, therefore, limited, but the allocation of resources is ultimately determined at head office. A global corporation organizes its activities on a worldwide basis so that its competitive position in one country is affected by its operations in other countries. Strategic decisions are retained at the core and the future development of the entire corporation is planned as an integrated whole regardless of international frontiers (see Dunning, 1974; Channon and Jalland, 1978). Despite the limitations of the typology employed in figure 5.2, the heterogeneous organizations which it represents share two unifying characteristics that

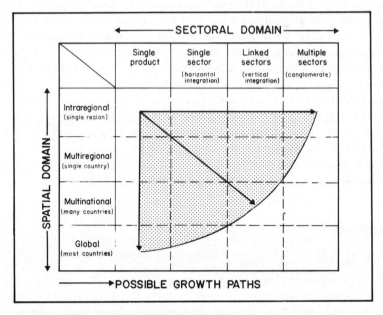

Figure 5.2 A typology of large business organizations

together make it meaningful to describe 'the large (industrial) enterprise as an area-organizing institution' (Hayter and Watts, 1983, p. 157). First, they all operate facilities at more than one location. Second, these facilities are component parts of a more or less integrated corporate system which ensures that the location and function of individual establishments can only be explained within the context of the organization as a whole.

We have already seen in chapter 2 how the emergence of corporate forms of industrial organization undermined the validity of normative location theory with its focus upon the single-plant entrepreneur. Considerable effort has been made to come to terms with this situation, and this is reflected in the literature in attempts to understand the role of the large industrial enterprise as an influence upon the changing geography of manufacturing and, therefore, upon spatial patterns of economic development and social welfare. Despite the lack of any clearly established framework specific to the 'geography of enterprise', it is possible to identify three themes within this largely empirical body of literature. First, efforts have been made to analyse the role of spatial factors in the growth of multiplant enterprises. Second, many studies have attempted to describe and explain patterns in the spatial structure of established firms. Third, the static or declining level of manufacturing employment in most developed economies has recently inspired efforts to identify the role of such firms in the process of deindustrialization by focusing upon the strategies of rationalization and contraction which induce locational adjustments within the corporate system. It is important to stress the interrelationships between these different aspects of the 'geography of enterprise'. The spatial structure of large industrial organizations is in a constant state of flux; processes of growth and decline may be occurring simultaneously, with factory closures taking place in one part of the corporate system at the same time that new investments are being made elsewhere. These issues are explored in the next two chapters, which adopt a spatial perspective on the growth (chapter 6) and internal structure (chapter 7) of corporate systems.

Further reading

Chandler, A.D. 1977: *The Visible Hand: the Managerial Revolution in American Business*. Cambridge, Mass.: Harvard University Press.
Hannah, L. 1983: *The Rise of the Corporate Economy*, 2nd edition, London: Methuen.
Wilkins, M. 1986: The history of the European multinationals: a new look. *The Journal of European Economic History*, 15, 483–510.

6
Spatial Aspects of Corporate Growth

The growth of large industrial enterprises was considered in general, macro-economic terms in the preceding chapter. Emphasis was placed upon the position of such enterprises relative to smaller firms and upon the basic forces responsible for the emergence of large forms of industrial organization. This chapter transfers the focus of attention away from the question of why firms grow to the issue of how they grow, with particular reference to the role of spatial factors upon the nature and direction of growth at the level of the individual enterprise.

Strategies and methods of corporate growth

A distinction may be drawn between *strategies* and *methods* of corporate growth. The former are concerned with the direction of expansion and the latter with the mechanism by which growth is achieved (figure 6.1). Although the two concepts are inextricably linked, the choice of strategy takes logical precedence since the growth path of the enterprise relative to its initial association with a particular type or sector of manufacturing activity is determined by this decision. *Integration* implies that corporate development follows a sequence which represents a 'natural' extension of the firm's existing activities, whilst growth through *diversification* occurs as a result of involvement in a progressively wider range of apparently unrelated sectors of the economy. This distinction seems unambiguous, but it is not always so self-evident when the nature of integration and diversification are examined in more detail.

The logical basis for integration varies and figure 6.1 distinguishes between horizontal and vertical strategies. Horizontal integration essen-

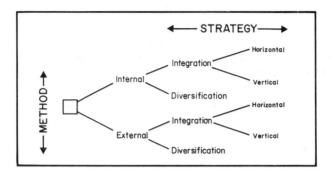

Figure 6.1 Strategies and methods of corporate growth

tially involves more of the same by expanding the firm's market share in its existing product line. Such a strategy is frequently associated with efforts to secure a more powerful position within a particular market. Vertical integration represents a step towards diversification by successfully adapting and applying existing attributes of the firm to new products and markets. These attributes are generally related to the technical and marketing skills of the firm and may be exploited in both backward and forward directions. Backward integration takes place when a firm becomes involved in operations previously the responsibility of its suppliers, whilst forward integration is achieved by extending its activities in the opposite direction to control the outlet for its product. For example, a move into oil refining by a chemical company would represent backward integration to secure the supply of its petroleum-derived raw materials. A move into plastics fabrication would be a case of forward integration, since a large proportion of the output of the petrochemical industry is ultimately transformed into plastic consumer goods such as buckets and bottles.

Although the factors determining the direction of corporate growth are complex, there is evidence that the extent and significance of horizontal and vertical integration is related to stages in the development of both firms and industries. Analysis of patterns of merger activity in the US since 1895, for example, suggest that successive peaks at the turn of the century, in the 1920s and in the 1960s were each associated with different types of corporate growth strategy (Lloyd and Dicken, 1977, p. 366). Horizontal integration appeared to be the principal objective in the 1890s and early 1900s; vertical moves characterized the 1920s; corporate diversification was the principal goal in the 1960s. Attempts to identify a similar pattern in the UK have been less convincing, and Prais (1976, p. 67) maintains that mergers of the horizontal type have consistently remained the most important category. Certainly there is some evidence of a reaction against diversification during the 1980s as several large companies such as British Petroleum and Philips have abandoned activities which are peripheral to their traditional lines of business. Despite the difficulties of generalization, however, the three-stage sequence in the evolution of large enterprises suggested by Bannock (1971) provides an intuitively reasonable framework for understanding the relationship between the various strategies. Bannock argues that the early development of such enterprises is based on the elimination of competition through horizontal integration. This is followed by a period of consolidation involving both backward and forward integration. Once a dominating position is secured in a particular sector, maintains Bannock, diversification is the only way in which rapid corporate growth may be sustained.

The empirical support for this hypothesis is ambiguous, especially regarding the intermediate stage of vertical integration (cf. Tucker and Wilder, 1977; Williamson, 1981), but there is little dispute concerning the importance of the final stage of diversification. Despite the fact that some very large organizations retain a clear identity and association with a particular manufacturing sector, 'there is a strong relationship between size and diversification' (Utton, 1979, p. 90). Business histories confirm that diversification frequently becomes the most important growth strategy once a firm has established a certain size through a combination of horizontal and vertical integration (see Chandler, 1962; Channon, 1973). However, the distinction between these strategies is by no means clear. In practice, most firms diversify into industries with which they have marketing and, especially, technical links. Research and development, for example, often results in product or process innovations which, although initially inspired by the demands of the firm's existing activities may be applied in other sectors (Grant, 1977).

Despite such apparently logical steps towards corporate diversification, a rather different kind of growth is apparent in the emergence of conglomerate corporations involved in widely different sectors of the economy. Indeed, once the concept of a single-product firm is abandoned, strategies of vertical integration and conglomerate growth may be regarded as opposite ends of a spectrum representing different degrees of diversification. The phenomenon of conglomerate diversification during the 1960s and 1970s was a feature of many developed economies (Canada, Royal Commission on Corporate Concentration, 1978; Beattie, 1980; Hill, 1983), although it was a characteristic of the Japanese economy before the Second World War where the *zaibatsu* ('financial cliques') were very influential in many sectors. This tradition has continued in the post-war period with the transformation of the *zaibatsus* into *sogo shoshas* ('trading companies') epitomized by the diverse branches of the Mitsubishi group (Young, 1979). Similar trends have promoted the development of corporations such as Grand Metropolitan and Hanson Trust in the UK and Textron and Litton Industries in the US which, although very large by any criteria of corporate size, are not clearly identified with any particular economic sector. This lack of identity is often reinforced by the adoption of a holding company structure in which ultimate control is vested in an executive board, but the various subsidiaries within the corporate empire continue to operate more or less independently of one another. However, the fact that mergers and takeovers have played an important role in the growth of such corporations has compromised their anonymity (see Meeks and Whittington, 1975; Gribbin, 1976; Goudie and Meeks, 1982), not least because of adverse publicity generated by factory closures associated with the restructuring of the enlarged organizations (Bluestone and Harrison, 1982a).

Emphasis has so far been placed upon the various *strategies* of corporate growth, but reference to the role of mergers and takeovers in the development of conglomerates draws attention to the significance of the different *methods* of growth. There are two such methods (figure 6.1). The first is where growth is achieved internally, financed by the retention of funds or new share issues and reflected in the expansion of existing and/or the establishment of new production facilities. The second is where growth is achieved by acquiring the assets of other firms. (The second method is associated in both the academic literature and the public mind with such terms as 'acquisition', 'merger' and 'takeover'. For the purposes of this book, 'merger' and 'acquisition' are treated as synonyms and used in preference to the less neutral 'takeover'). The relative significance of these two methods is difficult to assess and there are wide variations between both industries and firms. Once a merger has occurred, accounting practices generally obscure the performance of the acquired unit within data for the enlarged organization. In these circumstances, it is possible to measure the initial contribution of the acquisition to the growth of the firm, but not its continuing contribution. Nevertheless, Aaronovitch and Sawyer (1975) estimated that between one-third and one-quarter of the growth rate of large firms (i.e. with assets exceeding £5 million in 1957) engaged in manufacturing and distribution in the UK between 1958 and 1967 could be attributed to acquisitions. This period, however, coincided with high levels of merger activity and several observers have noted evidence of a cyclic pattern in such activity. Merger 'booms' with similar periodicities seem to have occurred in many developed economies. Golbe and White

(1988) demonstrate peaks in the US at the turn of the century, in the late 1920s and early 1930s, and, on a much smaller scale relative to the size of the national economy, in the 1960s and the 1980s. Information for the UK, Canada and Australia, for example, is less comprehensive, but the experience of all these countries in the 1960s and 1980s has been similar to that of the US (see Newbould, 1970; Canada, Royal Commission on Corporate Concentration, 1978; Taylor, 1984; Scouller, 1987). The existence of such merger 'booms' is important because it suggests that in addition to variations between firms and industries, there is a historical dimension to the relative significance of internal and external methods of corporate growth.

Most larger firms employ both methods of growth in the course of their development. There are, however, several reasons for believing that external growth is particularly important to the largest and fastest-growing enterprises. Generally speaking, acquisition enables the growth-motivated firm to achieve its objectives more rapidly than by reliance upon the internal approach. It is, therefore, not surprising to find that studies in both the US (Weston, 1961) and the UK (Evely and Little, 1960) suggest that there are few firms which achieve powerful positions within individual sectors and/or the economy without resorting to external growth at some stage. This conclusion emphasizes that the relative significance of internal and external methods of corporate growth is closely related to the issue of concentration at both the industry and the aggregate level. High levels of external growth clearly imply the absorption of smaller by larger firms. In the case of the UK, Utton (1971) argued that more than 40 per cent of the increase in concentration in manufacturing between 1954 and 1965 was due to mergers. Although the technical difficulties involved in making such an estimate are formidable, the balance of both UK and US evidence led Curry and George (1983, p. 247) to conclude that 'mergers have been the dominant factor in increasing concentration'. Thus the macro-economic trends in industrial organization described in chapter 5 are at least partly a consequence of a shift towards external methods of corporate growth, as dominant firms have consolidated their positions within the economy by using mergers as a means of achieving rapid diversification (see Meeks and Whittington, 1975; Goudie and Meeks, 1982).

The geography of corporate growth

Although economists usually measure corporate growth in financial terms – and it is possible to conceive of an enterprise achieving absolute and relative growth within an industry or economy simply by expanding the output of a single facility – such growth normally implies the addition of new factories and, therefore, a change in the geography of the firm. It is the evolving distribution of the various elements that make up the corporate system which is the principal focus of geographical interest in the growth of large enterprises. It has already been noted (chapter 5) that relatively few businesses achieve the transition from the constellation of small firms which make up the organizational periphery of the economy surrounding the select group of large enterprises at the core. However, if we focus our attention on the exceptional cases which have successfully followed this path, it is apparent that a substantial proportion of the employment and productive capacity of the firm is often concentrated in a particular region. The importance of this region can usually be traced to the origins of the enterprise, which typically appears to spread outwards from this focus as it develops. Using employment data for 1972, Watts (1980b) demonstrated that, despite operating plants in most regions of the UK, both the Cadbury–Schweppes and Dunlop organizations were most strongly represented in the West Midlands. Case studies of the evolution of individual enterprises have confirmed the impression of outward growth provided by static descriptions (see Moore, 1973; Rees, 1974; Taylor, 1975; Watts, 1980b). The progressive dispersal of activities may ultimately lead to a fundamental shift in the corporate centre of gravity away from its original geographical base. Bassett (1984), for example, shows how the policies of Imperial Tobacco during the 1970s and 1980s reduced the significance of its traditional Bristol-based activities within the overall corporate structure. The notion of a focal region at a national scale is paralleled at the international level by the dominance of the home country in the case of such global corporations as ICI (Clarke, 1985) and Philips (Teulings, 1984), although the extent of this dominance may be diminished in just the same way that the allocation of capital investment between regions may alter the geographical 'balance' of smaller corporations operating within a single country. Despite such spatial adjustments, it is reasonable to suggest that growth is accompanied by a gradual extension of the area within which the firm operates. This *operational space* is defined by the firm's linkages with customers and suppliers; its expansion is accompanied by a lagged development of new factories, warehouses and offices, resulting in the transformation of the enterprise into a progressively more widely dispersed multiplant operation.

There are several reasons for expecting such a pattern. The influence upon the geography of new firms of the inter-relationships between practical considerations and a general desire to minimize risk and uncertainty was emphasized in chapter 3. Similar considerations suggest that subsequent expansion involving the establishment of new manufacturing sites will typically occur within a reasonable distance of the initial plant. This distance will reflect the widening operational space of the enterprise which itself contributes to the accumulation of information about the business environment and, therefore, the increase in confidence necessary for the transformation from single- to multi-plant operation. Practical considerations also frequently limit the distance between a new branch and an established site. This distance varies from case to case, but there is no doubt that the desire to be within, for example, a day's drive by truck is frequently a constraint upon the choice of location. This may be due to important linkages between plants which are organized as an integrated production system (see chapter 7), or to the desire to reduce costs by allowing a 'mother' plant to perform various functions such as materials purchasing for satellite operations. Texas Instruments, for example, has adopted an explicit pattern of technology centres and satellites in the United States. Product development is the responsibility of the technology centres which are associated with at least one satellite manufacturing plant (Schmenner, 1982, pps. 133–4). An even more important influence than such production arrangements upon the geographical expansion of corporate systems is the successive development of market areas. Most small single plant firms serve local markets. In industries with high distribution costs such as food processing, beverages and paper products, corporate growth is often achieved by establishing new plants to enable the enterprise to progressively extend its activities from local, to regional, national, and, in some cases, foreign markets. This kind of sequence, which is confirmed by the importance of market factors in the location decisions of multi-plant firms (see table 3.3), clearly implies a direct link between corporate growth and geographical expansion.

Internal growth allows the evolving geography of the corporate system to be carefully planned, and position relative to existing facilities is often an explicit consideration in selecting a location for a new branch plant (see table 3.3). Where growth is achieved by external methods, such planning is more difficult since the location of facilities is inherited from acquired firms. It has already been argued that external growth has played a very important part in the development of most large industrial enterprises, and there is no doubt that, in most cases, it is the economic, financial and technical characteristics of individual firms which determine their attractiveness to others. Nevertheless, there is evidence at various scales that the resulting geography of the enlarged enterprise has a bearing upon such decisions, which 'implicitly involve a spatial search for acquisition or merger candidates' (Green and Cromley, 1984, p. 291).

Various studies have emphasized that such a search is geared towards achieving a steady extension of the operational space of the firm away from its core region. Leigh and North (1978b) argue that many firms in the UK plastics industry have expanded through the consecutive development of regional markets, a process accelerated in many cases by the acquisition of firms already established in these markets. A similar process is described by Watts (1980b) in tracing the growth of the principal UK brewing enterprises from their essentially regional origins into national concerns. In order to achieve this transformation, these enterprises necessarily extended the geographical range of their merger activities through time. This phenomenon was also observed by Healey (1983) in a study of locational change in small- and medium-sized multiplant firms in the East Midlands clothing and textile industries.

In a very different context, attempts have been made to define and identify change in the merger fields of firms with headquarters in New York, Los Angeles and Chicago (Green and Cromley, 1984; Green, 1990). Figure 6.2 indicates the areas within which 25 and 50 per cent of all the acquisitions by these firms were located in the specified time periods. It is clear that the extent of the merger field focused on each city has tended to increase, but there remains a heavy bias towards nearby acquisitions as emphasized by the 25 per cent zone. This type of distance-decay relationship in acquisition behaviour may also be observed at the international scale. Just as mergers may play an important role in transforming a regional firm into a national concern, so the same approach may be used to facilitate the transition to international operations. Indeed, 'acquisitions and mergers have become an increasingly important route to international expansion' (Channon and Jalland, 1978, p. 207) and studies of this phenomenon again suggest that expanding firms adopt spatially conservative strategies by initially seeking out merger candidates in geographically adjacent or culturally similar environments. Ray (1971) noted a distance-decay relationship between the location of US-owned manufacturing plants in Canada and the head offices to which they report. Not only were these plants highly concentrated within a zone adjacent to the US border, but the proportion controlled from head offices in Chicago, Detroit and New York was much higher than for more distant centres of corporate power such as Los Angeles. Ray did not distinguish between internal and external methods of corporate growth in contributing to the strong presence of US-owned companies in the economic core of Canada, but Hayter (1981) shows how acquisitions and joint ventures have allowed US capital to become heavily involved in the forest products industry of British Columbia.

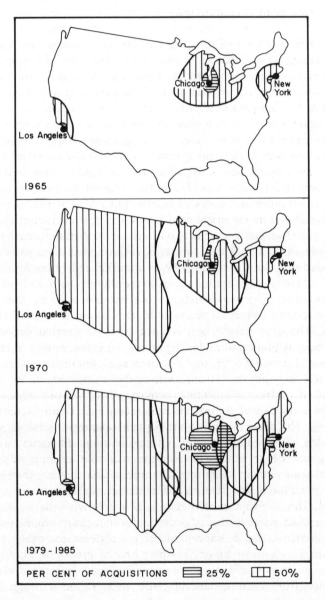

Figure 6.2 Acquisition fields of firms in Chicago, Los Angeles and New York in 1965, 1970 and 1979–85
Source: Green, 1990

Spatial models of corporate growth

The spatial evolution of growing multiplant companies as represented by the changing distribution of the various factories and other facilities which make up the corporate system is clearly affected by the chosen combination of strategies and methods of growth and also by historical circumstances unique to individual firms. McNee (1974, p. 51) describes the development of a hypothetical industrial enterprise from a small family firm to the status of 'a giant among corporations'. His imaginary account provides a perceptive insight into the dynamics of corporate growth, not least because it demonstrates the significance of idiosyncratic behaviour and chance events. At the same time, however, McNee's review of 'the life and times of International Gismo Inc.' suggests the existence of certain empirical regularities and this has encouraged others to identify characteristic spatial patterns of corporate growth.

Taylor (1975) and Watts (1980b) have developed models of corporate expansion from local or regional to national spheres of operation. Figure 6.3 is derived from Taylor's (1975) study of the UK iron-foundry industry. The diagram depicts a country divided into four regions containing large industrial agglomerations and smaller secondary urban centres. The hypothetical firm is assumed to be created within one of these large agglomerations (in region 2). This assumption is consistent with our knowledge of the circumstances conducive to new firm formation as 'spin-offs' from existing businesses are more likely in established centres of economic activity where various agglomeration economies also reduce the uncertainties facing such ventures (see chapters 3 and 4). The decisive step to multi-plant operation is taken when the firm adds a second plant (P2) within the same agglomeration as its initial plant (P1) to further develop the local market. Expanding to the regional scale, the firm sets up sales offices, first to serve the secondary centre in region 2 and then in the principal agglomerations in regions 3 and 4. This tentative expansion is later confirmed with the acquisition of the production plant (P3) of a competitor in region 4, the establishment of a new sales office in that region and the conversion of the sales office in region 3 into a warehouse. The firm breaks into the market of region 1 with the establishment of two sales offices and the sequence of expansion from local to national scale of operation is completed with the construction of a branch plant (P4) in region 3 and a warehouse in region 1.

Although the sequence outlined in figure 6.3 excludes the international scale, many national firms export their products to foreign countries. This is reflected in figure 6.4 which incorporates the transition from

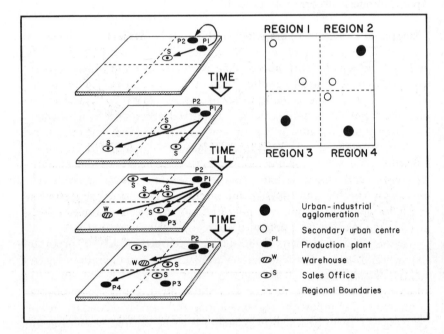

Figure 6.3 A spatial model of corporate growth from local to national operations
Source: Taylor, 1975

'home country' to overseas operation (Håkanson, 1979). Stages 1 and 2 of this model parallel the ideas incorporated in figure 6.3, but stage 3 represents the penetration of overseas markets which are usually developed via a network of sales agents acting on behalf of the corporation. As sales increase, company-owned offices are established in major overseas markets, and these may be followed by manufacturing plants as a combination of increasing transport costs and trade barriers make it more difficult to meet growing overseas demand from domestic production facilities. Indeed there is a tendency for the relative importance of 'domestic' operations to decline as multinationals extend the geographical range of their activities. For example, over 70 per cent of worldwide employment in the British chemical giant ICI was concentrated in the United Kingdom in 1970, but this proportion had fallen to less than 50 per cent by 1988.

The stimulus to foreign investment in Håkanson's model is the development of new markets. This, of course, is only one of several possible motives for such investment (Agarwal, 1980; Ballance, 1987;

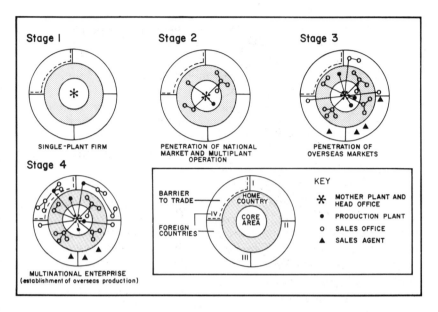

Figure 6.4 A spatial model of corporate growth from regional to international operations
Source: Håkanson, 1979

Dunning, 1988). The desire to secure corporate access to key raw materials and to take advantage of low labour costs, for example, is becoming much more important (see chapters 7, 8 and 11). Nevertheless, case studies of individual firms provide empirical support for the kind of sequence outlined by Håkanson. Tugendhat (1973, p. 204) quotes a US consumer goods company which expressed its foreign investment strategy in the following terms: 'If we can look forward to a certain level of sales, we won't hesitate to invest.' This philosophy was, for example, a potent factor in the massive influx of US manufacturing investment into Western Europe during the 1950s and 1960s (see Groo, 1971; Forsyth, 1972; Blackbourn, 1974; Rees, 1974). By the 1980s a few global corporations had reached the ultimate stage in this process of international expansion. This elite group 'sees the world as one market, not ... as a collection of national markets, and operates a long-term strategy, orchestrating and integrating the strategies of a diverse web of local subsidiaries' (Clarke, 1985, p. 47).

Despite their differing empirical origins, the various spatial models of corporate growth display certain basic similarities. In particular, they suggest that the growth of the enterprise will be accompanied by a progressive expansion in the geographical range of its marketing and productive activities. Even at an international scale, there is a tendency for firms to invest first in countries adjacent to their home base and only later in more distant locations. Franko (1976) showed that, during their formative stages, many continental European multinationals established facilities in other European countries. The Japanese were similarly cautious, making their first overseas investments in countries such as Indonesia and the Philippines before moving further afield (Giddy and Young, 1982). Kravis and Lipsey (1982) analysed the spatial pattern of foreign investment by US firms in six manufacturing sectors. Despite their economic and cultural differences, Canada and Mexico were consistently placed near the top of lists of countries ranked in terms of the number of US firms manufacturing within their territory. These patterns suggest that 'proximity to the United States would seem to be the most important consideration' (Kravis and Lipsey, 1982, p. 205) in determining the location of foreign production facilities. This conclusion emphasizes the general point that, whatever method of corporate growth is used and at whatever scale the process is considered, there are important practical reasons, related to the cost of operating in environments remote from head office, which encourage a typically gradual expansion away from the firm's historical core.

Most spatial models of corporate growth implicitly or explicitly assume that it takes place through horizontal integration from a single-product base. In these circumstances, market area extension is the logical approach to growth, although this strategy is most appropriate in industries serving widely dispersed customers and less relevant where the enterprise is primarily concerned with supplying intermediate or producer goods to other firms. Furthermore, the importance of diversification in the development of the largest enterprises has already been emphasized, and the addition (frequently by acquisition) of new and very different elements to the corporate system may result in a more complex spatial pattern of growth. It is also important to recognize that, despite the sequential nature of the various models, change is not always a one-way process and even the largest corporations may find it necessary to restructure their operations in a manner which involves withdrawal from certain markets and factory closures (see chapter 7). Many firms experience contraction, decline and death. Others have a relatively stable existence, remaining small- to medium-sized members of the periphery of Averitt's (1968) dual economy. Indeed the kind of development sequence suggested by Håkanson is exceptional, and significant thresholds exist which inhibit the successive transition of firms from local to regional to international scales of operation (Taylor and Thrift, 1982c). The size distribution of firms may, therefore, be conceived as a layered, broad-based pyramid in which fewer and fewer firms make the move from one level to the next. Viewed in a historical perspective, the upper levels of the pyramid have, perhaps, become narrower relative to the base with the emergence of a very small number of truly global corporations.

Conclusion

This chapter has analysed the macro-geography of the growing enterprise as reflected in the changing distribution of its various facilities. It has been implicitly assumed, however, that these facilities are identical in nature and function and that the evolving geography of the enterprise can be adequately expressed in terms of an undifferentiated point pattern. Such an assumption is contrary to the reality of complex, multi-facility corporate systems which include manufacturing plants, research laboratories, offices, warehouses, distribution terminals and so on. The next chapter is concerned with the internal geography of these corporate systems.

Further reading

Averitt, R.T. 1968: *The Dual Economy: the Dynamics of American Industry Structure*. New York: Norton.
Channon, D.F. 1973: *The Strategy and Structure of British Enterprise*. London: Macmillan.
Green, M.B. 1990: *Mergers and Acquisitions: Geographical and Spatial Perspectives*. London: Routledge.
Watts, H.D. 1980b: *The Large Industrial Enterprise*. London: Croom Helm.

7
Corporate Spatial Organization

Each large business organization has its own distinctive geography, which may be represented on a map indicating the distribution of its various facilities. The complexity and geographical extent of these distributions are obviously related to the degree of diversification and the overall size of the enterprise. Various case studies have explored these issues in the context of individual enterprises. Most of these have focused upon the distribution of production sites at the national scale (see Krumme, 1970; Chapman, 1974; Le Heron and Warr, 1976), although others have adopted a more comprehensive view of the enterprise by taking account of non-manufacturing sites such as research and development (R & D) establishments and offices (see Rees, 1972; Hayter, 1981). More recently, attention has focused upon the international dimension of corporate spatial structure by examining the relationships between the various elements which constitute the global systems of such household names as ICI (Clarke, 1985), Philips (Teulings, 1984), General Motors and Ford (Bloomfield, 1981).

Despite the difficulties of deriving generalizations from case studies which differ widely in their content and approach, such studies have contributed to important changes in the nature and scope of industrial geography. First, there has been a growing realization that the location of manufacturing plants cannot be explained simply in terms of the variables incorporated in normative location theory (see chapter 3) but, in the case of establishments which are part of multiplant enterprises, must also be seen in their organizational context. This view has been reinforced by the identification of locational hierarchies within corporate systems which suggest that the various elements of the systems display consistent spatial relationships to one another with different types of activity or function associated with different kinds of location. Following from this, the fact that the manufacturing operations of large business organizations are supported by a substantial and growing proportion of white-collar workers in offices, laboratories and other establishments has contributed to a broadening of the scope of industrial geography. Production remains the principal focus of concern, but the definition of what constitutes the system of production has been extended to incorporate non-manufacturing activities. Finally, despite their emphasis upon the internal structure and spatial relations of individual corporate systems, analyses of change within such systems have necessarily taken account of external influences, thereby providing a link between the organizational scale and developments at the industry or macro-economic level.

This chapter attempts to identify the basic principles influencing the geography of such systems. It begins by showing how certain aspects of location theory, despite its emphasis upon the small single-plant firm, are relevant to the spatial organization of multi-plant enterprises. This is followed by discussions of the relationships between the administrative and spatial structures of large business organizations; the implications of management hierarchies for the relative location of white- and blue-collar jobs; the influence of the technology of production upon the distribution of factories and of employment; and finally, the way in which these systems are modified through a continual process of locational adjustment inspired by changes in the operating environment of the enterprise.

Market areas, distribution costs and location

The concept of market areas and their relationship to plant location was discussed in chapter 3 with reference to the work of Lösch (1954). As originally conceived, market area analysis derived an optimal distribution for an industry of single-plant firms serving customers assumed to be evenly spread on a homogeneous plain. The same principles may, however, be helpful in understanding the spatial arrangement of factories owned by a large multi-plant firm operating within an industry characterized by high distribution costs to a dispersed market (Gough, 1984). Several industries fall into this category including various branches of food, drink and tobacco as well as cement and brick manufacture. Facilities such as bottling plants, breweries and bakeries are typically widely dispersed to serve their markets (Foust, 1975) and various studies have used census and survey data to demonstrate their relatively high distribution costs (see Chisholm, 1971; McKinnon, 1989, p. 10). Furthermore, large multi-plant enterprises are often significant players in these industries (see table 5.3) and 21 of the top 100 industrial corporations (ranked by sales) in the United States in 1988, for example, were primarily involved in the manufacture of food, drink or tobacco products. Thus firms such as Pepsico, Kraft and Anheuser–Busch are faced with the problem of devising an optimal plant location strategy to serve the national market for their soft drinks, food products and beers respectively.

The analysis of Lösch is based upon the assumption that the price to consumers will reflect manufacturing plus transport costs so that demand may be expected to fall with increasing distance from the point of production (figure 3.3). In practice, however, many firms adopt uniform delivered pricing in which customers close to the factory pay exactly the same as, and therefore effectively subsidize, distant customers. Several studies have emphasized that this practice is widespread (Greenhut, 1981; Norman, 1981). It simplifies accounting by avoiding the necessity to quote separate prices for each delivery and, more significantly, it means that firms within oligopolistic industries avoid competing with one another on the basis of price. This latter implication has important consequences for locational strategies. It means that changes in plant location designed to reduce the costs of serving the market will not adversely affect market share so that firms may act independently of competitors in this respect. This simplifies the location problem. If it is assumed that a firm is supplying an entire national market in the absence of price competition, its total revenue may be regarded as fixed so that profits are maximized when total costs are minimized, regardless of the actions of its competitors. This is achieved by establishing a system of plants of such a size and spacing that average delivered costs are minimized for each plant.

Figure 7.1 identifies the key variables and their interrelationships. It makes several assumptions: that production costs are the same in all locations; that transport costs vary directly with distance; that demand is evenly spread; that a uniform delivered pricing system prevails; and that the firm accepts a price determined by the market. In these circumstances the capacity/location problem is reduced to a trade-off between production cost savings associated with larger, fewer factories, and the transport cost increases resulting from serving a more extensive market area from each of these plants. The outcome of this trade-off in figure 7.1 defines the optimum plant capacity (OC) and market radius (OR) at the lowest position on the average cost curve. This position is obviously determined by the respective shapes of the production and transport cost curves. The former reflects the generally accepted and empirically proved relationship that unit costs fall as output increases, but at a diminishing rate. These economies of scale at plant level were discussed in chapter 4 and a specific example from the petrochemical

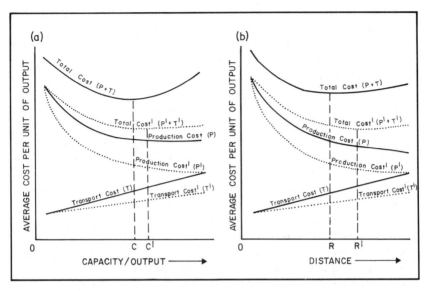

Figure 7.1 Optimal capacity and market area for plant serving dispersed consumers
Source: Gough, 1984

industry is described in chapter 8 (figure 8.6). Transport costs in the diagram do not start at zero because of loading charges at the factory. The assumption of direct proportionality to both volume carried (figure 7.1a) and distance travelled (figure 7.1b) is an oversimplification (see chapter 3). Nevertheless, the basic principle that total average costs will continue to decline as long as production costs are falling more rapidly than transport costs are increasing remains valid whatever the precise form of the transport cost curve.

As expressed in figure 7.1, the solution of the capacity/location problem seems simple, but in reality is more complex. This is reflected not only in the development of appropriate mathematical techniques to tackle it, but also in their use by specific multi-plant companies. H J Heinz, for example, began using such methods as early as 1953 to optimize transport flows between its factories and warehouses in the United States (Henderson and Schlaifer, 1954). Anheuser–Busch, a St Louis-based company, uses a similar technique to link its breweries throughout the country to approximately 1000 distributors (Schmenner, 1982, pp. 126–9). An analysis of Coca Cola bottling plants in south-western Ontario indicated that the actual distribution of these plants corresponded closely to the optimal solution (minimizing total system costs) predicted by a computer model, suggesting that the company had used a similar approach in devising its location strategy (Osleeb and Cromley, 1978).

The solution to the capacity/location problem is unique to a specific set of circumstances defined by the interaction of the level and spatial distribution of demand with the prevailing production and transport cost curves. These circumstances change, however, and the company is faced with the problem of adjusting its operations accordingly. Such adjustments are not easy to make in view of the fact that capital is tied-up in existing facilities so that, at any given time, the corporate system is unlikely to correspond to the optimal solution. In figure 7.1 demand is assumed to be evenly distributed around the production point. Even if this situation existed in reality, the density of demand may be expected to change through time in response to population and/or income growth. This would allow a larger output to be sold within a given radius of the plant, leading to a lower production cost curve with a more gradual slope. Viewed in a different way, it would allow a fixed level of output to be sold within a reduced market area, leading to a lower and less steeply rising transport cost curve. Such changes imply a re-arrangement in the size and spacing of plants serving established markets. On the other hand, the expansion of demand in other areas may reach a threshold level which justifies the construction of a new factory, a process exemplified by the market area extension approach to corporate growth discussed in the previous chapter.

Figure 7.1 indicates the way in which change in the production and transport cost curves may modify the optimum capacity and market radius. For many industries, the point at which the production cost curve becomes horizontal (i.e. when economies of scale are fully exhausted) has shifted to the right in the direction of larger plants. This is not a universal trend, but it is certainly an important one. Curve P_1 reflects this change in figure 7.1a. As far as transport costs are concerned, we have already noted the overall decline in the real costs of movement as technology has advanced (see chapter 3). The lower and shallower transport cost curve (T^1) in figure 7.1 indicates this and the aggregate effect of these influences is apparent in the revised average total cost curve ($P^1 + T^1$). The consequences for optimal capacity and market area are shown by OC_1 and OR_1 respectively. Clearly, these suggest the concentration of production in fewer, larger plants to serve a given level of aggregate demand. Such a trend has been demonstrated in various case-studies of multi-plant firms involved in industries such as brick-making (Gleave, 1965), fluid milk processing (Gough, 1984) and brewing (Watts, 1980b; pp. 214–45).

It has so far been assumed that products are distributed directly from the factory to the retail outlets. This is the exception rather than the rule and a study of a sample of food manufacturers in the United

Kingdom emphasized that the bulk of their output was channelled through complex distribution systems before reaching the store shelves (McKinnon, 1989, p. 53). These systems are not necessarily owned and operated by the manufacturer and distribution may be carried out by specialist firms. The majority of large business enterprises prefer to retain control of these functions, however, so that the various warehouses and depots are as much a part of their corporate systems as the factories to which these facilities are linked. Figure 7.2 indicates the principal elements in the distribution system of an oil company. It is based upon the operations of Shell UK Ltd, but is typical of other, similar companies. The diagram emphasizes the hierarchical structure of the system and the relationship of load-size to mode of transport. Thus large customers are supplied direct from the refinery using bulk transportation by rail, coastal shipping or, in some cases, designated pipelines. These modes are also used to supply the terminals at which products such as fuel oil and gasolines are stored. Medium-sized customers, such as petrol stations, are then supplied directly by large road tankers in single-drop loads. These vehicles also supply the distributor depots from which deliveries are made to low-volume customers such as individual households. Smaller road vehicles are used for this purpose and a tanker may make several 'drops' on a single journey. In the case of Shell UK, this final step in the chain is, formally, external to the company, although it retains control of the system because it owns most of the depots which are leased to local contractors.

The spatial expression of this hierarchical distribution system is evident in figure 7.3 which also reveals major changes in the number and location of the key points within the system between 1976 and 1990. The maps exclude the numerous distributor depots and focus upon the refineries and terminals. Three types of terminal are identified. 'Wet' terminals are owned and operated by Shell and include facilities for the receipt, storage and road loading of bulk petroleum products. As far as Shell is concerned, 'dry' terminals include only such service functions as office accommodation, parking and (in some cases) maintenance facilities for road tankers. These are, however, usually located adjacent to the 'wet' terminals of other companies which have agreed to supply products to Shell, normally on a reciprocal basis. A similar situation exists at 'pick-up' terminals, to which Shell vehicles have access, but where the company has no facilities of its own. These 'pick-ups' are usually made as a second load by a road tanker in the course of its daily operations and are intended to avoid the necessity for a longer return journey to its base.

The most striking feature of figure 7.3 is the reduction in the number of nodes within the system. This is typical of other companies serving the UK market and is largely due to the failure of demand to match the

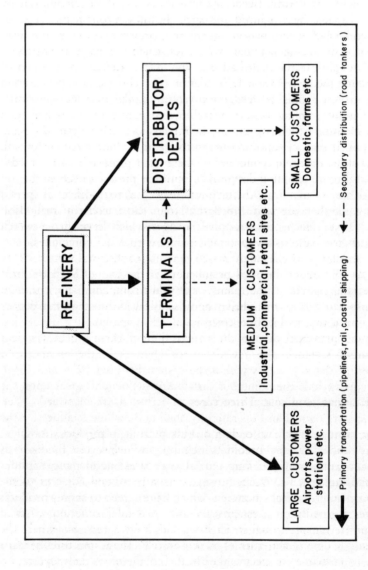

Figure 7.2 Oil products distribution system

optimistic projections of the 1960s when many of the terminals were established. Indeed, the demand for oil products fell sharply after the oil price 'shocks' of 1973 and 1979 and was, by 1983, broadly similar to the level prevailing twenty years earlier. In these circumstances, refinery capacity was reduced and Shell shut down four plants between 1976 and 1985. There was corresponding pressure to reduce the fixed costs of maintaining terminals which remained the same regardless of their throughput and Shell had only 12 'wet' terminals by the end of 1990, compared with 32 in 1976 (figure 7.3). This implies an extension to the market radius or delivery 'envelope' served from each terminal and, therefore, an increase in variable transport costs. This has been offset, to some extent, by the use of larger (38- rather than 32-tonne) road tankers for deliveries to distributors and medium-sized customers. Furthermore, the scale economies of these vehicles have been reinforced by careful route planning designed to optimize the use of the motorway network and to maximize the proportion of total road deliveries carried in big tankers. Even more important than these technical responses, however, have been organizational changes which have increased the significance of various swap arrangements with other companies. This has meant that approximately 20–25 per cent of the total volume of oil products sold under the Shell brand name in the United Kingdom may be ultimately traced to the refineries of other companies. This practice is widespread within the industry and has allowed the major companies to minimize the distribution costs involved in maintaining a national marketing presence, despite the contraction of their production and distribution systems.

Organizational and spatial structures

Despite their relevance to certain aspects of multi-plant operations, the ideas discussed in the preceding section and especially the role of transport costs, provide a very partial understanding of the geography of corporate systems. Deeper insights may be obtained by explicitly focussing upon the links between organizational and spatial structures. Corporate growth is necessarily accompanied by the development of appropriate organizational structures to administer and co-ordinate the increasingly diverse activities of the enterprise. These structures tend to evolve in response to specific problems and therefore differ from one enterprise to another. They are also subject to periodic review and modification. Nevertheless, it is possible to identify a number of general types which tend to be related to stages in the development of the large industrial enterprise. The functional form of organization (figure 7.4a)

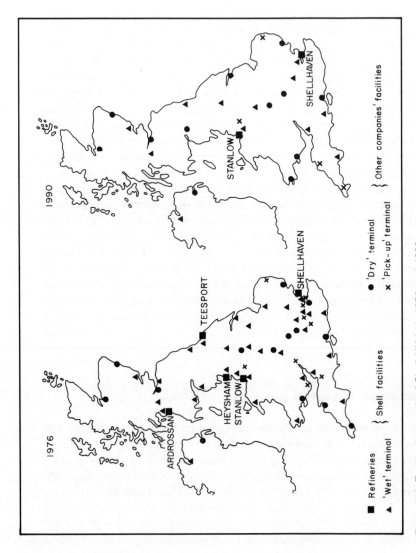

Figure 7.3 Terminal network of Shell UK Ltd, 1976 and 1990
Source: Shell UK Ltd

is based upon the subdivision of the various tasks of management into more specialized activities such as production and marketing. The multidivisional form (figure 7.4b) is a characteristic response to the problems generated by diversification, which is itself frequently associated with corporate growth (chapter 5). In these circumstances, responsibility for particular product lines is allocated to different divisions. In figure 7.4c, the company is organized on a territorial basis. Holding company structures (figures 7.4f) are often a consequence of rapid diversification by means of external growth. They are therefore frequently associated with conglomerates, although the experience of holding companies has not always been successful and many tend to return to the multidivisional form when the level of the acquisition activity is reduced. Any one of these structures, initially associated with operations at the national scale, may be adapted to cope with the problems resulting from the overseas extension of marketing and production activities. The patterns in figures 7.4d/e, which are characteristic of many of the very largest global organizations, build upon the principles of functional and multidivisional structures, by establishing a bureaucracy which is based on both area and product or function.

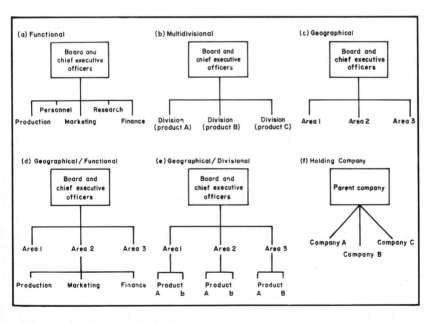

Figure 7.4 Possible organizational structures

The structures in figure 7.4 are obviously oversimplifications, and an almost infinite range of variation on these themes exists between different companies (see Stopford and Wells, 1972; Channon and Jalland, 1978). Viewed from a historical perspective, however, certain general trends may be perceived. A move away from the functional in favour of the multidivisional structure has been especially noticeable amongst the largest corporations. The latter form was pioneered in the US at the turn of the century (see Williamson, 1981), but it has found increasing favour since the 1950s (see Channon, 1973; Galbraith and Nathanson, 1978). The development of more complex structures, exemplified by figures 7.4d/e is a relatively recent phenomenon linked to the emergence of truly global manufacturing corporations during the last twenty years or so.

The diagrams in figure 7.4 are paralleled by the charts which large corporations produce to assist employees identify their position within the organization. A less descriptive and more analytical view of the internal structure of business organizations has been provided by Simon (1960). He suggested that such organizations typically have a three-tiered hierarchical structure. At the bottom are the manufacturing activities together with associated routine administration supporting these activities at plant level. In the middle are the co-ordinating functions which bind together the various elements of the enterprise. At the top are the strategic decision-makers who formulate the goals and objectives of the organization and also monitor its performance. This kind of hierarchy is common to all of the structures in figure 7.4, although it tends to become more highly developed as the organization increases in size and is, therefore, more clearly seen in multidivisional and global corporations. Simon's conceptualization is significant because it not only defines *position* within the organization, but also carries the implication of differential *status*.

Simon was particularly concerned with lines of authority and flows of information within organizations in the abstract sense. He was, therefore, little interested in the physical units (i.e. the offices and factories) within which the various activities take place and between which information flows are channelled. Once this concern with administrative structures is translated into physical terms it is possible to consider the question of the relative location of each of the various levels in Simon's hierarchy (see Hymer, 1972). In figure 7.5a there is no geographical separation between them; strategic and production functions are carried out at one location, and there is no necessity for the intervening tier of co-ordinating activities. This is typical of the small single-plant firm. Generally speaking, as firms increase in size, more complex functional and spatial divisions of labour are created. Thus in figure 7.5b administrative functions are devolved from headquarters to regional offices which have direct responsibility for independent subsystems of manufacturing plants. In figure 7.5c both strategic and routine decision-making is concentrated at head office, from which a complex network of interdependent production facilities is controlled. These hypothetical examples underline the point that organizational and spatial structures are very much interrelated, and there has been a growing awareness of this connection in the geographical literature (see Keeble and McDermott, 1978; Wood, 1978; Taylor and McDermott, 1982). This literature falls into two general categories. The first focuses upon the consequences for economies of the organizational and spatial structure of multiplant enterprises, and the second seeks to understand the internal geography of such enterprises.

The distribution between cities and regions of the economic benefits generated by the activities of industrial enterprises is related to their spatial structure. Pred (1974, 1977) drew attention to the organizational dimension as a variable influencing the role of such enterprises in the transmission of growth impulses from one place to another. He emphasized, in particular, the way in which decisions affecting the future of individual plants, and therefore the communities in which they are

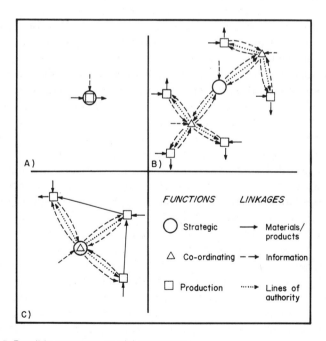

Figure 7.5 Possible corporate spatial structures

located, are frequently made in head offices which are remote, in every sense of the word, from those directly affected by them. Ultimate authority may lie not only outside the boundaries of the region but also, in the case of multinational and global corporations, beyond the frontiers of the country. These implications of corporate spatial structures are explored more fully in chapters 9, 10 and 11.

It is important to appreciate the dynamic nature of organizations, and there is evidence that highly centralized systems of management become difficult to sustain as the scale and diversity of corporate activities increase. Several writers have suggested that more flexible and decentralized structures will be adopted (see Brooke, 1979; Toffler, 1985). These may take the form of loose federations of largely independent companies, bound together only by the extensive collection of information at the centre. Alternatively, corporate structures may come to be regarded as essentially transient, assembled for specific purposes and rapidly changed to take advantage of new opportunities. Various pressures are pushing large organizations in these directions. Political concern over their power and influence and their relationship with nation states suggests that the role of head office in decision-making will either become less important or, at least, less visible. Greater competition resulting from the entry of corporations from differing national backgrounds into international markets will increase the importance of quick responses, which are difficult to achieve when freedom of action is constrained by the obligation to refer a problem to head office. Rapid rates of technical change in certain industries are probably the most important stimulus to the development of administrative structures which increase corporate flexibility. For example, new manufacturing technologies using computers to control robots are reducing the economic advantages of assembly-line methods relative to batch production. Although there is a clear trend towards greater concentration in the rapidly evolving international electronic and telecommunications industries (OECD, 1983d), detailed study of the internal structure of such giants as IBM and Matsushita suggests that efforts have been made to achieve global co-ordination and national flexibility simultaneously, centralizing some activities and decentralizing others.

These trends affecting the internal structure of large enterprises have implications for their relationships with their external economic environments. At the regional scale, they present opportunities to overcome some of the undesirable features of the branch plant syndrome (see Watts, 1981). The incorporation of higher-level functions such as research and development at sites previously restricted to production helps to provide a wider range of job opportunities as well as to emphasize the comparative autonomy of operations previously very much dependent upon decisions taken at head office. The same kind of arguments apply at the international scale. It has been suggested, for example, that Canada's relatively poor export performance in manufactured goods is partly related to the fact that a high proportion of industrial output is controlled by the subsidiaries of foreign (mainly US) companies producing standard products for the domestic market (Britton, 1980). One solution to the problem is world product mandating (Science Council of Canada, 1980). This involves allocation of responsibility for the manufacture and worldwide marketing of a specific product by a multinational or global corporation to a particular plant or national subsidiary. This kind of corporate devolution of power is consistent with the predictions of Toffler (1985) regarding the future form of the largest industrial enterprises. Despite these emerging trends, the fact remains that existing patterns of economic activity in sectors dominated by big corporations still largely reflect hierarchical systems of management. The remainder of this chapter, therefore, focuses upon the spatial structure of such systems.

Organization and location: patterns of office employment

Implicit in hierarchical organizational structures is a distinction between those individuals directly employed in manufacturing and those engaged in related administrative operations. A major proportion of the employees of any large business organization, even if it is primarily associated with the manufacturing sector, is involved in non-production activities. For example, it has been estimated that this figure is approximately 60 per cent in the case of the US-based General Electric Company (Ginzberg, 1982) whilst only one person in seven in the US workforce of the Xerox Corporation, which is the nation's second largest (in terms of value of scales) manufacturer of scientific and photographic equipment, is a production worker (Hansen, 1988). Although these cases may be exceptional, there is abundant evidence of an upward trend in the relative importance of employment in such producer services as accountancy and marketing. Approximately one-third of all employment in the manufacturing sectors of the UK and the US is accounted for by office-based tasks and the proportion appears to be growing in both countries (Gudgin et al., 1979; Rees, 1983). Several factors have contributed to this shift in patterns of employment. The substitution of capital for labour has tended to reduce the number of production jobs, whilst the increasing sophistication of manufactured goods and accelerating rates of technical change have led to the expansion of R & D activity which falls into the non-production category. The rise of large business organizations has itself probably contributed to the trend as the proportion of staff engaged in the day-to-day co-ordination and control of their diverse activities tends to increase with corporate size (see Pondy, 1969; Child, 1973). Indeed, these changes *within* large business organizations are just one aspect of a general increase in the share of service employment within developed economies – a trend which has prompted speculations regarding the nature of a new 'post-industrial' society (see Gershuny and Miles, 1983).

The ratio of non-production to production employment is less significant from a geographical point of view than the relative location of these activities. Surveys in the US (Noyelle and Stanback, 1984) and the UK (Gudgin et al., 1979; Marquand, 1983) have revealed significant regional variations in the importance of non-production employment. South-east England has a particularly high proportion, whilst the north-east United States displays similar employment characteristics. Many variables have contributed to these patterns, but the tendency for large business organizations to place their white-collar employment in distinctly different locations from their blue-collar jobs is a major contributory factor. The concentration of strategic head office functions in relatively few metropolitan centres is a particular characteristic which has been observed in many countries. Numerous studies have been carried out using lists of the largest 500 or 1000 business organizations within different countries. These data sets usually identify the headquarters location and the principal activities of each corporation. It is, therefore, possible either to consider large organizations in aggregate or to isolate those specifically associated with manufacturing. Since they are often published on a regular basis, these lists also allow any changes in patterns of headquarters locations to be recorded.

The concentration of corporate headquarters in a single city is, perhaps, more pronounced in the United Kingdom than in any other country, and the dominance of London appears to be increasing (Goddard and Smith, 1978). In many countries, two centres of corporate control may be identified, typically with one much more important that the other. This type of relationship exists in Canada between Toronto and Montreal (Semple and Smith, 1981), in New Zealand between Auckland and Wellington (Le Heron, 1977) and in Sweden between Stockholm and Göteborg (Pred, 1977). In the case of Australia, Sydney and Melbourne have a more equal relationship (Taylor, 1984), whilst Hamburg, Frankfurt and Düsseldorf are the most important centres in West Germany, although these cities are closely followed by several others including Essen, Cologne and Hanover (Strickland and Aiken, 1984). Figure 7.6 shows the distribution of the headquarter offices of the top 100 (ranked by sales) industrial corporations in the United States in 1988. The height of the columns indicates the importance of the various cities and states in terms of their respective shares of the total assets of the top 100 and in terms of the absolute number of corporations which are headquartered within them. Thus Michigan is more important on the former scale because it is home to some of the very largest corporations such as General Motors, Ford and Chrysler (see table 5.1). Studies have suggested that the overall pattern in the United States has been more fluid than most countries as individual cities have changed their relative positions in the hierarchy of headquarters locations (see Borchert, 1978; Rees, 1978b; Stephens and Holly, 1981). Nevertheless, the north east in general and the New York metropolitan area in particular have retained their long-established primacy (figure 7.6). Despite variations from one country to another, the overriding locational characteristic of corporate headquarters is their association with cities at the top of the various national urban hierarchies.

This association is related partly to the general factors which have promoted the growth of large business organizations (see chapter 5) and partly to the hierarchical structure of national urban systems which make metropolitan centres especially attractive locations for the kind of activities carried out within corporate head offices. Expansion through mergers and takeovers encourages concentration of non-production employment as a result of the internalization within a single enterprise of functions that were formally duplicated in separate organizations. Leigh and North (1978b), for example, demonstrate that the overall dominance of London in the British economy has been reinforced by the tendency for metropolitan-based firms to take over provincial ones rather than vice versa and similar trends have been observed in Canada (Green and McNaughton, 1989). This centralization is further promoted by the attraction of London and Toronto to the more successful provincial firms which may shift their head offices to these cities. The latter phenomenon is difficult to explain, but is presumably related to the perceived advantages of a metropolitan location. These advantages incorporate a wide range of agglomeration economies (see chapter 4) which ultimately rest upon the fact that head offices are essentially engaged in information processing. Furthermore, these offices are distinguished from those at lower levels within corporate hierarchies by the greater emphasis which they place upon the assembly and analysis of information from sources external to the organization such as government departments and financial institutions, which are themselves concentrated in major, and especially capital, cities. Despite the availability of sophisticated communications technology, numerous surveys have emphasized the continuing importance of personal business meetings, especially at the higher levels of corporate bureaucracies (see

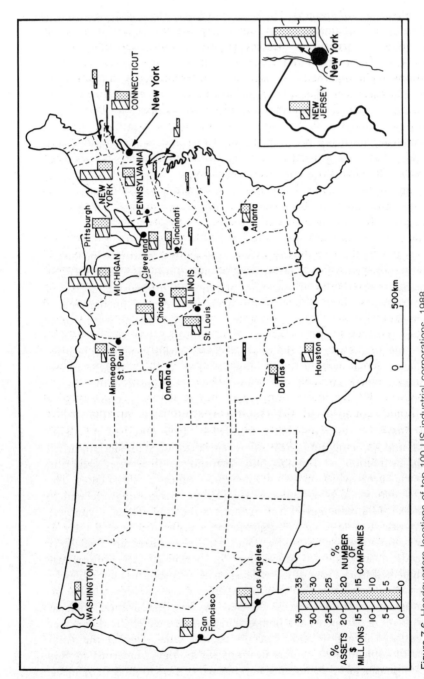

Figure 7.6 Headquarters locations of top 100 US industrial corporations, 1988
Sources: Fortune, 25 April 1988

Tornquist, 1970; Goddard, 1973, 1978). Where these meetings involve contacts with counterparts in other organizations, the benefits of geographical concentration become apparent. Numerous other advantages have been attributed to metropolitan centres as head office locations including their easy access to international communication networks, their general properties as information-rich environments, and the cachet attached to a prestige head office address (see Pred, 1977; Crum and Gudgin, 1978). Advances in communications technology undoubtedly have the potential to weaken some of these attractions, but they may also be used to reinforce the dominant position of head office by allowing more effective monitoring of operations throughout the organization. Given the inertia of an established head office, it is not surprising that, on balance, the centralizing influence seems to be more powerful (see Goddard et al., 1985; Hepworth, 1986).

The concentration of white-collar jobs within or near major metropolitan centres is often reinforced by the distribution of corporate R & D activities. Despite wide variations between sectors, and therefore between firms, in the commitment to R & D, innovation plays an important role in the growth of large industrial enterprises, as has already been argued (see chapter 5). Basic research geared towards the development of new products is especially important in securing long-term corporate growth. This type of activity is usually carried out in purpose-built facilities which are separate from the production units of the enterprise. These facilities are very unevenly distributed whatever the scale at which they are viewed. On the international level they tend to be concentrated in the 'home' countries of the major corporations, a situation which contributes to the dependence of Third-World countries on terms acceptable to the advanced industrial nations (see chapter 10).

At the national level, they tend to be highly clustered in particular regions. Figure 7.7 expresses the share of total US industrial R & D expenditure in 1985 in each state relative to its share of national manufacturing value added in the same year. States with a score exceeding one, therefore, have higher R & D expenditures than expected relative to this yardstick; those with a score of less than one have lower than expected R & D expenditures. With the exception of Idaho, which must be regarded as an anomalous case based upon very low absolute values, figure 7.7 reveals a similar general pattern to the distribution of corporate headquarters in figure 7.6, although the geographical concentration of R & D expenditures is even more striking. Indeed, five states (California, New York, New Jersey, Michigan and Massachusetts) accounted for more than 50 per cent of the total in 1985, with over 22 per cent being spent in California alone (National Science Foundation, 1988).

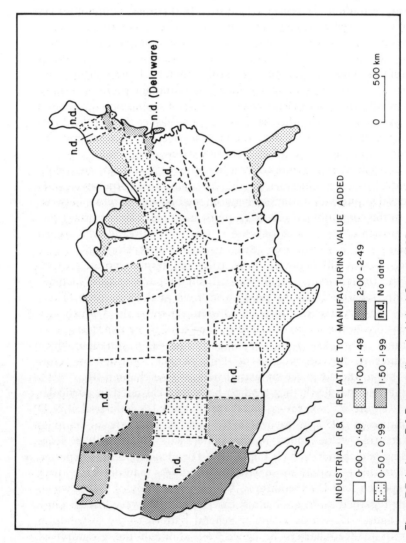

Figure 7.7 Industry R & D expenditure in United States, 1985
Source: National Science Foundation, 1988

This pattern does not, of course, simply reflect the attractiveness of particular states to corporate R & D facilities and it is strongly influenced by industrial structure. It is not surprising, for example, to find such heavy R & D expenditure in California in view of the importance of the research-intensive aerospace industry in the state. At the intra-state level, R & D facilities tend to be associated with major cities, especially the New York, Los Angeles and Boston metropolitan areas (Malecki, 1979, 1980). A similar orientation towards major cities, especially capital cities such as London (Howells, 1984), Tokyo (Sargent, 1987) and Paris, is apparent in other countries, although this orientation is diminishing in some cases as a result of government efforts to encourage a dispersal of corporate R & D to other regions (see Brocard, 1981; Cooke, 1985).

Despite differences of detail, certain clear patterns emerge from the various studies of the location of corporate R & D establishments (Lund, 1986). The most important single factor seems to be proximity to head office, thus reinforcing the tendency for top jobs to be concentrated in certain metropolitan regions. This association reflects the importance of basic research as an influence upon strategic decisions affecting the future direction of corporate growth, and direct contact between research staff and senior management is obviously facilitated by their proximity. Even so, it is unusual for head office and the principal R & D establishment to be on the same site. The former is more likely to be in the central area of the city, whilst the latter is typically found in attractive suburbs on the fringe of the metropolitan area. This situation is related to another important influence upon the location of R & D facilities – the life-style preferences of their staff. These preferences seem to include a set of climatic, recreational and cultural attributes which combine to produce a residential environment which is attractive to highly qualified R & D personnel. The particular qualities of such environments are difficult to define, but there is no doubt that they exist. It is partly a social phenomenon. As Massey (1984, p. 142) puts it: 'Living in Newbury (UK), or rather just outside Newbury, makes you feel better, confirms your standing in society.' In the US, it is places such as Palo Alto, California, and Cambridge, Massachusetts, which have the desired 'ambience' (Malecki, 1984). Personal economic advantage may reinforce this ambience. Job switching frequently accelerates the rise up the salary ladder, and this is made easier when a move from one company to another involves no change of residence.

The two principal variables influencing the location of basic research facilities are fundamentally different. Proximity to head office is a matter which is essentially internal to the organization, whereas the labour factor is an external consideration. These factors may pull in opposite directions. In France, the emergence of a major research centre on the Côte d'Azur, remote from head office in Paris, has been attributed to the sun-seeking habits of senior staff (Brocard, 1981). Similarly, in devising a classification of corporate R & D locations in the US, Malecki (1980) identified a number of important centres such as Lincoln, Nebraska, and Austin, Texas, which have developed, despite their lack of corporate headquarters, on the strength of the research environment offered by their universities. Such cases are, however, the exception rather than the rule and there is no doubt that basic R & D, if not necessarily located in the largest cities, is normally found within their immediate sphere of economic and cultural influence.

In reviewing the contribution of head office and basic R & D establishments to non-production employment within corporate systems, it is important to make a clear distinction between their numerical and their strategic significance. It is very difficult to obtain company-specific breakdowns of non-production employment by occupational category, although it has been estimated that approximately 10 per cent of non-production employment in UK manufacturing in 1971 was accounted for by managerial, professional and scientific staff (Gudgin et al., 1979, p. 136). Within any one multiplant enterprise it is safe to say that the majority of non-production employees will work in regional offices, branch plants and depots. Similarly a major proportion of R & D staff is involved not in basic research but in the development of existing products and processes. These activities are often dispersed to individual manufacturing sites. In numerical terms, therefore, the bulk of non-production employment in any large industrial enterprise is not concentrated at the corporate core. However, it is clear that the most important jobs are. Furthermore, it is also evident that the strategic functions of many different organizations are frequently located in the same metropolitan centres. These organizations have, by creating locational hierarchies of functions which demand different kinds of skill, also created a spatial division of labour. This division is not only based upon the existence of different levels of authority within corporate bureaucracies, but is also further refined by technological considerations which are most relevant to an understanding of the location of factories within corporate systems.

The product cycle

The question of plant location relative to raw materials, markets and the factors of production was considered in chapter 3 and the influence of other firms was reviewed in chapter 4. Such variables are part of the external economic environment within which the firm operates. However, in the case of multiplant enterprises they may be internal to the organization. Thus individual plants are frequently linked together by input or output relationships so that the reference points of a Weberian location polygon are determined by the existing spatial structure of the enterprise. In many circumstances the various factories operated by a multiplant enterprise perform very similar functions and have a common relationship to head office (figure 7.5b). This situation is characteristic of industries in which growth is achieved by geographical extension into new market areas (see chapter 6). It is also associated with industries, such as brewing and soft drinks, in which distribution costs are high and proximity to potential markets is therefore important. The basic principles of plant location are much the same whether or not a production facility is an isolated unit or part of a wider corporate system. The principles were discussed at the beginning of the chapter.

By no means all corporate production systems fit the pattern of figure 7.5b in which individual factories may be regarded as clones supplying identical products to their own market areas. Many large organizations assign specific roles to their various factories and it is possible to identify technology-based locational hierarchies within corporate systems as well as the administrative hierarchies described in the previous section. Two basic and related concepts – the product life cycle and the spatial division of labour help us to understand such hierarchies.

The product-cycle concept is derived from early work by Kuznets (1930) and Burns (1934) who suggested that the production history of specific sectors follows a typical sequence. Others extended the idea by arguing that these trends in output are accompanied by characteristic changes in the technology of production (Utterback and Abernathy, 1975). Figure 7.8 combines these two aspects of the concept by identifying three stages in the product life cycle. The commercial launch of the product is preceded by its initial discovery and development. This is followed by the rapid sales growth of stage 1. If the product is protected by patent, the company responsible for its discovery may enjoy an effective monopoly during this period which is also characterized by efforts to improve the qualities of the product. These efforts imply frequent changes in manufacturing process and product specification. Methods of production tend to be labour intensive but, owing to its novelty, the product commands a high price in the market place and there is little pressure to reduce costs, especially in a monopoly situation. Circumstances are very different in stage 2. Patent protection for the innovating firm may have lapsed and emphasis is placed upon low-cost, standardized, mass production technologies as efforts are directed towards the expansion of sales. By stage 3, potential markets have all

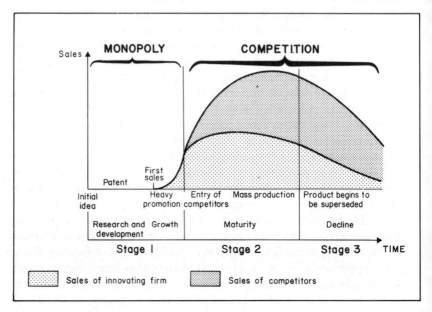

Figure 7.8 A typical product cycle

been reached and stiffer competition is faced from alternative products. This competition induces further downward pressures upon costs, but eventually markets are lost to the new products and manufacturing capacity is steadily reduced.

The geographical dimension of the product-cycle model is related to two mutually reinforcing effects which tend to encourage dispersal away from the initial centre of production in stage 1. First, as products become standardized, the need for skilled labour is reduced and the emphasis upon cost reduction in stage 2 encourages attempts to maximize economies of scale in large plants and a search for cheap labour. Second, agglomeration economies and linkages become less important during maturity, thereby weakening the attractions of the metropolitan locations with which new products are usually associated. These arguments were first applied at the international scale (see Vernon, 1966; Hirsch, 1967; Moran, 1979). Various attempts have been made to account for the rise of the newly industrialized countries as a consequence of the diffusion, through the medium of multinational corporations, of manufacturing operations associated with the second and third stages of the product cycle (see Hamilton and Linge, 1981).

Although this phenomenon cannot be explained solely in these terms (Schoenberger, 1988b), there is no doubt that countries such as the US and Japan represent sources of industrial innovation at an international scale and that manufacturing operations based on these innovations spread outwards from these core countries. The validity of this interpretation is emphasized by the fact that much concern has recently been expressed in countries such as the United Kingdom (Pavitt, 1980) and Canada (Britton, 1980, 1981) about their role as recipients rather than initiators of new technology. For example, a substantial proportion of manufacturing capacity in the UK electronics industry is accounted for by branch plants of foreign multinationals applying technologies developed elsewhere (Cooke et al., 1984).

It is not only at the international scale that the product cycle has been invoked to account for changing patterns of industrial location. The shift of manufacturing employment away from traditional industrial centres and major cities towards peripheral regions and small-town environments has been a feature of most developed countries in recent years (see Keeble, 1980; Keeble et al., 1983; Savey, 1983; Rees, 1983). In the United States especially, this redistribution has been linked to, amongst other factors, the product-cycle concept as multiplant corporations have transferred stage 2 and 3 activities from the Manufacturing Belt to states with lower wage rates in the south and south west (Hansen, 1979; Norton and Rees, 1979; Rees, 1979). Generally speaking, this argument has been based upon the circumstantial evidence of aggregate employment changes, and few studies have traced the regional dimension to the diffusion of products through individual corporate systems. One exception is a study by Oakey et al. (1980) relating to intra-corporate transfers of manufacturing innovations in the United Kingdom; this emphasized not only that the south east, because of its dominance of R & D was the major source of these innovations, but also that a substantial proportion of them were first applied in manufacturing plants in the same region. This tends to support the proposition that, as a result of the way in which multiplant enterprises organize their activities over space, certain regions have a high proportion of their manufacturing jobs concentrated in operations associated with the first stage of the product cycle whilst others have a very different employment structure. In the US computer industry, for example, New England and California dominate in the research, development and design of new products, but the assembly of machines and peripherals such as terminals and printers is much more widely dispersed throughout the country (Hekman, 1980a).

There is no doubt that the location strategies of many large companies have been shaped by the logic of the product cycle, but several writers have emphasized the limitations of the concept (see Storper, 1985; Walker, 1985; Taylor, 1986). Large-scale, mass production has never been a feature of many industries. Even in those industries such as motor vehicles which do seem to fit the model there is some evidence of a shift away from high-volume, standardized production towards more distinctive 'customized' items aimed at specific niches in the market (Schoenberger, 1987). This trend is related to the introduction of new methods of production which combine computers and robotic equipment to create what have been termed flexible manufacturing systems. Unlike the familiar assembly lines associated with the motor vehicle industry, these systems are able to switch, within certain limits, easily from one model to another. Such developments emphasize that the kind of 'natural' technological trajectory assumed by the product cycle model may be radically altered. Furthermore, by creating a demand for highly-skilled technicians to operate and, especially, to maintain such equipment and by promoting methods of production which increase the importance of linkages with specialist suppliers, flexible manufacturing systems contradict key features of the product-cycle model. However, the overall significance of such systems for industrial location is a matter of debate (Gertler, 1988; 1989; Schoenberger, 1988a; 1989) and the product cycle remains a useful aid to our understanding of the geography of multiplant enterprises, provided it is not regarded as a universal explanation.

Spatial divisions of labour

The shift in the location at which products are manufactured as they pass through the life cycle is not the only sense in which the technology of production is relevant to an understanding of the spatial organization of corporate systems. Multiplant enterprises frequently establish frag-mented production systems which involve the spatial separation of the various stages in the manufacture of a particular product. 'Stage' in this sense refers not to steps in a life cycle through time, but to steps in a sequence of linked activities leading to the manufacture of a product at a given time. Such sequences or part-process structures represent applications of the familiar economic principle of the division of labour. This principle has played a very important role in the organization of production within capitalist societies, and the progression from cottage industry to modern factory has tended to involve greater and greater specialization of function at the level of the individual worker (see Perrons, 1981). The epitome of this process is the assembly line concept pioneered by Henry Ford. Although the tasks of individuals working on such lines are very narrowly defined, their combined efforts result in the manufacture of a finished product such as a motor car under a single factory roof. The principle of the division of labour is taken a significant stage further by the establishment of part-process structures in which the various tasks are geographically separated so that the motorway networks and shipping routes which link them effectively become integral parts of the assembly line. This type of system has long been established on a regional scale within major industrial agglomerations such as the UK West Midlands, where the motor vehicle industry has traditionally depended upon metal-working and engineering trades for the supply of components (Wood, 1976). Similar networks focused upon the principal car makers such as Toyota and Nissan may be observed in Japan (Sheard, 1983), whilst Volvo has linkages with subcontractors dispersed throughout Sweden (Fredriksson and Lindmark, 1979). Although part-process structures may, therefore, be established by constellations of firms which are legally independent entities, such structures are often internal to multiplant organizations, so that economic relationships between regions and nations are becoming strongly influenced by intra-corporate transactions (Ettlinger, 1984).

These transactions vary considerably in their nature between enterprises and industries and also in the geographical scale over which they take place. The individual elements of a corporate part-process structure may be dispersed between regions within the same country (see Massey, 1984) or between many countries. International systems may operate on a continental scale, as exemplified by the attraction of investment by organizations based in the European 'core' to 'periphery' countries such as Ireland, Greece and Portugal (see Seers et al., 1979), or on a truly global scale as multinationals divert some of their activities to the Third World (see Fröbel et al., 1980). Not all manufacturing operations can be fragmented in this way, and part-process structures tend to be associated with sectors, such as electronics and motor vehicles, which are dominated by large enterprises and also characterized by assembly-type activities in which complex finished products are made up of many individually simple components.

Although the electronics industry displays tremendous variation both in the nature of its products (ranging from pocket calculators to military equipment) and in its forms of organization (ranging from individual entrepreneurs to global corporations), it is in the manufacture of consumer goods such as TV sets and video recorders that locational hierarchies based upon the fragmentation of the production process within large corporate systems are most clearly seen. These hierarchies based upon the fragmentation of the production process have been established at a global scale, with R & D activity concentrated in, for example, the US and Japan; the manufacture of complex but standardized parts in second-rank countries such as the UK; and final assembly operations in, amongst other places, China, Mexico and Taiwan. The labour factor is decisive in this structure. Highly trained scientific personnel are required in the development of new products, whilst the attraction of, for example, the Scottish new towns to US investment in electronics seems to be the availability of a relatively sophisticated labour force resulting from a well-developed education system (Hood and Young, 1980). Such a workforce is well equipped with the intermediate technical skills needed for the manufacture of semiconductors. However, such skills are not required to assemble these components into finished products. It is, therefore, hardly surprising that corporations based in the US, Western Europe and Japan began in the late 1960s to locate the final stages of many of their operations in the low-wage countries of South-East Asia (see Grunwald and Flamm, 1985; Dicken, 1986; Ballance, 1987).

It is not only direct labour costs measured in terms of wage rates that have played an important role in determining the relative location of the various elements in corporate production systems. The quality and productivity of labour is often more important from a corporate point of view (see Storper and Walker, 1989, pp. 154–82). For example, Ford's public comparisons between the output of its West German and British car plants, especially Dagenham, have frequently emphasized the better performance of workers in the former country. Indeed, the motor vehicle industry illustrates the way in which the strength of trade union organization may influence the evolution of corporate production systems. The early car plants were fully integrated operations which incorporated the entire spectrum of activities from foundry to assembly line and also manufactured an extensive range of models geared to the requirements of their particular national markets. However, with the introduction of models which are common to many countries, and with continuing interest in the concept of a 'world car' it has become possible for the giant motor companies to establish more complex, specialized and dispersed systems of production (see Bloomfield, 1981; Holmes, 1983). This is apparent in the evolution of Ford's European operations since 1950 (figure 7.9). The Spanish-built Fiesta, for example, incorporates parts from other Ford plants in West Germany, the United Kingdom, Belgium and France. The motives for establishing such a network are essentially linked to the interrelationship between economies of scale and the division of labour. Scale considerations have been important in the motor vehicle industry ever since Henry Ford introduced assembly line techniques in his Detroit factory. Their significance has been reinforced by the trend towards standardized models serving international markets. An important consequence of corporate efforts to take full advantage of scale economies has been the progressive subdivision of the various stages of production into more specialized operations. This in turn has made it possible to locate these operations in different places, and it is in selecting these locations that the labour factor has become important. Indeed, with reference to Ford, Ward (1982, p. 451) maintains that 'labour-related issues have been the cornerstone of the company's development policy since the late 1950s, exerting a strong influence over locational strategy'.

The significance of labour is related to the tradition of trade union militancy which has been a common feature of long-established centres of car production as far apart as Detroit, Coventry and Turin (see Friedman, 1977). The corporations which dominate the car industry have attempted to weaken the power of the unions by reducing their dependence upon these centres through policies of dispersal which have occurred at both national and international scales. In the United States, General Motors adopted a 'southern strategy' soon after the Second World War by diverting investment to states where the power base of the United Auto Workers was non-existent (Bluestone and Harrison, 1982a). Similar motives are alleged to have influenced Fiat in decentralizing some of its activities away from Turin to the Mezzorgiorno in the early 1970s (Massey, 1984). Parallel policies have been pursued at an international scale, and management's perception of a potentially co-operative labour force probably influenced Ford's decision to establish assembly plants in Portugal and Spain during 1970s (Ward, 1982). The political dimension to corporate location strategies in the motor vehicle industry is further emphasized by the practice of dual sourcing. Recognizing the vulnerability of an interdependent production system to disruption, it is not unusual for large corporations to sacrifice economies of scale for the additional security offered by the establishment of duplicate facilities in different locations. Despite labour difficulties at its Dagenham and Halewood plants, Ford, for example, was able to increase its share of the UK car market in the early and mid 1970s by importing components and finished cars from Spain and West Germany. Dual sourcing is just one of many short-term operational flexibilities which may be incorporated within multiplant systems. However, these systems must also be flexible in responding to long-term changes in economic circumstances, and such adjustments may radically alter the geography of the enterprise.

Locational adjustment within corporate systems

It is clear that, at a particular time, corporate production systems have distinctive spatial structures based upon the interaction of technical, economic and organizational factors. By adopting an historical perspec-

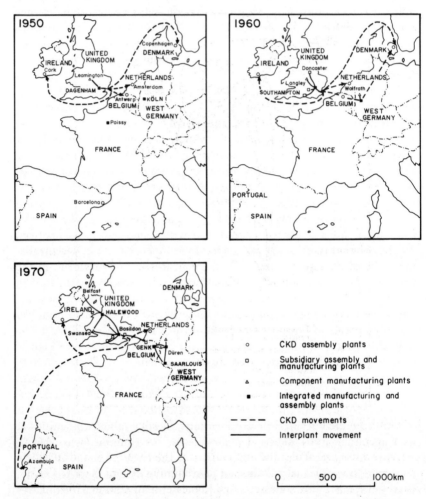

Figure 7.9 Operations of Ford Motor Company in Western Europe, 1950–1990
Source: Bloomfield, 1981 and data supplied by Ford Motor Co

tive, however, it soon becomes apparent that these structures change through time. Such changes may, of course, be associated with corporate growth (see chapter 6) and be reflected in the addition of new facilities, but in recent years many economies have experienced the other side of the coin – contraction and factory closure. These experiences have been analysed in several studies which have explicitly focused upon the link between the fortunes of regional economies and the policies of large, multiplant corporations. These studies have taken the form of both

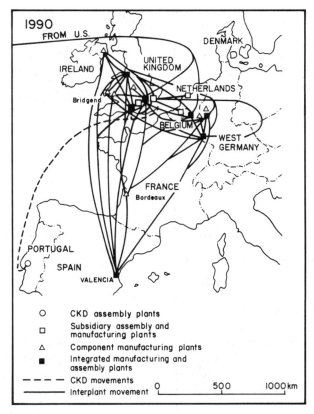

The following labels appear on the map:

1990
FROM U.S.
DENMARK
IRELAND
UNITED KINGDOM
NETHERLANDS
Bridgend
BELGIUM
WEST GERMANY
FRANCE
Bordeaux
PORTUGAL
SPAIN
VALENCIA

○   CKD assembly plants

□   Subsidiary assembly and manufacturing plants

△   Component manufacturing plants

■   Integrated manufacturing and assembly plants

— — —   CKD movements

————   Interplant movement

0   500   1000 km

Figure 7.9 Continued

general reviews (see Bluestone and Harrison, 1982a, 1982b) and specific analyses of individual corporations and communities (see Heron, 1975; Lloyd and Reeve, 1982; Bassett, 1984; Healey and Clark, 1984). The results of these studies tend to deny the often emphasized resilience of old-established industrial areas and their built-in resistance to decline which is assumed to rest upon various cumulative and acquired advantages (see Estall and Buchanan, 1980). Derelict sites and empty factories in such traditional manufacturing centres as Pittsburgh and the UK Black Country suggests that this resilience is less substantial than originally thought (see chapter 9). The withdrawal of major corporations is frequently decisive in undermining the economic base of such areas, and these withdrawals are just one aspect of the substantial and probably accelerating rates of capital mobility associated with the activities of large business organizations.

The relative ease with which capital may be transferred from one part of the corporate system to another is one of the benefits of scale. This kind of flexibility is obviously not available to the single-plant firm and the range of options, in both a geographical and a sectoral sense, is directly related to corporate size. Such flexibility confers not only economic advantages but also political benefits. The mobility of capital contrasts with the immobility of labour; this situation may be exploited by companies in their dealings with the unions, as the example of the motor vehicle industry demonstrated. The relative shift of manufacturing employment in the United States from the Manufacturing Belt to the south and south west has been reinforced by the phenomenon of 'running away from the unions' a strategy which is much easier to adopt in the context of the multiplant enterprise (Bluestone and Harrison, 1982a; Peet, 1983). At an international scale, global corporations may adopt similar tactics in negotiating with governments. Corporations such as ICI (Hudson, 1983) and Ford (Ward, 1982) have extracted substantial concessions in the form of capital grants, tax concessions and support with infrastructure investment from various European governments faced with the threat of capital transfers to other countries. These transfers may take various forms. Occasionally capital equipment may be moved, as when Chrysler shifted tools and machinery from its Coventry plant to other corporate sites in France, Spain and South America (Friedman, 1977), or even an entire factory may be dismantled and relocated. More commonly they involve less dramatic, but no less significant, shifts of financial resources within the corporate system. Thus profits made at one facility may be redirected elsewhere. Similarly, certain establishments may be starved of investment, resulting in their depreciation and ultimately their closure, whilst others are simultaneously undergoing major re-equipping and expansion. Such possibilities emphasize that change in the internal spatial structure of corporate systems is reflected not only in the addition of new plants in times of growth (see chapter 6) but also in periodic modifications to the status and function of existing sites. Such modifications are embraced within the concept of locational adjustment, which is defined by Watts (1980b, p. 115) 'to include reorganizations where the number of plants of an enterprise remains the same or is reduced while their capacities, products or linkages are changed'. By excluding the addition of plants to a corporate system, this definition represents a rather narrow interpretation of locational adjustment, but it is widely used in the geographical literature and we will, therefore, follow established practice.

Figure 7.10 identifies various forms of locational adjustment in the context of a hypothetical enterprise manufacturing four products and operating four separate sites. It extends Watt's definition of locational adjustment to incorporate employment as a further variable, but does not deal with the question of linkage changes. A broad distinction may be drawn between adjustments which have no impact on the geography of the enterprise as reflected in the number and distribution of its facilities and those which do induce such changes. Reorganizations at plant level may bring about an *intensification* in the use of labour which results either in job losses or an increased output without a corresponding increase in employment. Such reorganizations may involve minor changes in working practices or more radical shifts in the relative balance of capital to labour in the production process. Although they may have substantial effects on employment, the changes remain internal to individual manufacturing sites, and the position of these sites within the corporate system remains unchanged in both a geographical and a functional sense. By contrast, *specialization* does alter their functional roles by concentrating different product lines at specific sites (figure 7.10b). *Concentration* and partial disinvestment involves closure of certain sites, but not necessarily a reduction in overall capacity since the losses resulting from shutdown in one location may be more than offset by new investment in one or more of the remaining plants. Even more fundamental changes in the geography of the enterprise occur when existing factories are abandoned and replaced by output at an entirely new site. In this case, *rationalization and relocation* involves a reduction in both the overall output and the employment of the enterprise. The various strategies indicated in figure 7.10 are neither mutually exclusive nor exhaustive. In practice an enterprise may, over a relatively short period, reorganize its operation by a combination of all four strategies. It may also expand or reduce its product line without changing the total number of plants. Figure 7.10 must therefore be regarded as only a very general indication of the range of options available to a multiplant enterprise in adjusting its corporate system to cope with changing circumstances.

On one level, locational adjustment may be regarded as a more or less continuous process within any large enterprise. Such adjustments might include minor changes in levels of output or switching from one supplier or another. This type of flexibility is accommodated within the routine operating procedures of the enterprise. More significant from a geographical point of view are adjustments in response to major, sudden or unpredictable stresses placed upon the enterprise. It is convenient, although in some respects artificial, to distinguish between stresses which are internal to the enterprise and those which derive from external sources.

Locational adjustments are frequently associated with the reorganization of corporate systems following the acquisition of one company by

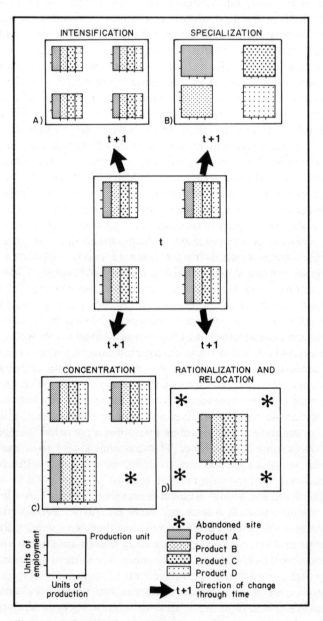

Figure 7.10 Possible forms of locational adjustment

another. Such ownership changes effectively 'relocate' the acquired plant (or plants) within a different corporate context, and its future prospects will be strongly influenced by the role which it assumes within the expanded system. This role is not necessarily determined by economic considerations alone. The various elements of multiplant enterprises often compete for resources in an essentially political internal bargaining process. The significance of such conflicts obviously depends upon the extent to which strategic decisions are centralized and the level of managerial autonomy at plant level. Nevertheless, recently acquired facilities are frequently vulnerable because they do not have an established position within the corridors of corporate power. British Leyland's decision to close down its car plant in Milan in 1975 only three years after its acquisition from Innocenti is, for example, interpreted by Grunberg (1981) as a consequence of the Italian subsidiary's lack of influence within the parent company.

Takeovers are usually regarded with apprehension by those employed in facilities which suddenly become part of another corporate system. This apprehension is often justified and there is abundant evidence that factory closure frequently follows acquisition (see Steed, 1971; Hayter, 1976; Le Heron and Warr, 1976; Watts, 1980b). Bluestone and Harrison (1982a) argue that the growth of many conglomerates in the US such as the Lykes Corporation and Ling–Temco–Vought has been achieved by ruthless and cynical closures of acquired factories which fail to meet rigidly defined criteria of profitability. This view regards conglomerates as the corporate equivalents of financiers with factories acquired and disposed of in the same way as stocks and shares. Although this interpretation of corporate behaviour may be valid in certain cases, it would be wrong to adopt an entirely negative view of the consequences of takeovers, which may have beneficial effects on individual plants. For example, a petrochemical complex operated by a single-plant enterprise at Carrington on the outskirts of Manchester was acquired by Shell in 1954. The site was subsequently expanded and developed during the next twenty years much more rapidly than could have been achieved by its seriously under-capitalized previous owner (Chapman, 1973). Green and Cromley (1982) quote a similar case in the US where the colour television division of Motorola was given a completely new lease of life following its acquisition by Matsushita of Japan. The diversity of experience revealed by case studies of individual enterprises has been confirmed by more general surveys of takeover activity which have focused upon the effects at plant level of absorption into a larger corporate system (see Leigh and North, 1978a, 1978b; Erickson, 1980a; Ashcroft and Love, 1989).

The absence of any general conclusions regarding the effects of mergers upon acquired facilities is not surprising. These effects may be expected to differ depending upon the motives for the takeover and upon the broader situation of the industry in which it takes place. Merger activity in the UK shipbuilding industry immediately after the First World War, for example, was inspired by boom conditions as independent firms were combined into larger regional groupings based on individual rivers such as the Clyde and the Tyne (Todd, 1984). Those same traditional centres have experienced very different conditions since the 1960s when a spate of 'defensive' mergers occurred as a prelude to a reduction in shipyard capacity. This example emphasizes that the impetus to merger activity is usually provided by forces which are external to the enterprise. Where merger is followed by locational adjustment, which we have already defined to exclude net additions to the number of plants operated by the enterprise, it follows that these forces are usually negative from the viewpoint of the company. For example, its markets may be contracting as a result of either a general decline in demand for its products or stiffer competition. Faced with such circumstances, the enterprise may attempt to reduce its costs and/or its capacity. Both of these responses will necessarily bring about changes in the internal structure of the corporate system.

Various strategies may be adopted in an attempt to reduce costs. Closures are for most enterprises a last resort, and less drastic measures involving changes in methods of production are usually tried first. Indeed, the interrelationships between changes in methods of production and changes in the geography of individual enterprises are very complex (see Krumme, 1969a). Corporate 'survival plans' which require specified levels of production to be achieved with reduced labour forces have become a fact of life in many manufacturing sectors faced with foreign competition. Chrysler in the United Kingdom and General Motors in the United States undertook major reorganizations during the 1970s which resulted in substantial job losses. These measures were mainly inspired by the challenge posed by imported cars in their respective national markets. Intensification (figure 7.10) does not automatically result in redundancies. It may simply involve working harder by speeding up production lines and reorganizing working practices, leading to higher output with the same input of labour. Improvements in productivity are frequently linked to new investment. This may be introduced either to complement the existing labour force or to partly replace it. Massey and Meegan (1982) outline changes in the technology of biscuit-making in the United Kingdom which have involved a move away from the traditional labour-intensive methods of baking towards highly automated systems of production. The exploitation of economies of scale is another common approach to the reduction of costs. This also often results in job losses. It may also encourage the redistribution of functions between factories within a corporate system as specific products are concentrated in particular factories (see Healey, 1981). Where changes in technology lead to larger individual units of production, there may be cost advantages to be gained by concentration and partial disinvestment or by the establishment of green-field sites (figure 7.10). The London Brick Company, for example, embarked on a major investment programme during the 1970s to establish a new generation of large, technically advanced brickworks. The result of this programme was a substantial reduction both in the company's labour force and in the number of its sites, although its aggregate level of output fell only slightly (Massey and Meegan, 1982).

A dictionary definition of rationalization implies more efficient use of resources, but the term has become synonymous in common usage with the reduction of capacity by factory closures. Many circumstances may force an enterprise to take this step. A company operating within an otherwise expanding industry may lose out to its competitors. More commonly, rationalization is associated with adverse trends at the sectoral or macro-economic level which affect all producers within an industry (see Grass and Hayter, 1989). Massey and Meegan (1979), for example, analysed the implications for enterprises and their factories of a restructuring of certain branches of the heavy electrical engineering industry in the UK in the late 1960s and early 1970s. These changes, which resulted in widespread factory closures and major job losses, were a response to a shrinking market for such equipment as transformers and switchgear used in electricity generation. Excess capacity may result from over-optimistic projections of demand and/or anticipated market shares. Many companies were involved in the European oil refining for these reasons during the late 1970s and the early 1980s. Their problems were partly self-inflicted, especially in the petrochemical industry where the search for economies of scale led the major companies to construct larger and larger production units in the hope that they could each capture a greater market share at the expense of their competitors. Chronic over-capacity has been the inevitable result of such policies (see Bacchetta, 1978). The nature of the product cycle ensures that individual products are eventually replaced by something better and, when this occurs, rationalization of capacity becomes necessary. The recent industrial experience of the United Kingdom, where industrial innovation has generally been lacking, provides many illustrations of painful corporate restructuring programmes resulting from falling demand for obsolete products. The replacement of electromechanical telephone equipment with electronic installations has, for example, necessitated major changes and factory closures with the Plessey group, which is one of three organizations which dominate the UK telecommunications industry (Peck and Townsend, 1984).

Conclusion

Case studies of locational adjustment within individual enterprises have consistently emphasized that such changes at corporate level are inextricably linked to changes in the wider systems within which these enterprises are set (see Massey and Meegan, 1979; Peck and Townsend, 1984). Thus, just as the location of the corporate systems of which they are the individual elements, so the evolution of these systems is related to events at the industry and macro-economic level. This part of the book has made the geography of the multiplant enterprise the focus of study; in the next part the level of resolution shifts towards the geography of industries.

Further reading

Bluestone, B. and Harrison, B. 1982a: *The Deindustrialization of America*. New York: Basic Books.

Grunwald, J. and Flamm, K. 1985: *The Global Factory: Foreign Assembly in International Trade*. Washington DC: Brookings Institution.

Massey, D. and Meegan, R. 1982: *The Anatomy of Job Loss*. London: Methuen.

Part IV
Industries and Regions

In this part the focus of attention shifts from the factory and firm levels which characterized parts II and III respectively to a consideration of the industries which are aggregations of these individual units of production and organization. A manufacturing industry is an artificial grouping of businesses which have some elements in common. Similarities of materials and/or technology often allow a sector's firms to be grouped together for research or policy purposes. Moreover, the age of an industry may have a bearing on its patterns of organization and location. Such changes within an industry may, in turn, have important consequences for the places with which it is associated. This part, therefore, provides a link between the logic of business and the logic of places, a link which is central to the policy issues discussed in part V.

8
The Spatial Evolution of Industries

In view of the principles outlined in earlier chapters, we may expect to find some evidence of order in the spatial pattern of the factories and firms which constitute an industry. Thus the location requirements of a bakery are very different from those of an oil refinery, and these differences will be reflected in the aggregate distribution of the industries of which they are the individual elements. We may also expect these patterns to change through time in response to such events as the development of new markets and advances in technology which alter the relative significance of individual location factors. Indeed the existing distribution of any industry is, to varying degrees dependent upon its age, an inheritance of former changes at factory and firm level – and numerous case studies have explored these relationships over various periods and at diverse geographical scales (see Bloomfield, 1978; Todd, 1984, 1985; Warren, 1973). More important than the details of these studies relating to specific industries are the insights which they provide into certain regularities underlying the spatial evolution of *all* industries. This chapter identifies these regularities by applying certain ideas, which we have already introduced in the context of factories and firms, to our analysis of the location of industries. However, before focusing upon this geographical problem, it is desirable to place our discussion within a broader perspective.

Innovation, industries and economic growth

It is generally accepted that technical change plays an important role in economic growth and the rate of progress seems to have accelerated sharply when viewed over the long perspective of human history (see Rosenberg, 1972; North, 1981). The Industrial Revolution is conventionally regarded as the watershed in this respect but the systematic application of science and technology through organized research and development is much more recent and has contributed to 'an inflection change in the supply curve of new knowledge' (North, 1981, p. 172) which has been reflected, over the last hundred years or so, in rates of economic growth which have been exceptional by earlier standards. Technical change is a complex process which embodies a wide spectrum of developments from minor improvements to fundamental advances. Incremental changes may have considerable cumulative significance but it is the discontinuous events, which have been described as 'technological revolutions' (Freeman, 1987), that have the most obvious impacts upon the structure of economies. Typically, these impacts include the creation of new industries and, in some cases, the destruction of established industries.

Casual observation of recent economic history suggests that particular sectors seem to serve as engines of economic growth at different periods. Innovations in cotton textiles, metallurgy and the pervasive influence of the various advances consequent upon the harnessing of steam power were, for example, characteristic of the Industrial Revolution. The steel industry and railways provided new impetus in the mid nineteenth century and this was followed by the impact of the widespread adoption of electricity and a series of overlapping, but successive sources of innovation associated with advances in, for example, motor vehicles, synthetic materials and electronics. Technical change, therefore, creates a temporal sequence of sectoral foci or 'poles' of economic growth (Perroux, 1961). Not only do these sectors and their constituent firms experience rapid growth, but they also induce further growth in related sectors. This *propulsive* effect is based upon backward and forward linkages as the industry generates new demands and new opportunities. Such characteristics are obviously desirable from a policy perspective and both national governments and regional development authorities seek to identify and to promote the prevailing and the next generation of high-technology or 'sunrise' industries (see chapter 11).

The interrelationships between innovation, the evolution of industries and economic growth have a geographical as well as an historical dimension. It is self-evident that there are wide variations in levels of economic development between countries and it has been suggested that the nature of the manufacturing sector changes in a systematic way as economic development takes place (see Chenery, 1960; Rostow, 1960). Cotton textiles is typically the first 'early' industry to be established and is followed by 'middle' and 'late' sectors such as rubber products and consumer durables respectively. These sequential relationships between industrial structure and economic growth, first associated with countries such as the United Kingdom and the United States, have also been described for countries which have industrialized later, right through from Italy and Sweden at the end of the nineteenth century to their contemporary equivalents such as Brazil and South Korea (see Rostow, 1978; Beenstock, 1983), the only major difference being a tendency for the process to accelerate as latecomers have been able to benefit from the pool of technology and experience accumulated by their predecessors. It follows that a particular industry may be a leading or propulsive sector in one country at the same time that it is in decline or has even disappeared in another. Thus the connections between technical change and economic growth imply a temporal sequence in the development of industries when viewed in historical terms and a corresponding dispersal when viewed from a geographical perspective. The following sections of this chapter further develop this geographical perspective, first with reference to a simple model which derives its inspiration from normative and behavioural concepts usually associated with the analysis of individual plant locations; second by focusing upon the relationship between technological and locational change; and finally by applying these ideas to a case study of the world petrochemical industry.

From plant location to industry evolution

Classical location theory is, as we have seen in chapter 3, essentially concerned with defining the 'best' location for the individual factory with respect to such criteria as costs, revenues and profits, but the normative approach also offers certain insights into the relative location of similar plants which, in aggregate, represent the spatial distribution of an industry. For example, the locational interdependence or market area ideas developed by Hotelling (1929) and Lösch (1954) imply a dispersed pattern and are appropriate to industries such as soft drinks manufacture in which distribution costs are high. On the other hand, Weber's (1929) model is most relevant to industries such as iron and steel which utilize bulky, localized raw materials and which tend to be concentrated at particular locations. Generally speaking, the least-cost model is probably most useful in the interpretation of contemporary spatial patterns at the industry level. Dispersed production was the rule before the Industrial Revolution when manufacturing was organized on a small scale in response to the demands of local markets. This pattern was radically altered by the technical and organizational changes associated with the introduction of the factory system. The basic units of production increased in size and the friction of distance was reduced by advances in transport systems. Thus the dispersed distribution of economic activity which preceded the Industrial Revolution was replaced by greater geographical concentration as particular industries became identified with specific areas. In these circumstances, it is not unreasonable to apply the least-cost approach of identifying a single optimal location for a given manufacturing activity such as a paper mill within a predetermined area, which may be defined at the regional or national scale, to an interpretation of the spatial evolution of the industry which is made up of many such establishments.

Figure 8.1 plots the development of a hypothetical industry through time. This representation combines elements of both normative and behavioural approaches to the analysis of industrial location (see chapter 2) and it attempts to provide a conceptual link between static analyses of the single-plant location problem and the infinitely more complex issues associated with the dynamics of industry patterns. An optimal location O, surrounded by spatial margins to profitability M, is identified for each of three successive times. To simplify the argument it is assumed that the industry is composed of single-plant firms and is established instantaneously at stage 1. At this initial stage, the distribution is random with respect to the optimal location, being determined by such chance factors as the place of residence of the entrepreneurs, who are assumed (perhaps unrealistically) to spontaneously acquire the expertise and knowledge required to enter the new industry. This knowledge is not necessarily sufficient to ensure that they all select a profitable location. Those firms lying outside the spatial margin to profitability (see chapter 2) will quickly go out of business. Others which are located just within the margin at stage 1 may have suffered the same fate by stage 2 as a result of unfavourable shifts in the boundary associated with changing technical and economic circumstances during the intervening period. In some cases, these changes may be dramatic, creating what Pred (1969) has referred to as parametric shocks. The development of synthetic fibres, for example, seriously undermined the market for the products of the cotton and other traditional textile industries. One response to the new competition was an attempt to dramatically reduce the costs of production, a strategy which led to the global redistribution of cotton-spinning capacity away from countries such as the United Kingdom to sources of cheap labour such as India. Parametric shocks may also be triggered by political events. The establishment of trading blocs such as the European Economic Community creates new market opportunities which may favour the concentration of production at fewer, bigger sites. Conversely, the fragmentation of larger political units into smaller independent countries, as illustrated by the Hapsburg Empire after the First World War, may have the opposite effect. Despite the unpredictability of such events, the logic of the model represented in figure 8.1

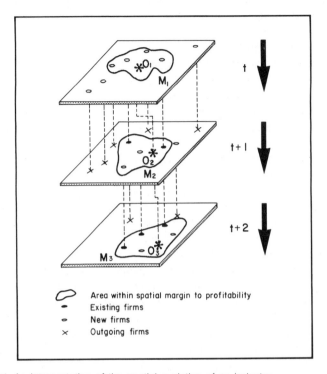

Figure 8.1 An interpretation of the spatial evolution of an industry

is based on a kind of economic Darwinism leading ultimately in stage 3 to an overall industry pattern that is more rational relative to the optimum. This view of industrial spatial evolution as a random or *stochastic* process constrained by the economic realities embraced within the concept of the spatial margin owes much to Pred's (1969) behavioural matrix (figure 2.1). Certain firms select locations within the spatial margin as a result of good judgement whilst others are simply lucky. The former adapt to the prevailing economic system, the latter are adopted by it. The distinction between the two types of survivor is, however, less important than the net result of their longevity – an industry pattern which displays an evolutionary tendency towards an economically rational spatial equilibrium.

It is one thing to identify such a tendency in theory, quite another to demonstrate it in practice. The kind of information required to test the model is very difficult to obtain. Although records are often available on the survivors, the failures tend to disappear without trace as far as documentary evidence is concerned. Further difficulties are associated with the complex nature of the variables involved. The evolutionary sequence identified in figure 8.1 implicitly relates to an industry manufacturing a single, uniform product. In reality most industries produce multiple products, each of which may have different locational requirements. Thus changing industry patterns cannot be related to a single optimum at any time. White and Watts (1977) attempted to overcome these difficulties by selecting an industry – the production of broiler fowls – with a single product and by concentrating their attention on its spatial evolution in a limited area, the East Midlands of England, over a period of less than twenty years from 1955 to 1972. On the basis of a detailed analysis of the economics of broiler production, they were able to demonstrate a clear tendency towards a more optimal pattern; plants established towards the end of their study period were more 'rational' in their location than those established at the beginning. Broiler production in the East Midlands is, of course, scarcely representative of manufacturing as a whole, but this study is perhaps the only published empirical test of the model outlined in figure 8.1.

The model emphasizes that the various firms are faced with the problem of selecting a location relative to an optimum which is, in effect, a moving target. Individual firms cannot, for obvious practical reasons, make continued short-term adjustments in their location, although they are often very successful in adapting in other ways to changes in their external environment. In a study of sugar-cane processing plants in Guyana and Jamaica, for example, Auty (1975) noted major differences in the cost structure in the older facilities associated with scattered plantations as compared with the larger modern operations in the urban centres which derived their raw material from several plantations. By running their machinery well beyond the 20 years normally used for depreciating costs and by paying very low wages the former were able to remain in business despite the competition from the more favourably situated urban plants. Such adaptability does not, however, invalidate the proposition that the kind of natural selection processes referred to earlier will have the long-term effect of producing a significant shift in the spatial pattern of an industry. The variables influencing this pattern are essentially the same as those which have already been identified in the location of individual plants (see chapters 3 and 4). Technical developments may alter the relationship between the various factors of production, leading to the substitution of capital for labour or to the use of differing combinations of raw materials. Advances in transport technology influencing both the assembly of inputs and the distribution of finished products may also modify cost and revenue calculations. The longer the period, the more likely it is that the key reference points in the determination of the optimum location will themselves shift as, for example, some raw material sources are exhausted and replaced by others and new markets develop in response to changing patterns of population and economic activity.

The iron and steel industry provides a good example of the operation of these variables because of the overriding importance of transport costs in the location decision together with the impact of certain technical changes upon the economics of steel-making. The bulky nature of both raw materials and finished products accounts for the significance of transport costs, but the relative importance of raw material and market factors has changed as a result of the progressive decline in the quantities of coal, iron ore and limestone required to produce a unit of steel. This trend has been reinforced by other developments, such as the upgrading of ores at their source and the introduction of 'unit trains' and bulk carriers which have reduced the real costs of raw material assembly. The importance of scrap, which obviously tends to be available in the major population centres, as an input to steel-making has also increased, further reducing the attractions of raw material sources. The impact of these influences upon the US iron and steel industry has been examined in various studies which have interpreted its spatial evolution with reference to shifting optima through time (see Warren, 1973; Hekman, 1978). Pennsylvania and Ohio have been the principal centres of the industry ever since 1850, largely as a result of the attractions of the coalfields of the northern part of the Appalachian plateau, but their dominance has declined steadily during the twentieth century (figure 8.2). Their combined share of US steel production fell from 63.4 per cent in 1893 to 31.2 per cent by 1987 whilst the Mid-West states of Indiana, Illinois and Michigan increased from 7.4 to 38.2 per cent during the same period (American Iron and Steel Association, annual reports). This westward shift created by the development of new steel-making centres along the shores of Lakes Erie and Michigan was mainly induced by the growth of new markets, a stimulus which has also led to the establishment of capacity in California.

The redistribution of an industry through time may be observed at the international as well as the national scale. Major changes have taken place in world leadership of the shipbuilding industry, for example. The abundance and low cost of timber along the Atlantic seaboard together with a buoyant domestic demand associated with the rapid growth of its merchant fleet made the United States the major producer during the first half of the nineteenth century. British supremacy from the mid nineteenth century to the Second World War was linked to the switch from wooden sailing ships to iron and steel steamships. This supremacy was technology-based and reflected the UK's pioneering role in such developments as the steam engine. As recently as 1950, the United

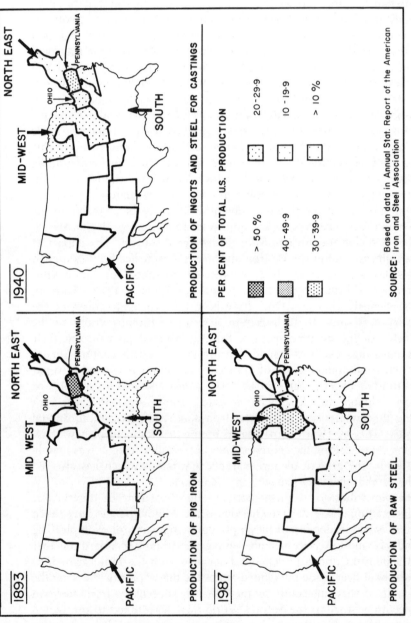

Figure 8.2 Changing distribution of US iron and steel industry, 1893–1987
Source: Annual Statistical Reports of American Iron and Steel Association

Kingdom and the rest of Western Europe accounted for approximately 90 per cent of new tonnage, but this share had slumped to 10 per cent by the end of the 1980s. Several factors have contributed to the rise of the new producers (see Todd, 1985; Sung Cho and Porter, 1986). However, there is no doubt that much lower labour costs have been especially important. These account for as much as 30 per cent of the total cost of building a vessel, and in a highly competitive international industry, efficient and low-cost labour has been a key source of comparative advantage to Japan and South Korea. China is expected to adopt a similar low-cost strategy to establish itself as a major producer by the end of the century.

The experiences of iron and steel in the United States and world shipbuilding emphasize the way in which the centre of gravity of an industry may shift in response to changing circumstances. These circumstances may be external to the industry, such as the appearance of new markets, but shifts in comparative advantage often have their origins within the industry. For example, the introduction of new methods of shipbuilding contributed to the pre-eminence of the United Kingdom in the late nineteenth century and then to the rise of Japan after 1960. These changes are obviously specific to shipbuilding, but certain regularities have been observed in many sectors which have encouraged attempts to interpret the spatial evolution of industries in terms of a life cycle. This concept is complementary to the stochastic model summarized in figure 8.1 because it identifies the role of technical and organizational changes which are internal to an industry in shifting the optimum location and, therefore, the spatial margins through time.

Life cycles and the location of industries

Innovation is central to the application of the life-cycle analogy to the development of industries. A distinction may be made between product and process innovations. The so-called 'law of industrial growth' was originally based upon an empirical study of historical trends in output in various US industries between 1885 and 1930 (Burns, 1934). The basic proposition states that industries tend to experience 'a period of experimentation, a period of rapid growth, a period of diminished growth and a period of stability or decline' (Alderfer and Michl, 1942, p. 14). It is product innovation which sets this cycle in motion, but each of these periods may be related to process innovations affecting the methods of manufacture (see Utterback and Abernathy, 1975; Magee, 1977). Indeed the argument at industry level is much the same as that applied to an understanding of the changing location within corporate systems of facilities for the manufacture of specific products at different stages in their development (see chapter 7). The technology of production seems to develop in certain systematic ways in apparently very different industries. Vernon (1960, 1966) argued that, because of the link between the technology of an industry and its location requirements, these similarities find spatial expression in characteristic distributions associated with industries in their youth, maturity and old age.

In theory the origin of an industry may be traced back to a key invention, but in practice it is rarely possible to attribute such a decisive role to a single discovery. Given the tendency for entrepreneurs to establish their businesses close to home (see chapter 3), it could be argued that the distribution of new industries is determined by essentially chance factors which contribute to the flashes of inspiration upon which they are based. However, there is no doubt that many inventions are a response to problems in existing industries and the individuals responsible for them are often involved with these industries. This type of relationship suggests that the distribution of inventive activity will tend to favour established industrial centres and there is abundant evidence to suggest that this was indeed the case during the nineteenth and early twentieth centuries (see Pred, 1966; Feller, 1975). On the other hand, established centres may stifle innovation through the adoption of restrictive practices and conservative attitudes (see Chinitz, 1961, chapter 9) and new industries to some extent create their own conditions for growth in new areas as exemplified by the replacement of the former fruit orchards of 'Silicon Valley' in California by electronics plants (Saxenian, 1985). In these circumstances, new industries may 'seem to "leapfrog" in space, establishing growth centers and new growth peripheries that are relatively insulated from existing highly industrialized regions' (Storper and Walker, 1989, pp. 11–14). Another factor influencing the locus of innovation is the distribution of corporate R & D facilities. We have already seen how the geographical impact of advances made in such establishments is determined by the spatial structure of the corporate systems to which they belong (see chapter 7). Such institutional R & D is becoming more and more important relative to the activities of isolated individuals as the principal source of technical change in industry (see Freeman, 1982). Nevertheless, even the largest enterprises recognize the potential significance of small research teams and ICI, for example, is pursuing a strategy of venture capital support for entrepreneurial, science-based firms in its promotion of new bio-technologies. There are good reasons for suggesting that the subsequent development of an invention, whether made by an individual entrepreneur or within a corporate organization, into a new industry will first be concentrated within a relatively limited area. The application and commercial development of an invention (i.e. the process of innovation) associated with young industries involves rapid technological change and firms are drawn to the source of such change in just the same way as to any other geographically fixed, scarce resource. This clustering is reinforced by the typically fragmented commercial structure of such industries as perceptive imitators copy and adapt the ideas of the pioneers. Agglomeration economies are especially important in an environment of small firms (see chapter 4) and the concentrations which they promote may in turn spawn new developments as advances in one industry stimulate growth in related sectors.

These features of young industries may be illustrated by both historical and contemporary examples. Although many factors, including the availability of water power and capital, have been identified to account for the early concentration of cotton textiles in the vicinity of Boston, Massachusetts, Hekman (1980b) argues that the decisive influences were a combination of entrepreneurial and mechanical skills which, in the context of the United States in the early nineteenth century, were unique to New England. At that time, the equipment required in the new mechanized mills stretched the technological capabilities of the embryonic machine-tool industry to the limit. Thus the textile producers needed to locate in close proximity to the machine shops which both provided and maintained custom-built equipment. More than any other nineteenth-century industry, machine tools demonstrated the maxim that necessity is the mother of invention as it faced and coped with the production problems of other industries. Indeed, it is generally accepted that machine tools played a vital role in the industrialization of the US and in promoting the emergence of the manufacturing belt as the economic heartland of the country (see Pred, 1966).

The silicon chip is equally versatile in the final quarter of the twentieth century, and clear parallels may be drawn between the concentration of textile mills to the south and west of Boston in 1840 and the existing concentration of electronics and computer-related activities in the Palo Alto/Santa Clara/San Jose corridor to the south of San Francisco (i.e. 'Silicon Valley'). Although the transistor, which is the basis of the modern electronics industry, was invented in the laboratories of a corporate enterprise, many other important technological advances were made in 'Silicon Valley' through the activities of scientist–entrepreneurs operating in converted garages and workshops (Saxenian, 1985). The development of electronics in the 1940s and 1950s was, therefore, characterized by the commercial fragmentation and geographical concentration typical of a young industry.

By the mid 1980s, many branches of the electronics industry and especially those concerned with the production of consumer goods such as stereo equipment and calculators had attained maturity. Several firms which began life as entrepreneurial ventures have grown rapidly to become major organizations, such as Hewlett–Packard and Texas Instruments. A much greater number of others have failed. The net result has been a radical change in the commercial structure of the industry as comparatively few large corporations have replaced the many small firms largely responsible for its initial development. These changes in organizational structure have been paralleled by developments in technology which have transformed production processes from the realm of the workbench to the assembly line. The impact upon the geography of the electronics industry of these technical and commercial dimensions of its progression from youth to maturity have already been referred to in chapter 7. The spatial division of labour within corporations occurs when individual products have reached the mature and old-age stages of their life cycles, and the aggregation of such systems of manufacture at the level of specific products and corporations leads to the emergence of distinctive patterns at the industry scale. In the case of consumer electronics, the tendency to transfer assembly operations to cheap labour locations in South-East Asia ensured that the geography of the mature industry of the 1980s is very different from that of the young industry of the 1950s.

The industry life-cycle model postulates a slackening rate of growth in output at the mature stage. Viewed on a global scale, trends in motor vehicle production suggest that this industry, for example, is at the mature stage of its life cycle and that its period of most rapid growth between 1945 and 1973 will never again be repeated (Bhaskar, 1980). Indeed, the annual world output (excluding the communist bloc) of passenger vehicles fell for the first time in 1979 (OECD, 1983b). However, more detailed analysis of this industry reveals some of the ambiguities of the life-cycle model. Figure 8.3 shows significant differences in output trends in North America, Western Europe and Japan. Levels of car ownership were already high in North America in 1950 by comparison with Western Europe and Japan. Rapid rates of output growth obviously became difficult to sustain as more and more families became car owners and the proportion of replacement relative to new demand (i.e. first-time buyers) tended to grow. Even greater geographical variations are likely to emerge towards the end of the century as the demand for cars takes off in various Third-World countries, some of which will follow the example of Brazil and seek to establish their own motor vehicle industries. The Brazilian industry may expect to grow at rates typical of youth despite the fact that it is using essentially mature technology. There are many different dimensions of maturity as applied to industries. It is possible to speak of maturity not only with reference

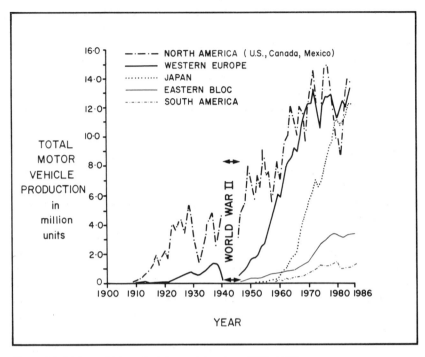

Figure 8.3 Motor vehicle output by world region, 1910–1986
Source: Motor Vehicle Manufacturers' Assocation of the US, *World Motor Vehicle Data 1988*, Detroit, Mich.

to technology and market characteristics, but also in organizational terms. In particular, there is a tendency for firm size to increase and the number of firms to decrease in the mature stage. All of these attributes of maturity are related but, because this phase may last a long time, it is very difficult and misleading to portray a definitive picture of its characteristics.

Two general situations leading to the stable or declining output stage of the industry life cycle may be identified. The first is an extension of the concept of market saturation; the second is associated with technological changes which lead to the displacement of one industry by another. As economies develop, certain structural changes take place which modify patterns of demand for the products of different industries. The relationship between growth processes at the macro-economic, industry and product levels are very complex (see Thomas, 1981b), but we have already noted a tendency for particular industries to act as engines of growth at specific phases in the development of national economies. The changing role of the iron and steel industry is a good example. There is a strong link between steel demand and levels of economic development which may be represented as a flattened, S-shaped curve. The form of the curve reflects the fact that the demand for steel is greatest in the intermediate stages of development as a result of the requirements of transport, engineering and construction activities. Major steel-using industries are relatively less important in the advanced economies, which place greater emphasis upon high-technology sectors such as telecommunications and aerospace and upon non-manufacturing tertiary and quaternary activities. Steel output is, therefore, relatively stable in many developed countries and even contracting in others at the same time that it is experiencing rapid growth in, for example, Brazil, South Korea and India (see Dicken, 1986).

Although the fortunes of the steel industry may wane as economies develop, there is no suggestion that its products will be entirely replaced by new materials in the foreseeable future. However, the experience of history emphasizes that the decline of one industry may be a direct consequence of the rise of another, often in an entirely different location. The collapse of the traditional linen textile industry of Northern Ireland during the 1950s and 1960s was, for example, related to competition from new synthetic materials such as nylon (Steed, 1974). Similarly, the village-based watch-making industry of the Swiss Jura has been virtually destroyed as a result of the replacement of traditional, precision-made mechanisms with quartz and electronic technologies which can be mass produced at much lower cost in the factories of Japan.

In many cases the decline of an industry is a long and, for the areas with which it is associated, painful process (see chapter 9). This process involves changes at firm and corporate level which, in aggregate, lead not only to a reduction in, but also to a redistribution of, production capacity (see chapter 7). The nature of this redistribution often varies depending upon the scale at which it is viewed. At a national level, contraction usually implies concentration of production at fewer sites. This process is often facilitated and accompanied by organizational changes as the stronger of the remaining enterprises take over the weaker. The restructuring and redistribution of various branches of the heavy electrical engineering industry in the UK during the 1960s and early 1970s exemplified these processes (Massey and Meegan, 1979). In this case, the changes were actively encouraged by the British government through the medium of its Industrial Reorganization Corporation in the hope that a more competitive, if smaller, electrical engineering industry would be the outcome. The Ministry of International Trade and Industry performs a similar function in Japan where, for example, the restructuring of the petrochemical industry since 1983 has been facilitated by the Ministry's role in co-ordinating the rationalization plans of the various companies. Such public intervention in regulating the contraction of declining industries is not unusual and may operate at an international scale. For example, various plans have been devised by the European Commission which have, in effect, attempted to share the misery involved in reducing capacity in such industries as synthetic fibres (Shaw and Shaw, 1983) and iron and steel (Commission of the European Communities, 1981) between its member countries. Although such schemes require a degree of political co-operation which is not always forthcoming, their broad geographical effect is again one of concentration at fewer centres.

At the same time that concentration is taking place within Western Europe, more and more countries are reaching the point in the relationship between their economic development and their steel consumption at which the establishment of their own industry is perceived to be economically and politically desirable. The contrasting experience of old and new steel producers ensures that whilst concentration may be the principal spatial dynamic within the former groups, dispersal is the rule at the international scale. Although the establishment of new national steel industries has eliminated some of the export markets of long-established producers, there is no direct link between the decline of the industry in Western Europe, for example, and its rise in Latin America and South-East Asia. The explanation for these contrasts lies more in the relationship between economic development and steel consumption than in any systematic transfer of investment, through the medium of the global corporation, from one part of the world to another. However, this kind of mechanism has played an important role in the redistribution of, for example, textile and clothing manufacture which, in many countries, displays all the characteristics of an industry in the declining phase of its life cycle.

The textile and clothing industries are closely related. Demand for their products is linked to levels of economic development. Whereas this relationship is determined by the changing requirements for capital goods in the case of iron and steel, it is regulated by the characteristics of household demand in the case of textiles and clothing. These products are fundamental necessities but, as the level of disposable income rises, the proportion spent on clothing tends to fall. Thus although it is one of the first industries to be established in any country, it is difficult to sustain rates of growth commensurate with general levels of economic expansion. Even stability has proved a forlorn objective as output, employment and capacity have all declined steadily in most of the advanced economies (OECD, 1983c). The activities of large corporations have been an important factor in these trends as production is being organized increasingly on an international basis (Dicken, 1986). Despite the efforts of governments in many developed countries to protect their own textile and clothing sectors by erecting tariff barriers, there has been a flight of corporate capital from the core industrial economies to the global periphery, attracted by lower labour costs which are especially important in an essentially labour-intensive industry. This shift has precipitated the relative decline of the industry in the core economies – which would have occurred anyway as a result of changing income-related patterns of demand – into an absolute decline as imports from the Third World have entered the markets of the US, Western Europe and Japan.

Attempts to relate the experience of specific industries to the life-cycle model emphasize its limitations. Its validity tends to diminish as both the sectoral and the spatial level of generalization increases. Gold (1964) demonstrated that whilst individual products may conform with the model, 'industries' are usually aggregations of products, each of which may be at different stages in their own life cycles. Similarly, an understanding of the evolution of industries cannot be divorced from an equivalent understanding of the economies of which they are a part. Despite the growing interdependence of the world economy, many industries still operate at a national scale and the same sector may be at very different stages in different countries. Furthermore, the life-cycle model implies a continuity of development which is often lacking. Radical changes in methods of production or external 'shocks' (affecting, for example, the availability of raw materials) may completely reorientate an industry within its cycle of development. The US automobile industry originated in the 1890s in numerous small workshops associated with the manufacture of such items as farm machinery and horse-drawn carriages and was, therefore, widely dispersed throughout the country (Boas, 1961). The introduction of Henry Ford's assembly line in Detroit in 1915 represented a fundamental departure from the craft methods previously employed. Not only did this event transform the geography of the industry, but it also amounted to a kind of rebirth in terms of its life cycle. Such events seem to be occurring with increasing frequency, with the result that individual product cycles in sectors such as electronics may have a duration of as little as five years. The acceleration of rates of change at the product level increases the already formidable difficulties of applying the life-cycle model at the industry scale. It is important, however, to place these difficulties in perspective. As with any model, the technology-based product/industry life cycle is, in a geographical context, only intended to provide a conceptual framework for interpreting the spatial evolution of an industry. Such a framework is helpful in proceeding from description to analysis, and this approach is adopted in the next section with reference to the petrochemical industry.

A case study: the petrochemical industry

Petrochemical manufacture is a segment of the chemical industry which is distinguished by its dependence upon petroleum-based raw materials rather than by the nature of its products. These products include chemicals such as ethanol which have a very long history of manufacture using traditional methods such as the fermentation of molasses. However, the switch to petroleum-based feedstocks in the chemical industry has been inextricably linked with the development and commercial manufacture of a whole range of new products. Some of these are chemicals, whilst others include the principal synthetic materials such as plastics, man-made fibres and rubbers which have both displaced established materials in existing applications and also created entirely new markets. It has been the buoyant demand for plastics in particular which has ensured that petrochemical manufacture has played an important role in the post-war economies of the developed countries. Thus, although petrochemical manufacture is strictly speaking a branch of the chemical industry, its importance in the development of materials which, despite being taken for granted in modern society, have only come into widespread use since the Second World War, provides ample justification for regarding it as an industry in its own right. One of the most distinctive characteristics of this industry has been its rapid growth, which has found physical expression in some of the most spectacular contemporary agglomerations of economic activity in places such as Houston, Rotterdam and Teesside.

An awareness of the technical basis of an industry is a prerequisite to an understanding of its location. In the case of the petrochemical industry this basis is provided by the principles of hydrocarbon chemistry, and the origins of the diverse products of the industry may be traced to a limited number of reactions involving certain key hydrocarbon compounds. These compounds may themselves be derived from two different raw material sources – oil and natural gas. Although the direct use of crude oil in petrochemical plants is technically feasible, such plants normally consume a range of fractions from heavy liquids to petroleum gases which are obtained from oil refineries. This association with oil refineries does not exist for those plants which use certain components of natural gas. The distinction between oil- and gas-based operations has an important geographical dimension; the European and

Japanese industries are largely dependent upon the supply of refinery feedstocks, whilst the US and some of the major new producers in the Middle East and Latin America rely heavily upon the use of natural gas. Despite their different starting-points, the subsequent processing of oil- and gas-based raw materials follows an identical sequence. In both cases the raw material is subject to cracking (i.e. thermal decomposition) to produce a series of intermediates, of which ethylene is by far the most important. These in turn represent the starting-point for a series of further reactions, leading to the production of such materials as polystyrene and acrylonitrile which find applications in the plastics and textile industries respectively. Some of these reactions and relationships are portrayed in figure 8.4, which provides a necessary if rudimentary technical framework for what follows.

Although the origin of the petrochemical industry cannot be attributed to any single discovery, it is generally accepted that it was born in the United States in the 1920s as a result of the independent research of several major oil and chemical companies including Shell, Esso, Dow and Du Pont. It has, therefore, been dominated from the very beginning by large organizations. Nevertheless its early location was, if not

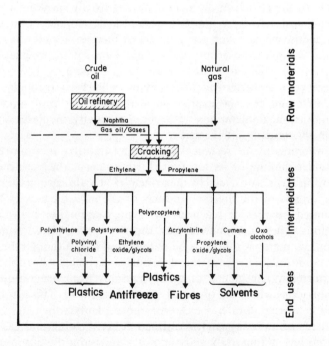

Figure 8.4 Principal processes and products of the petrochemical industry

determined by the distribution of individual entrepreneurs, strongly influenced by the geography of the enterprises associated with its initial development. The translation of processes pioneered in corporate R & D laboratories into commercial plants occurred first of all at existing manufacturing sites. These sites were often oil refineries because many of the early petrochemical plants in the United States converted gases previously burnt as refinery fuel into chemical products. Thus, by the beginning of the Second World War, the embryonic petrochemical industry consisted of a scattered distribution of isolated plants associated with the oil refineries as far apart as California and New Jersey and with natural gas deposits in several states including Michigan, West Virginia and Oklahoma. No other countries had established commercial-scale petrochemical facilities, although it should be emphasized that research in Germany and, to a much lesser extent, in the United Kingdom, during the inter-war years was to make a major contribution to the spectacular post-war growth of the industry. Indeed, many more key product innovations linked to the development of new synthetic materials such as polyethylene and polyvinyl chloride (PVC) were made in Europe than in the United States. However, the existence of its large petroleum and, more specifically, oil refining industry gave the United States a major raw material advantage which ensured not only that it was the first to manufacture chemicals from petroleum but also that it dominated the new industry for at least 25 years after the end of the Second World War.

Fears of possible shortages of strategic raw materials such as rubber provided an impetus to the development of the industry in the United States following the outbreak of war as efforts were directed towards the production of synthetic substitutes. The rapid growth of the 1940s and 1950s was accompanied by a significant shift in the distribution of the new industry, which became progressively more concentrated in major complexes along the Gulf coast of Texas. This concentration crystallized out of the previously scattered distribution of plants determined by the various influences of raw material availability from gas fields and existing oil refineries as well as the geography of corporate inventive and innovative activity. This trend is consistent with the model outlined in figure 8.1 in that the increasing importance of Texas represented a move towards a more rational pattern focused upon an optimal location in the Houston area, related to the availability not only of refinery feedstocks but also of abundant and cheap natural gas.

At the same time as the US petrochemical industry was becoming focused upon Texas, the technology was beginning to be introduced in other countries. An important permissive factor in the development of petrochemicals first in Western Europe and later in Japan was the massive post-war expansion in their oil refining industries. This expansion was primarily motivated by economic and political considerations relating to energy supplies, but it had the effect of making available the kind of feedstocks required by the petrochemical industry. Both oil and chemical companies were quick to seize this opportunity and the petrochemical industry maintained very high rates of growth in Western Europe during the 20 years from 1950 to 1970 and in Japan during the second half of the same period. Between 1960 and 1973, for example, the average annual growth in ethylene output in the developed market economies was 17 per cent – more than three times the rate for industrial production as a whole (OECD, 1985, p. 71).

Despite the significant time lags separating the establishment and rapid expansion of petrochemical manufacture successively in the United States, Western Europe and Japan, its aggregate rates of growth in these economies to 1970 were characteristic of an industry in the youthful stage of its life cycles. These were sustained by the interrelationship between high levels of demand for the products of the industry and the influence of various technical advances which reinforced this market-led growth. Chemical manufacture has always occupied a basic position in the industrial economy because of its role as a supplier of materials to other sectors. The chemical industry in general and petrochemicals in particular therefore benefited from the historically high rates of economic growth characteristic of the 1950s and, especially, the 1960s. However, further impetus to growth was provided by the way in which various products of the petrochemical industry such as plastics and synthetic fibres displaced traditional materials in many applications. This substitution effect was made possible by a series of important product innovations. Many of these, including polystyrene, polyethylene, nylon and PVC, were developed in the laboratory in the 1930s, but production on a commercial scale was initiated after the war. The rate of technical advance tended to slacken off in the post-war years and, in accordance with the product and industry life-cycle models, the emphasis switched towards process innovations designed to improve the qualities and reduce the costs of existing products. For example, much effort was devoted towards achieving economies of scale in the production of ethylene, the basic building block of the industry, and the average size of cracking unit in Western Europe more than doubled every five years between 1950 and 1970 (Chapman, 1973). These efforts, together with the declining real price of oil-based feedstocks, ensured that the average cost of ethylene to downstream plants fell steadily throughout the 1960s, further improving the competitiveness of its many derivative products (figure 8.5).

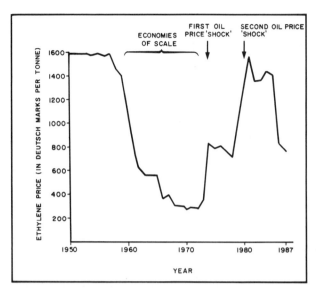

Figure 8.5 Contract price of ethylene in Western Europe, 1950–1987
Source: ICI plc

By the late 1960s, there were signs that the industry and its markets were approaching maturity in the developed economies. In particular, its growth rate relative to other sectors began to look less impressive. This was mainly due to the diminished opportunities for substitution and the onset of market saturation. The industry also failed to maintain the growth dynamic previously based upon product and process innovations. Few entirely new products have been introduced since 1960, whilst several of the industry's staples such as PVC and polystyrene have remained essentially unchanged for thirty to forty years. On the process side, the form of the scale/cost curve (figure 8.6) has limited the scope for further cost savings. However, at the same time that market-led growth was slackening in the established centres of petrochemical production, new markets were opening up elsewhere.

The demand for petrochemicals bears an S-shaped relationship to levels of economic development similar to that for iron and steel, and a number of countries such as Brazil were beginning to cross the threshold into the intermediate (accelerating) segment of the demand curve by 1970. These countries viewed petrochemicals as a key element in industrialization strategies based upon import substitution. By this time, petrochemical technology was relatively mature and widely

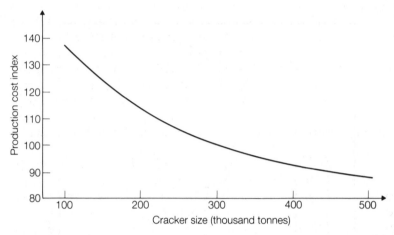

Figure 8.6 Economies of scale in ethylene production
Source: OECD

available for purchase from, for example, chemical engineering contractors. In these circumstances, the governments of several developing countries including Brazil, Mexico and Taiwan directly promoted the creation of national petrochemical industries. The gradual dispersion of the industry at the international scale implicit in such market-led investment was, however, dramatically accelerated by the entirely new set of circumstances created by the world oil price increases of 1973 and 1979.

These events, especially the second round of increases, have had a profound effect upon the economics of petrochemical manufacture (Auty, 1984). This effect is exemplified by the case of ethylene. The variable costs of energy and feedstock as a proportion of the total cost of producing this intermediate from a typical cracking plant located in Western Europe increased from 46 per cent in 1973 to 85 per cent by 1980 (OECD, 1985, p. 45). It is, therefore, not surprising that energy and resource costs became a more important consideration in the location of basic petrochemical facilities. Whereas the industry has, at the international scale, been essentially market oriented, the optimum location has shifted towards countries with abundant supplies of cheap natural gas. The magnitude of this shift will depend upon the kind of pricing policies adopted by the gas producers and by the vagaries of the international oil market. These are difficult to predict because they will be determined by political as much as economic circumstances. Taking ethylene production capacity as an index, table 8.1 and figure 8.7 summarize past and probable future changes in the global distribution of the petrochemical industry. The 'others' include both resource-rich countries such as Saudi Arabia in which the industry is geared to serving export markets and large market countries such as Brazil where domestic demand has been the principal impetus to development. Figure 8.7 emphasizes that rather than a single life cycle, it is possible to recognize a succession of spatially disaggregated life cycles for a single industry.

The redistribution of the industry has been a consequence not only of the construction of new petrochemical capacity, but also of the closure of older plants. Viewed in terms of our evolutionary spatial model (figure 8.1), the industry was required, during the early 1980s, to adjust to a new optimum location. For Western Europe and Japan, this involved a spate of defensive mergers and market-sharing agreements, often with the tacit approval or active encouragement of national governments, designed to facilitate the shedding of capacity and the restructuring of the industry (Bower, 1986). These measures adversely affected regional economies such as Teesside which had become heavily dependent upon petrochemicals (Hudson, 1983). Indeed, the industry that twenty years earlier was widely regarded as a potential catalyst of regional economic growth (Chapman, 1984) seemed to be just another basic industry in decline. This decline is unlikely to be terminal, however; even with the challenge of the new producers, the industry will remain an important element within the structure of the developed economies. Nevertheless it remains firmly the mature stage of its life cycle in these economies, where the long-term future of the chemical industry appears to lie in raw materials and energy sources other than petroleum and in entirely new directions such as biotechnology.

Conclusion

The case of petrochemical manufacture emphasizes that, despite the apparent intertia of capital equipment tied up in factories and other

Table 8.1 World distribution of ethylene capacity, 1950–1990

	1950 (%)	1960 (%)	1970 (%)	1980 (%)	1990 est. (%)
US	98.1	74.4	48.0	41.6	36.0
Western Europe	1.9	21.8	32.6	33.8	34.0
Japan	–	1.1	13.7	12.8	11.0
Others	–	2.7	5.7	11.8	19.0
Total	100.0	100.0	100.0	100.0	100.0

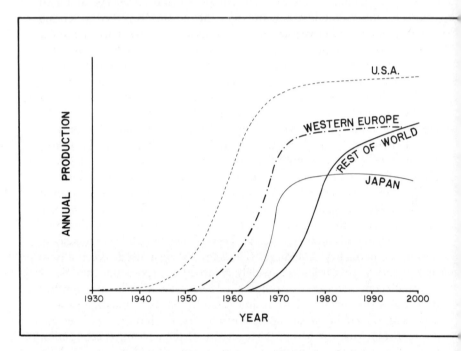

Figure 8.7 Ethylene capacity by world region, 1940–2000

facilities, the geography of individual industries is never static. Locational shift may be inspired by technical and organizational developments which are internal to an industry, or by changes – such as the international oil price increases of 1973 and 1979 – in the external macro-economic environment in which it operates. The nature of these influences and their effects will obviously vary from one industry to another. Nevertheless, the evolutionary models outlined in this chapter have suggested that certain common themes may be identified and that these models may be usefully applied to an interpretation of the changes, at a variety of geographical scales, in the distribution of a specific industry. However, they fail to take account of relationships between industries. The early development of petrochemicals, for example, was facilitated by advances in chemical engineering technology originally associated with oil refining, whilst the availability of petroleum-derived synthetic materials such as nylon and polyethylene in turn encouraged the growth of new industries responsible for converting these materials into consumer goods. These connections exemplify the place of the petrochemical industry within a mutually beneficial technological system which played an important role in the post-war boom during the 1950s and 1960s. They also emphasize the need to interpret the evolution of individual industries with reference to changes in other industries. This will become apparent in the next chapter which is concerned with the development of industrial areas.

Further reading

Malecki, E. J. 1983: Technology and regional development: a survey. *International Regional Science Review*, 8, 89–126.

Storper, M. and Walker, R. 1989: *The Capitalist Imperative: Territory, Technology and Industrial Growth*. Oxford: Blackwell.

Vernon, R. 1966: International investment and international trade in the product cycle. *Quarterly Journal of Economics*, 80, 190–207.

9
The Evolution of Industrial Areas

Just as companies and industries go through development phases, so also do the industrial areas of which they form a part. An area's evolution has far more flexibility because it may be a reflection of a wide variety of sectors and firms, but there are nevertheless elements of the life-cycle idea that are quite appropriate in analysing long-term regional change. As firms get older they often stop growing, or even decline and die. Similarly, buildings and infrastructure deteriorate, whilst technical change ensures that equipment ultimately becomes outdated and inadequate. The economic vitality of a region clearly depends upon compensating replacement and renewal processes. Such rejuvenation is by no means inevitable; changing circumstances may favour or adopt some regions at the expense of others (see Alchian, 1950; Tiebout, 1957a; Walker, 1975). Bearing in mind the dangers of pursuing the life-cycle analogy too far, the following chapter adopts this framework by looking successively at the factors which contribute to the 'birth' of industrial areas, their subsequent growth, ageing and, in some cases, rejuvenation. These ideas are then illustrated with reference to the economic history of two very different industrial areas.

Initial advantage

The reasons for the initial development of manufacturing in an area are as diverse as the location factors discussed in chapter 3. Clearly, 'natural' advantages of resource or relative location have played a major part in the development of many industrial areas. The historical significance of the coalfields in Western Europe and the United States was emphasized in chapter 1. In certain circumstances, cheap labour has attracted investment into an area from external sources. Johnson (1985) suggests that textile and apparel industries drawn to the south eastern United States by this location factor have successively shifted within the region to more remote locations in search of the lowest labour costs, but that they have helped to initiate the process of economic and industrial development in the communities with which they have been associated. Whilst this has certainly happened in some cases, the benefits of a low-wage strategy of industrialization are debatable and Cobb (1982) notes that the commitment to this approach in the southern United States tended to limit the growth of per capita incomes and, therefore, the opportunities for attracting activities to serve local and regional consumer markets. The production of goods and services for such markets is important in the development process as Gilmour's (1972) study of the early growth of settlement and industry in southern Ontario demonstrates.

Low incomes not only limit demand, but also tend to stifle initiative and entrepreneurship. Whatever 'natural' advantages an area possesses, the exploitation of these advantages depends upon the actions of individuals with the vision to recognize them. The significance of such qualities in the development process is illustrated by the emergence of Birmingham and the Black Country as a major centre of innovation and economic activity during the Industrial Revolution. In 1750, this was a relatively unimportant part of Britain; its local market was small, and many other areas had similar or even better natural resources for the new industries. There was already an industrial tradition, but mainly of a craft nature employing hand tools in workshops. Even mining operations remained very limited until they began to employ steam engines to control drainage problems associated with deeper mining. This, from about 1720, increased the capital investment needed for mining and led to a decline of smaller operations (Court, 1938, pp. 161–4). Certainly, however, the West Midlands had a tradition of independent business, perhaps encouraged by lack of guild controls in an area which had been unimportant in medieval times. Court (1938, pp. 54–5) believes that the scatter of small centres may have preserved the area from these essentially urban monopolies. In any case, even in Birmingham, 'no restrictive influences existed either to hamper the introduction of new trades or to prevent freedom of entry into any particular branch of manufacturing or commerce' (Wise and Johnson, 1950, p. 174).

The openness of West Midlands society was perhaps the factor which gave the area an edge over many others. Ultimately, it allowed the rise of some good entrepreneurs; encouraged the immigration of others, including James Watt; fostered the development of a remarkable meeting ground, the Lunar Society and encouraged a high rate of inventiveness.

The Lunar Society (see Hooper and Walker, 1983) took its name from the date of its meetings, these being on the nearest Monday or Tuesday to a new moon. Regular participants initially included Matthew Boulton (son of a buckle manufacturer) and Erasmus Darwin (grandfather of Charles), who was a doctor at Lichfield, both of whom had strong interests in a wide range of scientific problems. Later these were joined by Josiah Wedgwood, the famous potter; James Watt, who moved from Scotland to work with Boulton; James Keir, another Scot, who ran a chemical works; and the chemist Joseph Priestley, who came to Birmingham as pastor of the New Meeting House. During the 1790s deaths, business pressures and departures undermined the society and it gradually faded away. The interesting feature of this group is that some members were primarily businessmen and others doctors or scientists, but all concerned themselves with a wide range of investigations; they had a thirst for knowledge and a desire to solve problems, both theoretical and practical. Boulton and Watt were primarily involved in developing and exploiting Watt's ideas on the steam engine, and their factory at Soho attracted visitors from all over the world; they complemented each other because Watt was a technician and experimenter while Boulton had a flair for promotion and project planning (Schofield, 1963, pp. 149–50).

The role of individuals in the economic success of the West Midlands during the nineteenth century finds contemporary parallels in attempts to understand the factors which influence, and to develop policies which promote innovation and entrepreneurship. We have already emphasized the existence of spatial variations in rates of small-firm formation and drawn attention to some of the variables responsible for this phenomenon (see chapters 3, 4 and 8). Interest in the geography of small firms during the 1980s was encouraged by a dominant political philosophy, at least in the United Kingdom and the United States, which stressed individualism and self-help. This ethic has certainly focused more attention upon this aspect of economic growth than is warranted by the absolute numbers of new jobs created by expansion in the small-firm sector. Nevertheless, the activities of scientist–entrepreneurs played a significant role in the early development of the electronics industry in the United States, for example, and also in the emergence of Silicon Valley as a distinctive industrial area. Malecki (1988) emphasizes that the specialized technical and professional skills characteristic of 'high-technology' industries are not widely available. Indeed, they tend to cluster in specific areas, reinforcing their already favourable prospects for growth. In this respect, Silicon Valley and other modern centres of innovative economic activity may be regarded as the contemporary equivalents of Birmingham and the Black Country in the late eighteenth century.

Circular and cumulative causation

Once the development process is under way, a number of features have a strong tendency to reinforce the further growth of a well-established industrial area. These are best discussed by reference to figure 9.1. Myrdal (1956) formulated the principle of circular and cumulative causation, which contradicted the prevailing view that in the long run regions would tend towards an equal level of prosperity. In economic theory, market forces should favour less-developed areas because their factor prices are low, but in practice, argued Myrdal, the opposite more commonly takes place. What is more, the disparities widen over time: the process is cumulative.

In figure 9.1 four cycles can be seen, giving the circular aspects of the process. These are:

1 The effect of increased income, via new wages, on local opportunities in business and on community wealth. The rising local markets encourage more service firms, shops, etc., making it possible to create new jobs in those sectors too. Thus there is a so-called multiplier effect – one job in the original sector creates others elsewhere – and this new wealth also provides more income in the community for the public provision of infrastructure and community services. All this, of course, makes the area more attractive to manufacturers in the next period. The process can be guaranteed to take place to some degree, but it is possible that nearly all of the newly created income actually leaks away from the area (leakage results when people spend their income elsewhere and thus provide no encouragement to local businesses). The new income provides opportunities, but it must be remembered that businesses have thresholds below which they cannot operate profitably, and the demand for some goods and services must be quite high before it can sustain a business. Thus, this multiplier process can only reach its full form in quite large cities.
2 New jobs in the industry usually increase the pool of trained labour. Local people are trained or others are brought in from elsewhere; either way the community benefits. With time and job turnover, the number of qualified workers increases and educational institutions may do their part to provide even more.

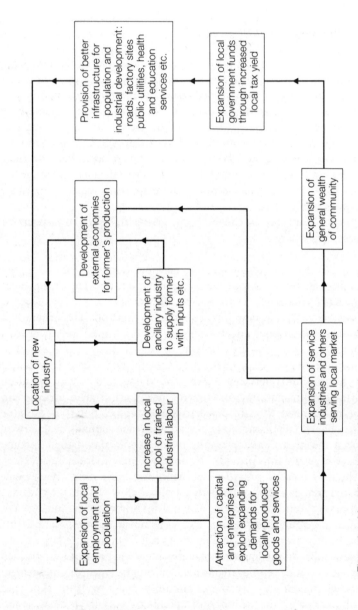

Figure 9.1 Myrdal's process of cumulative causation
Source: Keeble, 1967

Thus, manufacturers in later periods can see a larger, more qualified local labour force, which may be an important location factor.

3 Some industries require many raw or semi-finished materials, components and/or a variety of business services. Not all companies buy these from others, but there is often a market created. If a large company (or, over time, many small related ones) locates in an area, then it may be an attraction for linked ancillary companies to also locate there. These linkage effects can be an important element in strengthening an agglomeration (see chapter 4), although they are common only for a minority of industries such as metal and machinery complexes.

4 External economies derived from the build-up of ancillary industries are also strengthened by the general improvement of business services in the area. Thus both localization and urbanization economies increase (see chapter 4).

Although not shown in figure 9.1, another cycle might be expected to show up after several periods. New inventions and innovation related to the major sector should become evident and, if urbanization economies strengthen sufficiently, these may also extend to other industries, including new ones.

Meanwhile, in the vast majority of areas not experiencing expansion, this cumulative pattern of growth in industrial and metropolitan centres brings more disadvantages than advantages. The negative (i.e. 'backwash' or 'polarization') effects include strong competition in manufactured goods, which may undermine older craft activities or more primitive manufacturing, as well as takeovers of local business. The opportunities for investment and work draw away the more enterprising individuals and their capital, leaving many places in a much weaker economic state than before. Only where a region has food, natural resources or semi-finished products demanded by the growth area can the process be expected to have positive (i.e. 'trickle-down' or 'spread') results. Then indeed an upward spiral may be initiated that gives beneficial, if restricted economic gains.

The tendency for development processes to produce both areas of growth and areas of stagnation or decline has encouraged increasing reference in regional theory and policy to cores and peripheries, dependency and domination. In considering such issues, the theoretical statement by Friedmann (1972) is used here as a basis. Rather than focusing on sectoral specializations or on linkages, this work concentrated strongly on questions of control and domination. Self-determination is obviously desirable from many points of view, but it also brings benefits in economic structure and job creation. Friedmann's formulation first notes the crucial role of innovation in the development process. Innovation may take various forms; these are not all necessarily the result of inventive activity within the society, for they may be borrowed or imitated from elsewhere. A complete process is characterized by Friedmann (1972, p. 87) in the following way:

> The cumulative effect of successive innovations is to transform the established structure of society by attracting creative or innovative personalities into the enclaves of accelerated change; by encouraging the formation of new values, attitudes and behaviour traits consistent with the innovation; by fomenting a social environment favourable to innovative activity; and by bringing into existence yet further innovations.

A successful innovator obtains competitive advantage and, frequently, power. If the innovation is socially compatible the innovator is usually rewarded, but there are other cases in which innovators may be in conflict with the existing authority group (élite). Such conflicts may lead to the suppression of the innovators (counter-élites), to the latter's success in overthrowing the existing group, or to some intermediate solution. If the innovators gain control, however, there will be a considerable change in the social situation as authority–dependency relationships are transformed. These conflicts, derived from new economic situations, soon have a strong political dimension. For industrialization to take place, it has usually been essential to break the economic power of the land-owning classes and allow merchants and industrialists a role in the organization of society.

Returning to the environment in which such social changes take place, it can be noted that innovations tend to occur in a small number of centres, designated as core regions by Friedmann. Note that the core/periphery terminology used by Friedmann in a regional context is analogous to Averitt's use of the same terminology to describe the organizational structure of economies (see pp. 84–5). Corresponding to the authority–dependency relations amongst people and institutions are those between core regions and their dependent peripheries. While there may well be conflicts as a result of peripheral challenges to established authority, the core's position tends to be strong and self-reinforcing because resources, people and capital are continually drawn to it as a result of circular and cumulative causation. Thus conditions favourable to further innovations, such as a high degree of interaction, modern attitudes and a growing demand for new products, are fostered there as was emphasized in discussing the locational origin of new industries in chapter 8. Core–periphery relations are evident at several scales in 'a nested hierarchy of spatial systems' (Friedmann, 1972, p. 96). Thus a core can be observed at a world scale (chapter 10), but there are national cores and peripheries and, at the local level, they take the form of a metropolis with its surrounding region.

Core–periphery theory suggests that the inevitable disparities resulting from economic growth in one region will be reinforced by social and political elements in society as a whole. Furthermore, the powerful are not obliged to play the game of fair competition after they have attained their position. Marxist oriented writers such as Amin (1976) have stressed ways in which the capitalist system encourages regional disparity. Despite these tendencies for core areas to remain strong, the processes of cumulative causation do not necessarily operate indefinitely and there are many examples of formerly important industrial areas which have experienced economic decline.

Maturity and decline

Paradoxically, the very success of the firms upon which its prosperity was originally based may be responsible for the incipient decline of an industrial area. As these firms grow and become increasingly profitable, their owners will look for new investment possibilities. At first, the most likely step will be to build distribution centres or branch plants to serve new markets elsewhere. Although this takes funds away from the original location, it may also lead to a strengthening and expansion of headquarters jobs and facilities within the corporate core region. Moreover, as long as the company does well, good profits ensure that in the long run the inflow of funds should exceed the outflow. A greater danger of leakage from the local area takes place when investment into completely different sectors begins. This tendency towards diversification on the part of growing companies was noted in chapters 5 and 6. Diversification in a sectoral sense is frequently accompanied by geographical expansion, leading, over a long period, to a relative decline in the importance of the core region to the enterprise (see Owens, 1980; Watt, 1982; Teulings, 1984).

There are various limits to continuous growth. Physical factors may impose constraints. Hilly terrain and hard surface rock increases building costs, as does low-lying land subject to flooding. Generally speaking, few major industrial cities have developed in such environments. It is also possible that the supply of a critical local resource becomes exhausted. Economic pressures will tend to inflate costs as the expansion of infrastructure increases local taxation and land, labour and buildings all become more expensive. Furthermore, the logic of industry life cycles (chapter 8) implies that regions which become excessively dependent upon specific sectors inevitably find themselves associated with activities characterized by stable or declining production, using routine methods and requiring semi-skilled workers obtainable locally only at uncompetitively high costs.

The fate of such regions will partly depend upon the adaptability of the companies responsible for their original development. One strategy is the transfer of production to lower cost, peripheral regions, whilst retaining higher-order functions within the core. This will probably reduce the total demand for labour in the core region, but shift the emphasis towards higher skills. As already emphasized in chapters 7 and 8, organizational restructuring frequently occurs in mature and declining industries. This may result in the takeover of a regional firm by external interests which may in turn lead to a reduction in the scale of activities within the region and the loss of management functions (Acheson, 1972; Leigh and North, 1978a).

Over the long term, the success of an industrial area hinges upon the attraction and encouragement of new firms in a wide range of economic activities. However, very few industrial regions – as opposed to metropolitan regions where manufacturing is only one element in a diversified economic base – have succeeded in doing this over a long period of, say one hundred years. Indeed, contemporary studies of the geography of new-firm formation suggest that long-established industrial areas, dominated by one or two sectors and by a few large companies, tend to inhibit such developments (see Birch, 1979; Fothergill and Gudgin, 1982; Storey, 1982; Lloyd and Mason, 1984; Mason, 1987). This situation reflects many interrelated factors including the insistence of organized labour upon higher wages than small firms can afford, reluctance to take risks and an education system which trains people for existing jobs rather than encouraging them to think creatively about new business ideas.

Moreover, critical location factors change through time. These may favour and adopt an older region, but more likely they are disadvantageous, especially in relation to firms based on new technologies (see chapter 8). Heavy, traditional industries such as steel and chemicals often leave a legacy of polluted and blighted landscapes which are unattractive to potential investors in new industries (Hall, 1985a; 1985b). Typically, sectors such as computing, electronics and pharmaceuticals are associated with sophisticated cities with good universities, research laboratories and a favourable 'quality of life' in the broadest sense of the term; they are not necessarily satisfied even with the largest metropolitan centres, such as Paris, London and New York, which once attracted precision engineering, optics and other high-quality products.

Rejuvenation

The concept of rejuvenation suggests that, despite all the obstacles, some regions are able to adapt to changing circumstances. This is especially true of large metropolitan areas. Their strength appears to be based on centrality within the information system of a country, bringing them early news of both innovations and market opportunities. Pred (1977) extended Myrdal's principle of circular and cumulative development to show how early trading centres developed strong manufacturing and how they built up critical decision-making and control functions over a national economy. Figure 9.2 identifies the relationships promoting growth in an advanced national economic system containing a large metropolitan complex (C_1) and other metropolitan complexes ($C_2 \ldots C_n$) (see Pred, 1977, pp. 173–82). Pred's work demonstrates that the major centres were never just manufacturing cities, but have tremendous importance in finance, trade, education and business services, the combination of which provides the wealth to supply a high level of cultural amenities, educational facilities and attractive living conditions for those who can afford them. Frequently, especially in centralized countries such as France or Britain, the metropolitan city has massive political influence as well. Every kind of urbanization economy has made these cities attractive to a succession of firms in new manufacturing business, where new entrepreneurs need support of the most diverse type. The extremely varied labour supply of a large city, as well as its rich and diversified market, add to its favourable location for business. The key advantage of metropolitan centres is the diversity of their economies in both a sectoral and an organizational sense. Whilst specialization may offer important economic advantage to a region in the short-run, the long view suggests that diversification is necessary to ensure continuity of development as declining firms and sectors are replaced by more dynamic ones at earlier stages in their respective life cycles (Norcliffe, 1984a).

The rejuvenation of declining manufacturing areas has traditionally been a central objective of government regional policies and the nature and limitations of these efforts are considered in chapter 11. In some cases, attempts to change economic direction are inspired by the efforts of individuals within a region rather than by the external policy initiatives of central government. These attempts are frequently made in response to crisis situations. Workers or management may, for example, buy a

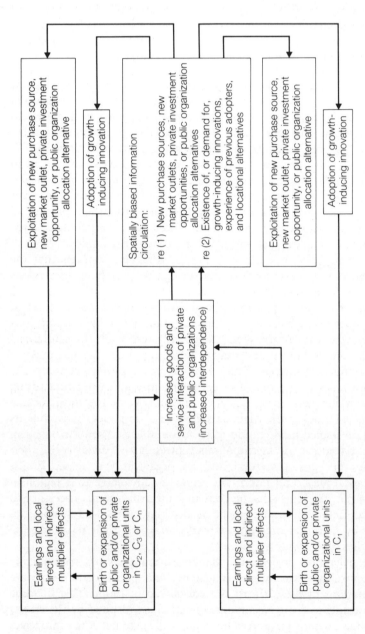

Figure 9.2 The circular and cumulative feedback process for large metropolitan complexes in advanced economies
Source: Pred, 1977

plant which a large corporation is planning to close. The outlook in these circumstances is not good and workers often make the mistake of continuing to manufacture a previously unsuccessful product (such as motorcycles at the former Triumph factory at Meriden, near Birmingham, taken over in 1974). Better long-term prospects may result when a larger plant disintegrates into smaller units, or when some of its skilled workers break away to form related activities. In Italy, the recent development of modern industrial districts has been very important in the central and north-eastern part of the country, known as the 'Third Italy' to stress its distinctiveness both from the poor south and the industrialized Turin–Milan–Genoa triangle in the north (Sabel, 1982, pp. 222–31; Goodman et al., 1989). In the area, each district specializes in a number of related items. Sabel (p. 220) describes it thus:

> In Tuscany, for instance, cloth is made at Prato, ceramics at Sesto and Montelupo; in Emilia–Romagna, knitwear is made at Carpi, ceramic tiles at Sassuolo, motorcycles at Reggio Emilia; in the Marche, shoes are made near Ancona; and in the Venetian hinterland, ceramics, plastic furniture, and sport shoes are made.

The firms involved in these activities vary widely in their working practices and technology; some are like nineteenth-century 'sweatshops' whilst others utilize advanced equipment, often based on micro-electronic communication and control devices. The latter are characterized by Sabel as a kind of 'high-technology cottage industry'. This activity has dramatically raised employment, per capita income and investment in parts of Italy since its emergence in the mid 1960s. Both Sabel (pp. 221–31) and Brusco (1985) stress that these industrial districts have managed to develop real independence, with no one firm able to control others and with all firms supplying several different markets. Moreover, there is a high degree of competition which keeps up efficiency and skill. This atmosphere also has the effect of increasing the pressure on labour costs and there is no doubt that the economic success of such operations rests upon their ability to hire and fire employees at short notice and to prevent unionization. The highly fragmented organizational structure of this system, together with the spatial dispersal of individual operations within the regional complex that makes up the 'Third Italy', facilitates this flexibility (Hudson, 1988).

Co-operative schemes are another alternative form of economic organization which has been proposed in response to economic crises at plant and regional level. They have not, however, been very successful in connection with manufacturing activities. Mondragon, in the Basque region of Spain, is a conspicuous exception. Its origins may be traced to the efforts of five engineers to persuade the local plant to introduce worker participation in line with the teaching of a local priest. When their requests were refused, they set up their own company, Ulgor, to make paraffin heaters and cookers in 1956 (Bradley and Gelb, 1983, pp. 12–19). Other co-operatives were formed around the same time and dealt with financial problems by setting up their own co-operative savings bank. The complex expanded remarkably so that by 1980, there were more than 80 industrial co-operatives employing some 1800 members in a diverse spectrum of activities including the manufacture of machine tools, refrigerators and other kitchen appliances, furniture, bicycles, electrical components and bus bodies. Some co-operatives are agricultural but the group is mainly industrial. About 10 per cent of total jobs resulted from conversion of existing firms to co-operatives; the rest involved job creation. Despite its achievements, it is debatable that the Mondragon experience may be regarded as a model for other regions as its success seems to be related to the strong sense of identity within the Basque community (Thomas and Logan, 1982).

Types of industrial region

Industrial regions may be classified in various ways. Many owe their distinctiveness to dependence upon a particular sector such as shipbuilding, textiles or chemicals. This close association between industries and regions, which produced clear geographical specialization, developed out of the changes initiated by the Industrial Revolution. Before these changes, areas had typically been more self-contained and, therefore, self-sufficient in economic terms. Remarkably persistent, the patterns introduced by the Industrial Revolution began to break down in the 1960s, mainly as a result of the decline of the industries concerned.

The spatial division of labour introduced by large corporations (chapter 7) created a new basis for economic regionalization as differentiation has come to depend less upon industries and more upon stages in the overall production process. Viewed in this way, high-order functions and activities are concentrated in relatively few metropolitan regions, whilst routine manufacturing operations are located in peripheral, low-wage regions. This kind of conceptualization may be applied to the organization of economic space within countries and also, at a different scale, to the system of production at a global level (chapter 10). The nature of labour and its interaction with the organization of production by large enterprises is the basis of this functional and geographical hierarchy (Lipietz, 1980).

Table 9.1 is another typology which attempts to consolidate some of the ideas introduced in this chapter. It focuses upon the dynamics of growth and decline, emphasizing the importance of such factors as the quality of education and the level of research activity. The terms adopted are generally self-explanatory. The label 'sunbelt' was originally coined to refer to the south and south-western United States, but it effectively conveys the image of the high-amenity environments with which many new industries seem to be associated. The classification is closely related to our previous discussion of the evolution of industrial regions in terms of a life cycle because it draws attention to the factors which help or hinder adaptation to changing circumstances. These factors may be further illustrated with reference to the experiences of two very different industrial regions.

A manufacturing area in decline: Upper Steiermark, Austria

The province of Upper Steiermark is located in south-east Austria and is focused upon the city of Graz. Its history has been closely linked to metals for several centuries. Certainly there have been and are other sectors – wood and paper, food and drink in particular – but its specialization is very old. Estimates of pig iron production exist from the fifteenth century, and many centres were established well before the Industrial Revolution in England. The key advantage of the area was its iron ore deposits, notably the very large iron mountain (Erzberg) near the town of Eisenerz. Charcoal was readily available at first from local forests, although even by the mid eighteenth century shortages were evident in places. A variety of furnaces, forges and metal-using crafts were located in many Alpine villages and towns on both the north and south sides of the central mountain ridge (Köstler, 1984, pp. 109–12), spreading into both Upper and Lower Austria.

Already in the early nineteenth century many of these locations were affected by the rapid changes in technology developed with the use of coal instead of charcoal in England. Many small units and outdated plants closed before 1850. Changes were even greater in the late nineteenth century as most of the smaller iron ore mines closed, iron and steel technology demanded a great scale increase to be efficient, and the lack of local coal increased material costs. As some plants expanded, the companies found themselves short of capital and a strong concentration process took place. In 1881, most of the primary iron and steel industry came under the control of the Österreichisch–Alpine Montangesellschaft (ÖAMG). Despite periods of poor business, pig iron

Table 9.1 A typology of industrial regions

1   Metropolitan

Diverse manufacturing within an even more diverse economy
High urbanization economies
Excellent, broadly-based education and research
High firm creation across broad spectrum of sectors
Moderate industrial growth resulting from decline of some sectors

2   Successful manufacturing region

More specialized manufacturing sector
High localization economies, less powerful urbanization economies
Excellent education and research focused upon principal sectors
Moderate new-firm creation focused on principal sectors
Some large plants and firms
Steady growth as result of successful sectors

3   Declining manufacturing region

Similar level of diversification to 2
Declining agglomeration economies
Education and research increasingly out of touch
Poor new-firm creation
Predominance of large branch plants
Decline

4   Sunbelt region

Concentration on new, especially high-technology sectors
Improving localization economies in principal sectors
Good amenities and living environments
Excellent education and research linked to high-technology frontier
High rate of firm creation
Most firms small and young
Fast growth

5   Peripheral regions, developing

Variety of sectors in mature stage
Virtually no agglomeration economies
Routine vocational education
No research
Limited firm creation, mostly branch development
Satisfactory or rapid growth

6   Peripheral regions, truncated

Variety of sectors, mainly in mature stage
Limited agglomeration economies
Excellent education, some research and development
Limited firm creation, mostly branch development

Table 9.1 Continued

Satisfactory or rapid growth, but opportunities failing to match educational
    levels or ambitions

7   Peripheral regions, undeveloped

Little manufacturing, mainly tied to resources or local markets
No agglomeration economies
Poor education, no research
Low rate of firm creation
Few local firms or branch plants
Little or no growth

Source: Adapted from Aydalot, 1984; 1985

production rose enormously in the latter half of the nineteenth century
and into the First World War. A great step forward was the opening
of the first modern blast furnace at Donawitz in 1891. In steel production,
Siemens furnaces spread widely in the area, and electric furnaces were
taken up very quickly after their invention in 1903 (Köstler, 1984,
pp. 122–40).

From 1914 until 1955, Austria, as a whole, experienced conditions that
were very unsettled and completely changed the economic environment in
which firms in the Steiermark operated. The aftermath of the First
World War led to the breakup of the Habsburg Empire, which disrupted
trading patterns in central Europe. This meant, for example, that Silesian
coal was now an import from a foreign state instead of from within the
empire (a free trade area of 52 million people). In addition, the
newly created countries (Poland, Czechoslovakia, Hungary, Yugoslavia)
pursued industrialization programmes designed to reduce imports from
such manufacturing areas as the Upper Steiermark. These difficult
circumstances were magnified by the worldwide depression of the 1930s.
In 1938 another new era began as Austria was taken into the Third
Reich and economically integrated into its war machine. The heavy
metals area received considerable business, but its competitive position
was undermined by a key locational decision taken by the Nazis. This
was the establishment of a large new integrated iron and steel complex
at Linz to the north of the Alps and on the major east–west route
through Austria. Although it was not fully built by the Nazis, this site
became a very efficient producer from the late 1940s.

The end of the war saw Allied occupation in Austria; the Steiermark
ended up in the British zone and escaped the problems of permanent
Soviet occupation. Nevertheless, the new political circumstances cut off

Eastern markets completely, and made coal supplies difficult for a while. Linz, also under Western allies (the Americans), was, by virtue of its location in the northern part of the country close to the West German border, better placed than Upper Steiermark to serve Western markets. Further problems resulted from a process of organizational concentration which saw effective control within the nationalized Austrian steel industry move away from Upper Steiermark. The impact of these processes was not evident during the expansionary 1950s and 1960s, but the economic situation deteriorated considerably during the 1970s. The number employed in mining, for example, almost halved between 1971 and 1981. The region had a lower growth rate than the national average and all the characteristics of an old industrial area – large plants, relatively high wages, a specialized economic base, low new-firm formation rates, poor productivity and a narrow range of skills (Steiner and Posch, 1985).

Palme (1984) emphasizes the difficulties involved in overcoming these problems. Little investment has been attracted from elsewhere, partly because of the peripheral location relative to the rest of Austria and partly because high wage levels have discouraged the establishment of branch plants. The small and scattered regional market limits the opportunities for locally-based developments and entrepreneurial activity has been stifled over a long period by the tendency of the large steel and paper plants to meet their own requirements for goods and services or to purchase them from outside the region (Tichy, 1984, pp. 205–8). Further discouragement to indigenous new firms stems from the almost total lack of urbanization economies which help to reduce the uncertainties facing any new venture (chapters 3 and 4). In short, the long history of specialization with increasing plant size and concentration, together with political events that have dramatically altered and worsened the area's location relative to actual and potential markets, have brought Upper Steiermark to a virtual economic dead-end. The problems are all too evident, but the solutions are much less apparent.

Decline and rejuvenation: New England in the twentieth century

New England was one of North America's great industrial regions in the nineteenth century. Starting with an almost ubiquitous pattern of craft industries covering most consumer essentials such as foodstuffs, clothing, footwear, farm and home tools, the region also had some urban-based specialities (silverware, fashion clothing, furniture, etc.) by mid century (Leblanc, 1969, pp. 12–81). The second half of the century saw an expansion of the factory system, unprecedented economic growth, and a concentration of production associated with steam power and larger factories. Towards the end of the century there was a failure of many small businesses and a growing concentration on textiles and shoes, in which the area dominated US production. In 1889, with only 7.4 per cent of US population, the region produced 16.4 per cent of value added in manufacturing and accounted for 18.5 per cent of all employment. Until the end of the First World War, New England increased its manufacturing, although it declined relative to the country as a whole (15.3 per cent employment, 14.3 per cent value added in 1919) – not surprising in view of New England's increasing peripherality as population spread westwards. In the inter-war years, however, manufacturing employment fell by 26 per cent (390,000 jobs) compared with a national reduction of only 3.2 per cent. Those sectors which had been the mainstay of the economy before 1914 collapsed and the future looked dismal because they still accounted for two-fifths of the region's workforce in 1940 (Estall, 1966, pp. 14–17).

Despite the poor prognosis, the decline relative to the rest of the United States seems to have ended by the late 1950s as further contraction in traditional sectors was offset by the rise of new activities. The biggest gains were in machinery, instruments and transportation equipment, all of which were relatively weak before 1939 (Estall, 1966). One of the major stimulants was war-time contracts, which not only went towards armaments and aircraft parts, but also encouraged electronics and communication equipment. New England has been able to share in a boom of research and development in a wide range of new electronic industries focused especially upon components and accessories for radar, telecommunications systems, electronic tubes, missile control and guidance systems and computing devices rather than upon final consumer products. It is not simply the presence of these sectors which is important, but also the fact that this presence includes high-level research and development functions as well as manufacturing operations. Four of the major US minicomputer firms (Digital, Data General, Prime and Wang), for example, have their corporate headquarters in Massachusetts.

The revitalization of New England's manufacturing has built on an aspect of a mature industrial area which can provide a way into the future – its skills and educational infrastructure. There has been no development from the old sectors themselves: they have adapted to quality production with very much smaller employment. Growth has come from building upon the advantages of mature educational institutions and research personnel capable of exploiting ideas to create new products and industries. This has implied locational change within the region, especially a move towards larger centres such as Boston.

This rejuvenation has been neither easy nor continuous. The earlier post-war developments were heavily dependent on the nation's military and space programmes, but demand from these sources has been reduced since the end of the Vietnam War, and the Boston high-technology complex was in decline in the early 1970s (Dorfman, 1983). Despite this, several sectors (especially electronic components and office machines) maintained rapid growth in the late 1970s, and this was based upon the success of many local companies operating under normal market circumstances. Characteristic of the growth is the rapid expansion of relatively young firms (established since the Second World War), numerous entrepreneurs and rapid rates of new firm formation. As in Silicon Valley, the process depends upon large numbers of highly qualified graduates from such institutions as the Massachusetts Institute of Technology, spin-offs of entrepreneurs from other high-technology companies and from research laboratories, and the growth of specialized infrastructure in the Boston area. Nevertheless, New England as a whole has had a long period of relatively high unemployment which has transformed it into a low-wage area, despite high living costs (Harrison, 1982). Moreover, Harrison shows that both inequality and instability increasingly characterize the job market. Of 159,000 workers losing jobs in traditional sectors (food, textiles, clothing, lumber, leather and shoes, furniture, paper and printing) between 1958 and 1975, only 18,000 had obtained new jobs in electronics, instruments or computer industries in New England and another 2000 elsewhere. Most were employed in the service sector by 1975 or were retired or unemployed. Apart from those in high-technology sectors, however, nearly all businesses were reducing job skill requirements; this resulted in an increasing divergence in income between rich and poor workers in New England. Instability is brought about by the larger number of part-time jobs, as well as by the nature of the high-technology sectors themselves.

New England was once one of the major centres of population in the United States, and its enterprising people built up many industries. But the country's population has moved further and further away, increasing the region's marketing problems; the labour force became too expensive for older sectors; and the buildings and infrastructures have required renewal. In consequence, the long-term path of the inter-war years pointed to increasing unemployment and/or emigration. Changes have not been complete – there are still older sectors and buildings, still unemployment – but a remarkable transformation has taken place which has been characterized as the 'Massachusetts Miracle' (Lampe, 1988). A lively modern industrial complex has grown up around Boston, and growth has spread out into the attractive smaller towns of southern New England. The region looks prosperous and provides a pleasant natural and cultural environment which should attract and hold the kind of entrepreneur and workforce to keep the renewal going. Whether the transformation can extend to all New Englanders or all parts of the region is debatable, however. Certainly the region has far more services now than it once did and the manufacturing sector has become smaller and more specialized, but it is unquestionably the case that the region's economy can face the future with more optimism than it could in 1940. With slow population growth it has been possible to maintain per capita incomes, and to expect the region's position relative to the United States as a whole to hold its own (Bolton, 1978, pp. 164–74).

Conclusion

The topic of evolution is rather neglected in industrial geography, and our discussion of the question of how industrial areas develop over time has necessarily been exploratory. Some conclusions arise, however, which seem to be important guides to policy questions. In the long run, areas need their own indigenous firms, and firm creation into new sectors to replace the levelling off of jobs in established ones. A situation dominated by large firms is dangerous and domination by large branch plants is even worse. A variety of firm ages and sizes provides the flexibility necessary to adapt to changing economic environments. Areas without innovation and entrepreneurs will always remain dependent, but even very powerful companies and established industrial areas are vulnerable to competition and the rise of new sectors, unless they keep close to the research frontier and continually improve their business practices. Adopting an historical perspective upon the interrelationships of industrial and regional development emphasizes that, notwithstanding the considerable forces of inertia implicit in the economic and political dimensions of 'cumulative causation', no region can take its future prosperity for granted.

Further reading

Hudson, R. 1988: Uneven development in capitalist societies: changing spatial division of labour, forms of spatial organization of production and service provision, and their impacts on localities. *Transactions, Institute of British Geographers (New Series)*, 13, 484–96.

Myrdal, G. 1956: *Economic Theory and Underdeveloped Regions*. London: Methuen.

Norcliffe, G. B. 1975: A theory of manufacturing places. In L. Collins and D. F. Walker (eds), *Locational Dynamics of Manufacturing Activity*. London: Wiley, 19–57.

Seers, D. (ed) 1981: *Dependency Theory: a Critical Reassessment*. London: Frances Pinter.

Steiner, M. 1985. Old industrial areas: a theoretical approach. *Urban Studies*, 22, 387–98.

Part V
Industrial Location and Public Policy

Following long-established practice throughout the world, we make the underlying assumptions in this part that public policy should attempt to improve the lot of the average person and that manufacturing is a sector of the economy which can be used to this end. There is room for a variety of opinion as to the extent of public sector involvement as well as the form it should take. Some of the differences of viewpoint will be evident throughout this part, but a wider discussion of the relationship between manufacturing and human welfare is left until the last chapter.

The topics chosen for detailed discussions are those which have caused the most widespread interest. We start by considering the relationship between national economic strategies and international trends in manufacturing. Every country has such a strategy, whether or not it is framed in formal plans, and its success will be strongly influenced by events in the international economy. Regional policy is also widely practised, and almost everywhere manufacturing is expected to play the critical role in modifying the regional balance of welfare. Our chapter on inner cities and metropolitan development is more restricted in its application to older industrial countries, but there are many lessons which more recently industrializing areas should learn from their experiences. Finally, we complete the book with the broader perspective of our living space and of human welfare in general.

10
The Evolving International Industrial Economy

There have been significant changes in the international distribution of manufacturing since the Second World War. It has declined in both absolute and relative importance within the economies of many nations with a long industrial tradition, whilst the experience of the so-called Semi- or Newly Industrialized Countries (NICs), has been very different. Almost everywhere, national policy-makers see manufacturing as a critical element in their economic planning, yet we seem to be 'in a period that is witnessing a weakening of many of the basic premises of industrial growth and structural change, one of transition characterized by considerable uncertainty on the part of industrialists and policy-makers' (UNIDO, 1983, p. 1). This chapter examines some of these issues. It begins with a descriptive review of international trends in manufacturing, including recent events within the developed and centrally-planned economies. In subsequent sections, the emphasis is placed upon the developing countries as attempts are made to identify the general factors which promote and inhibit their industrialization. These factors are then illustrated with reference to the very different industrial development experiences of South Korea and Nigeria. Finally, some of the major policy issues and uncertainties affecting future prospects for industrialization and economic development at the global scale are reviewed.

Trends in the world distribution of manufacturing

Official statistics on world industry are compiled, from national data, by organizations such as the United Nations Industrial Development

Organization (UNIDO) and the World Bank. Data for individual countries are frequently aggregated into three groups which are helpful in identifying general trends and in making comparisons:

Developed market economies These include the countries of Western Europe, the United States, Canada, Australia, New Zealand and Japan. Although the relative significance and the age of manufacturing within these countries varies widely, they may all be regarded as essentially free market economies.

Centrally planned economies These are members of the Council for Mutual Economic Assistance (CMEA), China and a few other countries which have traditionally opted out of the world market system except under very restricted circumstances. The data, however, often only include Eastern Europe and the USSR (i.e. CMEA), as other socialist countries fit the third group better.

Developing countries These make up the rest, often subdivided, because some clear distinctions have arisen. One subgroup is the *semi-industrialized countries* including Argentina, Brazil, Columbia, Egypt, Hong Kong, India, Malaysia, Mexico, Philippines, Republic of Korea, Singapore, Thailand and Turkey.

Figure 10.1 indicates changes in the shares of world manufacturing value-added of these three groupings since 1963. Table 10.1 provides a more disaggregated view, identifying subgroups. The principal trends are clear – a decline in the share of the developed market economies and an increase in that of the centrally planned and developing economies. These shifts have been achieved as a result of the differential growth rates shown in figure 10.2. In the post-war period to 1973, world manufacturing grew at historically unprecedented rates. These were not sustained after the first oil price 'shock'. Indeed, the contrast between the generally lower growth rates of the developed market economies before 1973 and the other two groups became even more pronounced after that date as manufacturing output within these economies actually fell between 1979 and 1982 (figure 10.2). It is important to emphasize, however, the continuing dominance of Western Europe, Japan and the United States. The huge imbalance between the size of the respective manufacturing bases in the developed and developing economies means that differential growth rates must be maintained for a very long time to produce any fundamental shift in the balance of economic power at the global scale. Thus the share of the developing countries increased from 7.8 per cent in 1963 to 11.4 per cent twenty years later (figure 10.1). The rate of change is, therefore, very slow and it is clear that UNIDO's goal of a 25 per cent share for

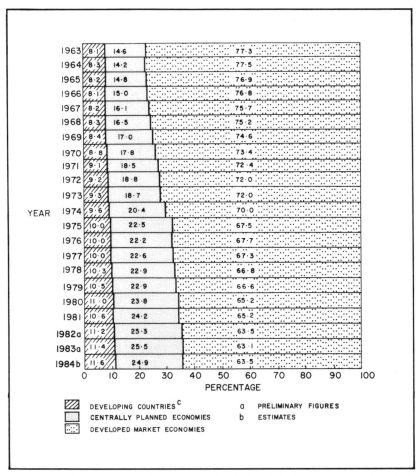

YEAR			
1963	8·1	14·6	77·3
1964	8·3	14·2	77·5
1965	8·2	14·8	76·9
1966	8·1	15·0	76·8
1967	8·2	16·1	75·7
1968	8·3	16·5	75·2
1969	8·4	17·0	74·6
1970	8·8	17·8	73·4
1971	9·1	18·5	72·4
1972	9·2	18·8	72·0
1973	9·3	18·7	72·0
1974	9·6	20·4	70·0
1975	10·0	22·5	67·5
1976	10·0	22·2	67·7
1977	10·0	22·6	67·3
1978	10·3	22·9	66·8
1979	10·5	22·9	66·6
1980	11·0	23·8	65·2
1981	10·6	24·2	65·2
1982a	11·2	25·3	63·5
1983a	11·4	25·5	63·1
1984b	11·6	24·9	63·5

PERCENTAGE

DEVELOPING COUNTRIES[c]   a   PRELIMINARY FIGURES
CENTRALLY PLANNED ECONOMIES   b   ESTIMATES
DEVELOPED MARKET ECONOMIES

Figure 10.1 Share of economic groupings (excluding China) in world manufacturing value added, at constant (1975) prices
Source: UNIDO, 1985

the developing countries by the end of the century, set in the Lima Declaration of 1975, will not be realized. Indeed, a World Bank estimate in 1983 suggested that this target would not be achieved until 2070 at prevailing rates of change (Leechor et al., 1983, p. 16).

Grouping the economies into three broad categories conceals both the absolute size of national economies as well as variations in their performance. Table 10.2 ranks the principal manufacturing nations, identifying those countries which accounted for at least 1 per cent of

Table 10.1 Estimated per cent shares of world manufacturing value added by economic grouping and subgroup, 1963, 1975 and 1981

Economic grouping	1963	1975	1981
	(at constant 1975 prices)		
Developed market economies	77.0	67.9	65.2
of which			
Canada and US	31.9	24.1	23.9
Japan	6.4	9.0	10.5
Other mature[a]	36.1	31.2	27.3
Recently industrialized[b]	2.6	3.6	3.5
Centrally planned economies	15.2	22.5	24.2
of which			
USSR	9.2	15.0	16.6
Developing countries	7.8	9.6	10.6
of which			
Semi-industrialized[c]	5.5	7.0	7.7
Others	2.3	2.4	2.9

[a] Australia, Austria, Belgium, Denmark, Finland, France, Germany (Federal Republic), Italy, Luxembourg, Netherlands, New Zealand, Norway, Sweden, Switzerland, United Kingdom.
[b] Greece, Ireland, Israel, Malta, Portugal, South Africa, Spain.
[c] Argentina, Brazil, Colombia, Egypt, Hong Kong, India, Malaysia, Mexico, Philippines, South Korea, Singapore, Thailand, Turkey.
Source: UNIDO, 1985

world manufacturing value added in 1985. It is misleading because it excludes the centrally planned economies for which comparable data are not available. Nevertheless, it emphasizes the dominance of the United States, West Germany and Japan and also draws attention to the insignificant contributions of the vast majority of nations which lie below the 1 per cent threshold. Amongst the developed economies, the fastest rates of growth have generally been achieved by some of the smaller countries such as Greece and Portugal, whilst the shares of the United States and the United Kingdom, for example, have fallen. The most important event, however, has been the rise of Japan despite its defeat in the Second World War.

In the case of the developing economies, table 10.1 emphasizes that the relatively small number of semi-industrialized countries were responsible for most of the gains achieved by this group as a whole. Indeed, the sources of growth were even more sharply focused upon a handful of rapidly industrializing countries in East and South-East Asia. By contrast, the shares of tropical Africa and Latin America have been stagnating. The least developed countries' share of world manufacturing

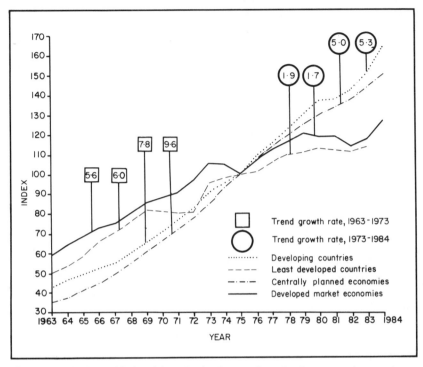

Figure 10.2 Indices of industrial production in manufacturing by economic groupings, 1963–1984 (1975 = 100)
Source: UNIDO, 1985

output is discouragingly small, especially in Africa. In 1981, they accounted for only 1.52 per cent of the manufacturing value added by all developing countries compared to 2.41 per cent in 1967 (UNIDO, 1985, p. 18).

The changing relationships between the major economic groupings expressed in terms of *total* manufacturing activity are, of course, the result of developments at the sectoral level. Despite a declining share of total manufacturing value added, the developed market economies still dominate in most sectors, especially paper, printing and publishing, chemicals, iron and steel, metals, machinery and transport equipment (table 10.3). The centrally planned economies are also strong in these sectors, but show a concentration in textiles and footwear as well as pottery and earthenware. Only in petroleum refining and tobacco products do the developing countries make a real impact. This is apparent in table 10.4 which identifies those industries in which the

Table 10.2 Shares of world manufacturing value added of principal industrial nations (excluding centrally planned economies), 1985

Rank	Country	Manufacturing value added ($ millions)	% of world total	Cumulative %	Growth rate 1970–1985 (at constant 1980 prices)
1	US	803,391	34.0		2.6
2	Japan	395,141	16.7	50.7	6.0
3	W. Germany	201,637	8.5	59.2	1.5
4	France	131,176	5.5	64.7	2.3
5	UK	102,555	4.3	69.0	−0.6
6	Italy	93,975	4.0	73.0	2.8
7	Canada	64,224	2.7	75.7	2.4
8	Brazil	58,089	2.5	78.2	5.5
9	Spain	39,056	1.6	79.8	2.5
10	India	28,942	1.2	81.0	4.6
11	Australia	27,660	1.2	82.2	1.3
12	South Korea	24,219	1.0	83.2	13.3
13	Netherlands	23,065	1.0	84.2	2.0

Source: UNIDO, 1988a

developing countries' share of manufacturing value added exceeded 10 per cent of the world total in 1985, drawing attention to those in which the developing countries seem to be gaining ground relative to the developed (market and centrally planned) economies. Generally speaking, their comparative advantage seems to lie in light industry and some resource-based industries, reinforcing the observations made in chapter 8 concerning the changing role of individual sectors as economies advance.

In some ways, trade figures are even more revealing than those indicating the size of the manufacturing sector, because they identify specialisms, strengths and weaknesses more clearly. The developed market economies have retained a dominant position in manufacturing exports, supplying over 80 per cent of the world total in every year since 1960 (table 10.5). In the meantime, the centrally planned economies' share has fallen since 1960 whilst that of the developing countries has increased. The total volume of exports (expressed by value), which declined for the first time since the Second World War as a consequence of the recession of the early 1980s, is dominated by very few countries. Three nations (i.e. Japan, the United States and West Germany) accounted for over 50 per cent of the manufactured exports of the developed economies in 1982 (UNIDO, 1985, p. 43). Similar domination is apparent within the much smaller export volumes of the developing countries. By the end of the 1970s, Asian countries generated three-quarters of the total manufacturing exports of the developing economies and just four countries – Hong Kong, Singapore, South Korea and Taiwan – accounted for 59 per cent of this total (Dicken, 1986, p. 40). There are significant differences in the geographical patterns of trade within and between the three broad economic groupings. Most of the manufactured exports (68 per cent by value in 1982) of developed countries are sold to other developed countries. In the case of the centrally-planned and developing economies the corresponding percentages were 59 and 38 respectively (UNIDO, 1985, p. 40). The greater external orientation of the developing economies is not surprising in view of the limitations of their own markets and the massive purchasing power concentrated in Japan, the United States and Western Europe.

The traditional pattern of exports of resource-based products from developing countries in exchange for manufactured goods is breaking down as the developed countries face growing challenges in their former preserves. The Asian NICs in particular have been remarkably successful in penetrating the domestic markets of the developed economies. The developing economies as a whole increased their share of total manufactured imports into the OECD countries (i.e. the developed market economies) from 4.4 per cent in 1964 to 13.5 per cent by 1985 (OECD, 1988, p. 19). The bulk of this growth was accounted for by only six countries (i.e. Brazil, Hong Kong, Mexico, Singapore, South Korea and Taiwan) which increased their collective shares from 1.6 to 9.5 per cent over the same period. The extent of the challenge posed by these NICs becomes even more evident when the sectoral composition of their exports is analysed. They initially concentrated upon mature, low-technology industries such as clothing and textiles and these two sectors alone accounted for almost 50 per cent by value of the manufactured imports into the OECD countries from the six NICs in 1964 (OECD, 1988, p. 21). The pattern was much more diversified by 1985 with increases in the contributions of electrical goods, data processing equipment and motor vehicles. Essentially, these countries have advanced into more sophisticated products. On a spectrum from 'low' through 'medium' to 'high' technology, more than 82 per cent of their manufactured exports to OECD countries in 1964 fell into the first category, 16 per cent into the second and 2 per cent into the third; by 1985, these proportions had changed to 53, 22 and 25 respectively (OECD, 1988, p. 24).

It is clear that significant changes have taken place in the distribution of industrial production and in the pattern of trade in manufactures at

Table 10.3 Estimated per cent shares of world manufacturing value added by economic grouping[a] for selected industries, 1965 and 1985 (at constant 1980 prices)

Industry	ISIC code	Developing countries		Centrally planned economies		Developed market economies	
		1965	1985	1965	1985	1965	1985
Food products	311[b]	17.0	19.7	24.1	29.1	58.9	51.2
Tobacco	314	35.8	37.5	14.8	18.8	49.4	43.7
Textiles	321	21.4	22.1	23.7	33.5	54.9	44.4
Wearing apparel	322	12.9	16.1	18.0	32.3	69.1	51.6
Footwear	324	14.5	18.7	16.9	33.7	68.6	47.6
Paper	341	7.3	10.8	5.5	7.8	87.2	81.4
Industrial chemicals	351	7.4	12.3	18.8	26.8	73.8	60.9
Petroleum refineries	353	24.6	34.6	10.8	17.6	64.6	47.8
Pottery, china and earthenware	361	10.2	12.7	12.6	26.6	77.2	60.7
Glass	362	10.3	13.6	9.5	15.9	80.2	70.5
Iron and steel	371	5.6	12.3	12.9	18.2	81.5	69.5
Metal products, excluding machinery	381[b]	7.8	11.3	5.2	13.2	87.0	75.5
Non-electrical machinery	382[b]	3.2	4.3	17.5	34.6	79.3	61.1
Electrical machinery	383[b]	5.4	7.0	7.4	11.1	87.2	81.9

[a] Excluding China.
[b] Variations in national reporting practices for ISIC 38 may create significant distortions.
Source: UNIDO, 1988a

Table 10.4 Industries in which developing countries accounted for more than 10 per cent of world manufacturing value added, 1985

Rank	ISIC code	Industry	% share
1	314	Tobacco	31.26*
2	353	Petroleum refineries	30.24*
3	321	Textiles	21.60*
4	369	Other non-metal mineral products	18.31*
5	311	Food products	18.12*
6	313	Beverages	17.57*
7	352	Other chemical products	17.25
8	324	Footwear	16.96*
9	323	Leather and fur products	15.16
10	355	Rubber products	14.98
11	322	Wearing apparel	14.82*
12	390	Other manufactures	12.70
13	356	Plastic products	12.68
14	331	Wood products	12.47*
15	362	Glass and glass products	12.35*
16	361	Pottery and china	11.99*
17	371	Iron and steel	11.93*
18	351	Industrial chemicals	11.90*
19	354	Petroleum and coal products	11.61*
20	372	Non-ferrous metals	10.98*

* Industries in which developing countries grew more than twice as fast as developed countries, 1980–85.
Source: UNIDO, 1988b

the global scale. We will now attempt to identify some of the principal factors responsible for these changes, whilst at the same time emphasizing that manufacturing remains poorly developed in the vast majority of Third World countries. The limitations of space make the discussion of these issues necessarily superficial and the list of further reading provides an introduction to the massive literature on this topic.

Factors promoting industrialization

An important principle in geographical specialization and trade, whether at regional or international level, is that of *comparative advantage*. Essentially this states that, given free and unhindered trade, places will tend to specialize in those activities for which they have particular advantages in comparison with others. Their special attractions may be environmental, such as a particular natural resource, or human, such as

Table 10.5 Estimated per cent shares of economic groupings in world exports of manufacturers (SITC 5–8 less 68), selected years

Year	Total (billion $)	Increase over preceding year (%)	Share of economic grouping (%)		
			Developing countries	Centrally planned economies	Developed market economies
1960	65.6		3.9	12.4	83.7
1965	103.0	10.6	4.4	12.3	83.3
1970	189.9	15.2	5.0	10.0	85.0
1975	500.1	9.1	6.3	9.3	84.4
1980	1090.2	15.9	9.1	8.1	82.8
1983[a]	1051.0	0.9	10.9	8.8	80.3

[a] Estimate.
Source: UNIDO, 1983, 1985

skilled or cheap labour. If trade takes place unhindered, it is beneficial for everyone that locational specialism takes place, as any economics textbook will demonstrate.

Trade theories are, like most others, based on assumptions which limit their validity. The commonly used Heckscher–Ohlin theory has many versions, but essentially takes the view that trade depends on factor endowment (Olsen, 1971, pp. 3–14). A country with cheap labour will benefit from concentrating upon goods requiring a high labour content, in comparison with a different country where labour is more expensive and capital is relatively abundant. Each country will capitalize on its advantage, and trade its surpluses. Of course, this trade will also be dependent upon the costs of moving the products, something which trade theory, despite its explicit concern with relationships between areas, neglects to take into account. Another limitation is linked to the question of the mobility of the factors of production. The emphasis upon differential factor endowments rests upon the assumption that these factors are only available at specific locations. In practice, capital and labour can be moved from place to place, although there are significant differences in the ease or difficulty and, therefore, the costs, of movement. These differences have important consequences for industrial location (chapter 3). The Heckscher–Ohlin model also fails to take account of economies of scale which may improve the competitiveness of a country even in the face of higher factor costs. This helps to explain the advantages of a country such as the United States, as well as the pressures for free trade zones to create larger markets. Despite the many limitations of the Heckscher–Ohlin trade theory, the concept of comparative advantage upon which it rests remains valid and is helpful in understanding some of the situations which have presented opportunities for industrialization in certain developing countries. The export of raw materials to the controlling imperial power was a characteristic feature of colonial economies. Following independence, many developing countries have accorded high priority to the industrial processing of indigenous raw materials. This strategy is based on the proposition that it is better to export materials in processed or semi-processed form because the economic benefits from these value-adding operations are retained at the source rather than lost to importing countries. One of the most significant recent examples of this approach has already been described in chapter 8 with reference to the petrochemical industry. Several oil-rich countries, notably Saudi Arabia, have attempted to exploit the comparative advantage offered by their cheap supplies of associated natural gas by establishing major export-oriented petrochemical complexes during the 1980s. Other activities which have been established within developing countries upon the basis of resource-endowment include a range of mineral smelting operations from aluminium to zinc as well as some forest and wood-processing industries.

Despite its logical basis in the principle of comparative advantage, resource-based industrialization is not without its problems as a development strategy. First of all, the essentially unpredictable nature of resource distributions means that it is not an option to many countries which have been unlucky in the 'resource lottery'. Furthermore, these basic activities tend to reflect rather than lead macro-economic trends and their growth rates have been unimpressive in recent years. Very often, they are vulnerable to events in the world economy over which national governments have little or no control (Auty, 1988). This problem is aggravated by the fact that developing countries must frequently rely on foreign multinationals for both the technology and the capital to exploit their own resources. This tends to create enclave situations in which any beneficial economic effects of these activities are highly localized at or near the processing site. It has also led to accusations that the multinationals themselves operate almost as imperial powers with more concern for their own commercial interest than the economic development of the host country. Extensive Japanese involvement in resource-based projects in East Asia and in Australia, has, for example, been interpreted in this way (Forbes, 1982).

The significance of labour as a location factor at plant level was emphasized in chapter 3 where the existence of regional variations in wage costs within countries was noted (figure 3.5). Such variations are, however, minimal compared with those *between* countries. Data problems make it difficult to measure accurately international differences, but there is no doubt that they are considerable. They have, for example, been very influential in shaping the development of certain branches of the electronics industry (chapter 7) and it is estimated that the average hourly earnings of workers in this industry in 1985 ranged from $9.56 in the United States to $1.21 in Taiwan, $1.03 in South Korea and $0.46 in India (*Financial Times*, 1987). It is important to appreciate that such comparisons take no account of the productivity of labour, which is itself determined not only by the quality of the workforce itself, but also by the tools at its disposal. Furthermore, it cannot be assumed that Indian workers, with far less education, training and industrial experience, can necessarily do the same job as their counterparts in the United States. Nevertheless, there is no doubt that several countries have attracted foreign investment on the strength of cheap labour and have actively promoted this as a key source of comparative advantage (Dicken, 1986, pp. 170–71). This advantage has, in some cases, been deliberately reinforced by policy measures. *Export processing zones*, for example, permit foreign companies to operate within specified parts of a country (usually port or border locations) on the basis of especially favourable trade and investment conditions – in particular freedom from the obligation to pay customs duties on imported components assembled into goods for re-export in factories sited within such zones. There are numerous examples of such arrangements within the developing world. One of the most significant in terms of the scale of industrial development is Mexico's Border Industrialization Programme, initiated in 1965. Under this scheme, approximately 1000 factories employing an estimated 310,000 people are located in various zones on the Mexican side of the border from Tijuana in the west to Matamoros in the east (United Nations, 1988, p. 170). Most of these factories serve the US market and many are owned by US companies which are attracted by the much lower wage rates in Mexico (House, 1982).

International variations in labour costs can only influence the location decisions of organizations that are able to switch investments from one country to another. The rise of the global corporation (as defined in chapter 5) has, therefore, been a necessary condition for the emergence of the so-called 'international division of labour' (Fröbel et al., 1980; Schoenberger, 1988b). This is simply the extension to the global scale of the principles outlined in chapter 7 linking the organizational structure of large corporations, changes in the technology of production associated with the product-cycle concept and spatial variations in the cost of labour. This extension has become possible because of advances in communication and transport technologies which permit the control and co-ordination of such dispersed corporate systems. There has been a kind of double dynamic in the rise of the NICS. On the one hand, the existence of low-cost and disciplined workforces within these countries was a decisive comparative advantage; on the other hand, the exploitation of this advantage has partly depended upon the competitive strategies of corporations based in the developed economies. In fact, the role of foreign investment in promoting industrialization varies widely from one country to another. Japanese companies have been the principal driving force in Singapore, for example, whereas internally generated capital has played a much more important role in South Korea. Nevertheless, the pattern of industrial development within many Third World countries has been influenced by the actions of enterprises based in Japan, North America and Western Europe. To what extent this influence has been entirely beneficial from a development perspective will be considered later in the chapter.

The links between innovation, technical change and industrialization have been explored in several earlier chapters (especially 7, 8 and 9). Viewed at the global scale it is self-evident that new technology tends to originate in the advanced industrial nations. Access to this technology is obviously relevant to the industrial prospects of the developing countries and there is a massive literature concerned with the role of technology transfer in shaping the economic and political relationship between the developed and developing world (see Mansfield et al., 1977; OECD, 1981). Much of this literature has emphasized the obstacles to technology transfer and we will return to this issue in the next section, focusing here upon the positive aspects of the process. As a general rule, technology becomes more widely available as it matures, a characteristic which has been exploited by several developing countries in establishing state-owned basic industries such as iron and steel, petrochemicals and textiles.

Innovators, often multinational corporations, naturally wish to maximize the commercial returns from their successful research and development activities. Technological monopolies are, however, inevitably transient. Patent protection eventually expires and imitators are often successful anyway in 'inventing around' this legal obstacle to diffusion. A point is eventually reached when the balance of power between the sellers and buyers of technology shifts in favour of the latter. This is exemplified by the case of petrochemicals. By the mid-1960s, the technology necessary to establish an indigenous petrochemical industry could be obtained from a wide variety of commercial sources. Many of these, including the consultancy firms responsible for process and plant design as well as the engineering contractors responsible for plant construction, were actively in the business of selling information. Unlike the multinational chemical and oil companies which had previously controlled much of the key technology, they were not faced with the problem of balancing licence income against possible losses from reduced product sales. As far as the consultants and contractors were concerned, the greater the number of producers, the greater the demand for their services. In these circumstances, countries such as Brazil and Mexico were able to acquire the technology to establish their own basic petrochemical industries in what had become, at least by comparison with earlier years, a buyers markets (Cortes and Bocock, 1984).

If the acquisition of technology is a prerequisite for industrial development, so too is the existence of a potential market, which may be domestic or foreign. The exploitation of indigenous natural resources or of cheap labour has provided some countries with routes to industrialization based upon the principle of comparative advantage. This principle implies dependence upon export markets, but it is important to acknowledge that domestic markets also provide opportunities. Much of the recent interest in the role of multinational and global corporations has obscured the fact that a major proportion of foreign direct investment is intended to serve the market of the host country. Indeed, there is a clear correlation between market size and the propensity of foreign companies to establish manufacturing facilities overseas as was emphasized in the discussion of spatial aspects of corporate growth in chapter 6.

In many cases, market-oriented inward investment by foreign companies has been encouraged by the erection of trade barriers as part of a deliberate policy of import substitution on the part of the governments of developing countries. Such a policy seeks not only to persuade foreign companies to replace imports from elsewhere within their corporate systems with production from locally-based branch plants, but, more importantly, to encourage domestic initiatives from the public and/or the private sector. Virtually all developing countries have employed import substitution to initiate industrial development, although the most successful have subsequently adopted a more outward looking, export-oriented strategy as the limitations of their domestic market become apparent (Donges, 1976). This suggests that a large domestic market is a considerable advantage in providing a valuable base from which to expand. Size is a question not just of population, but also of income levels (table 10.2). Companies in the United States, for example, can grow to a considerable size before even having to consider foreign markets. Expertise can, therefore, be acquired under familiar circumstances and financial resources built up to a point at which the growing company can cope with the inevitable setbacks involved in moving overseas. This is much more difficult for companies based in the Third World. Many developing countries have such rapid rates of population growth that they are unable to achieve enough personal wealth to create home markets for anything other than essential products. Relative to its huge population (765 millions in 1985), industrial production in India, for example, remains limited (table 10.2). Brazil and Mexico, on the other hand, are large countries with significantly higher levels of per capita income and their domestic markets have certainly played a significant role in encouraging industrialization. At the same time, the successes of Hong Kong and Singapore, with populations of 5.4 and 2.5 millions respectively in 1985, emphasize that a substantial domestic market is an encouraging rather than a necessary condition for industrial development.

Obstacles to industrialization

Despite the achievements of a few NICs, manufacturing remains poorly developed in the vast majority of Third World countries which face considerable difficulties in altering this situation. They typically lack the infrastructure required by industry that is taken for granted in developed nations. This infrastructure includes not only such elements as reliable utilities and transport facilities, but also the nature of the education system. Manufacturing skills and, especially, entrepreneurial and managerial talent are usually in short supply. Even factory work habits take time to acquire where the labour force has previously been occupied in a traditional agricultural sector. Education and training programmes are, therefore, important in improving development prospects, but are necessarily long-term investments which cannot be guaranteed to provide a comparative advantage at some distant future date.

In the discussion of the product cycle in chapter 7, it was emphasized that innovating firms retain a monopoly of the new technology during stage 1 (figure 7.4). Extending this period for as long as possible may confer considerable commercial advantages on the innovating firm and great efforts are made to stop proprietary information from passing to competitors. The same argument applies to the diffusion of technical information between countries. As already noted, innovating firms are generally based in the developed economies. Thus many of the technologies essential to industrialization in the Third World are controlled from elsewhere. This sometimes introduces a political dimension when governments restrict the freedom of their national companies to release their technology to potentially unfriendly countries. Such embargoes have, at various times, been imposed by the US government, for example, in relation to transfers to Eastern Europe and the USSR. Even where such political intervention does not occur, it is the commercial interests of the multinationals rather than the welfare of the developing countries which normally determine the rate of technology transfer. Eventually, innovating firms lose their monopoly and technologies become widely available. This process implies, however, that technology originating in the developed economies is already old by the time it reaches the developing nations. On the other hand, there is abundant evidence that, because of the limitations of their socio-economic infrastructure, many developing countries cannot effectively absorb new technology and there are numerous cases of prestige industrial projects which have never operated at anything like their design capacity.

Even if technology is available and production difficulties are solved, indigenous businesses in developing countries often face formidable marketing problems, especially in building up foreign sales. Assuming a good, competitive product in a free-trade environment, an entrant into a new foreign market such as the United States would be challenging established companies with existing marketing networks. These companies would certainly make life difficult for the new entrant. In these circumstances, it is not surprising that many developing countries attempt to assist the initial export efforts of indigenous companies by establishing state-funded trading companies.

As if the 'free' and 'fair' situation did not pose enough difficulties, success in world manufacturing and world trade in practice is even harder, and is highly influenced by political and historical circumstances which work to the detriment of the already disadvantaged. This had led many scholars to argue that, in fact, the operations of the richer countries have actually made things worse – that underdevelopment is not a state, but a process practised by developed countries on the rest of the world. Frank (1966), observing the Latin American scene, formulated this position and many dependency theorists have followed it. Frank (1975) argues that underdevelopment is not a natural state which can only be remedied by development processes emanating from the developed world. Rather it is part of the same process that created development elsewhere: it is an inevitable part of the capitalist system. Hymer (1972) writes of the 'law of uneven development'. Such scholars believe the developing world would be better off without any relations with developed countries. This view could hardly be more opposed to most economists, who view the spread of 'development' from the industrial countries as being beneficial and indeed the only real hope of improvement.

Dependency theorists argue that one-sided relationships were a feature of colonialism, when most countries of the world were dominated by very few. The colonies were exploited for their raw materials and foodstuffs, which were shipped to the mother countries in return for manufactured goods, cheaply produced by new mass-production methods. Any attempts by the colonies to change this pattern in the direction of self-sufficiency in manufacturing were squashed (Frank, 1975, pp. 39–42; de Souza and Porter, 1974; Slater, 1975). It is argued that, in fact, there were such ventures and that at least some of the colonies were capable of breaking from the pattern if allowed. Only a well-endowed coùntry such as the United States, which rebelled and broke ties early, was able to move strongly into independent manufacturing at a time when manufacturing was going through the critical period of the Industrial Revolution. Even rich countries such as Australia and Canada, which remained much longer under British control, never really broke away from a predominantly resource orientation to become major manufacturing countries.

Key aspects of dependent, peripheral economies are their reliance on exports of primary products and their general characteristic of extraversion (Amin, 1976, pp. 203–14). Amin argues that an 'advanced economy is an integrated whole' with dense internal linkages and marginal external ones, while for an undeveloped economy the position is reversed (p. 237). This is often reflected in the orientation of transport networks and the colonial infrastructural legacy has contributed to regional inequalities within many developing countries. In India, for example, the economic dominance of the port cities of Bombay, Calcutta and Madras, which became firmly established under British rule, has continued in the post-colonial era, partly because their inherited advantages made them attractive to further industrial development (Udhay-Sekhar, 1983). Whether strong independent growth can arise out of an initial primary export dependency is doubtful. The case of Canada is instructive. The white man entered the country in search of a series of products – fish, furs, and later wheat and lumber. The nature of settlement depended on the product. These staples (raw and slightly-processed items) in some cases required little permanent settlement and so provided a weak stimulus to development. Only with wheat did a widespread permanent population arise with demand for food, household goods, farm machinery, etc. (Watkins, 1963). This encouraged manufacturing on a small scale, but the majority of goods were imported. After Canada became independent in 1867 it was decided to promote manufacturing, and this was done by both protective tariffs and subsidies. As a result the sector flourished, but increasingly the new plants were foreign-owned. In the twentieth century the inflow has continued and has been supplemented by mergers and takeovers which have further extended this pattern so that over 50 per cent of domestic manufacturing production is accounted for by foreign-owned plants. Moreover, the sector suffers from what has been called 'truncation' (Canada, Government of, 1972; Hayter, 1982) – the chopping-off of much of the key decision-making and research functions from Canadian plants. So

Canada is relatively wealthy, but has little real independence in economic matters.

Despite the break-up of the political structures of colonialism since the Second World War, the economic relationships, forged over centuries, have proved more durable and the opportunities for developing countries are still highly restricted. Dependency theorists regard multinational and global corporations as agents of 'neo-colonialism'. These agents supply management and mature technology, but often at inflated prices; they take away profits and leave little that can contribute to long-term self-sufficient development (Müller, 1973). In most developing countries the political and economic élites – a tiny group of the very rich – benefit by supporting the system as it is and do not generally wish to make changes that will weaken their own position.

Thus, dependency writers see a core at the international level, which controls much of international business, and a periphery that has little influence on world affairs. The terms 'metropolis' and 'hinterland' are also used, but we will retain core and periphery in conformity with Friedmann's (1972) idea of nested hierarchies of cores and peripheries at different spatial scales (see chapter 9). Many would argue that international institutions such as the World Bank, the International Monetary Fund and even the United Nations do much to reinforce the pattern because they are strongly influenced by the richer countries. Certainly, richer countries act in their own interests as far as possible. The United States, from its position of economic strength, has been the greatest proponent of free trade in the post-war era, just as the United Kingdom took a similar position during much of the nineteenth century (Anell and Nygren, 1980, pp. 341–5). Nevertheless, when threatened by imports of cheaper and/or better products, the country has not hesitated to apply quotas or to use various forms of economic coercion to encourage investment in the United States itself. Economic interests within developed countries threatened by imports of manufactured goods such as clothing and footwear from cheap labour countries have often vigorously defended their positions by lobbying their respective national governments to provide protection. So developing countries have found it difficult to put a foot on the first rung of the ladder to more advanced products, never mind to begin a long climb up it.

But many factors which reinforce dependency hardly need any special or conscious promotion. Rather it would take mammoth forces to change them, because they are reinforced by two hundred years of development history. Financial institutions and their methods of assessing firms and projects, transport and commercial infrastructure, educational institutions and facilities, and even cultural opportunities, all weigh heavily in one direction. An educated population with a variety of special skills, inventors, entrepreneurs and managers of all types reinforces the pattern and makes its continuation likely. The activities of multinationals with their own core and periphery structures (chapter 7) have the same effect. Little systematic, malicious operation of the system is required.

It is also important that a recognition of certain common elements of dependency not be allowed to obscure the fact that there are great variations in countries which can be generally described as dependent. In size, population, culture and resources there are enormous contrasts, to say nothing of variations in infrastructure and colonial history (Seers, 1981). Some NICs have made great progress in expanding their manufacturing sectors, whilst others have lagged far behind. These contrasts may be illustrated with reference to the experiences of South Korea and Nigeria.

South Korea: a successful NIC

The modern state of South Korea was created in 1945 and its independent existence was subsequently threatened in the Korean War between 1950 and 1953. Bearing in mind the devastation caused by the war, its economic progress has been remarkable and the country ranked 12th in the non-communist world in terms of manufacturing value-added in 1985 (table 10.2). Although South Korea received considerable foreign, mainly US, aid in the immediate aftermath of the war, its economic achievements have been due to the country's own efforts. It is interesting to examine these efforts both as an illustration of the kind of measures employed by the more successful NICs and also to consider their relevance as a model for other developing countries.

South Korea's economic development has been characterized by a high degree of state intervention. In this respect, it is typical of the other NICs which may be described as *guided market economies* (Grice and Drakakis-Smith, 1985). The broad policy framework has been set within the context of a series of five-year economic development plans, starting in 1962. These plans not only set growth targets, but also established investment priorities for the successive planning periods. These priorities changed through time as attention was focused upon different manufacturing sectors. Nevertheless, heavy public investment in infrastructure, broadly defined to include utilities, transport facilities, education and housing, was a common element of all plans from the first, beginning in 1962, to the fifth, ending in 1986. Indeed, the proportion of total investment directed to these purposes was between 58 and 68 per cent throughout the 25-year duration of the first five plans (Enos and Park, 1988, p. 32).

Several forms of government intervention have been made to achieve the objectives set out in the economic development plans. Extensive government control of the financial sector has, for example, ensured that the allocation of investment funds has broadly matched the pattern set out in each plan. A number of state-owned corporations have been established to carry out key operations in strategic industries. Korea General Chemical Corporation, for example, is the pivot of the country's drive to create a sophisticated petrochemical industry. The government has also attempted to mobilize indigenous private capital and has actively promoted the formation of large industrial enterprises, such as Samsung and Daewoo, by the merger of smaller companies. Trade policy is yet another strand of the industrialization effort. Restrictions upon imports were especially important in protecting infant industries in the early stages. When the emphasis shifted towards external markets in later years, the provision of export financing and export guarantees, as well as the establishment of overseas information offices, assisted Korean products in penetrating new markets.

These policies have resulted in a series of stages in the industrialization of South Korea. The emphasis between 1958 and 1964 was upon import substitution of consumer goods. The switch to export-led industrialization occurred in 1964 and this strategy has itself involved successive shifts in the identity of priority sectors. Attention in the first and second five-year plans was focused upon light, labour-intensive industries such as textiles, footwear and toys. This reflected a desire to exploit the country's prevailing comparative advantage of labour that was cheap in international terms and also abundant as a result of land reform policies which encouraged a transfer from agricultural to industrial occupations. The emphasis upon light industries during the 1960s was reinforced by capital shortages which severely limited the scope for capital-intensive developments. The third five-year plan introduced a new phase of industrialization when attention shifted to heavy industries, including steel and non-ferrous metals, petrochemicals, machinery and shipbuilding. This was partly motivated by a desire to establish a foundation of basic industries; it was also an opportunistic strategy to the extent that it coincided with a Japanese policy decision in 1971 to reorientate its economy away from the very industries that South Korea was promoting. The Japanese policy was driven by concerns about pollution and raw material supplies in the case of industries such as iron and steel and petrochemicals. Sensing that this was a trend that would be followed by other developed countries moving into 'cleaner', knowledge-intensive industries, South Korea regarded activities such as steel and petrochemicals both as agents of change, likely to generate growth elsewhere within the economy as a result of their extensive linkages with other sectors (see chapters 4 and 11), and also as potential export earners.

The changing direction of industrial development in South Korea is reflected in figure 10.3, in the accelerated growth rates of fabricated metal products, machinery and equipment (which includes electronics and transport equipment) and the basic metals industry. By contrast, the food, textile and wood-products industries, which were more important in the early years, have slowed down. Further changes have continued beyond the 1984 end-date in figure 10.4. In particular, export growth in the basic sectors has been difficult to sustain in the face of a world recession. Even more important from the point of view of identifying general patterns of development has been the increasing competition in labour-intensive sectors from countries lower down the development ladder such as China, Pakistan, Thailand and the Philippines. The main response has been to move into activities that are more sophisticated in a technical sense. This is evident in electronics where relatively simple assembly operations account for a smaller proportion

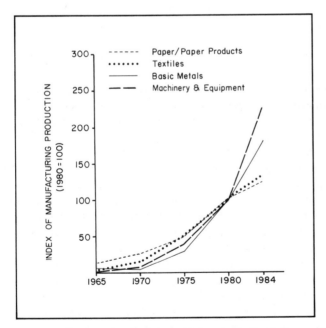

Figure 10.3 Indices of production for selected industries in South Korea, 1965–1984
(1980 = 100)
Source: OECD, 1988

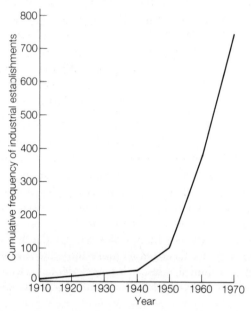

Figure 10.4 Number of manufacturing establishments in Nigeria 1910–1970
Source: Onyemelukwe, 1978

of total output, whilst the production of computers and peripherals, which is beyond the capabilities of lower-cost competitors, has become more important (see Scott, 1987).

South Korea's response to increasing labour-cost competition draws attention to perhaps the most significant aspect of its development policy. From the very beginning, great importance was attached to improving the quality of education and to the closely related issue of the acquisition and control of technology (Enos and Park, 1988). This is apparent in the rapidly expanding output of its educational institutions, especially in engineering fields. Furthermore, the state has always been closely involved in negotiations with foreign companies contemplating investments in South Korea. The objective has been to maximize indigenous control over the development of its industrial technology. The level of foreign direct investment has been severely limited as the government has, until very recently, insisted upon joint venture arrangements, allowing South Korea to 'purchase both the capital goods and the know-how, rather than letting foreign firms possess them' (Enos and Park, 1988, p. 39). This policy has been reinforced by high levels of government-funded research and development expenditure targetted upon specific sectors. The results of this are evident not only in South Korea's ability to refine imported technology and to manufacture sophisticated products, but also in the emergence of national firms, including Samsung and Hyundai, as global corporations which have actually succeeded in reversing the traditional flow of investment between the developed and the developing world by establishing their own production facilities in countries such as the United States and Canada.

Nigeria: dependent industrialization

Despite a population exceeding 100 million, the scale of manufacturing in Nigeria remains small and, to that extent, it is much more typical of the developing world than South Korea. Although the slave trade made an early impact on West Africa, formal colonial rule was established only in the late nineteenth century. The colonial power was interested mainly in farm produce, which came from peasants rather than plantations and allowed some Nigerians to prosper in both farming and trading as well as in petty commodity production generally, but British interests were firmly in control via the financial system. Moreover, British manufacturers wished to exploit the colonial market, and products imported into Nigeria often undermined the local monopolies which had been established by native craftsmen. Apart from a few branch plants established after the Second World War by companies that had previously been exporting to the country, modern manufacturing was almost non-existent in colonial Nigeria (Williams, 1976, pp. 11–25). Prior to independence in 1960 the British government 'had opened up new opportunities for political, administrative and commercial activities to the Nigerian bourgeoisie' (Williams, 1976, p. 28). Thus there was some preparation for the responsibilities of running a country, but it did not advance beyond more than a small proportion of Nigerians, and it was very brief. In manufacturing itself there had been almost no build-up of managerial, technical or entrepreneurial skills (Kilby, 1969).

Not surprisingly, then, foreign companies responded better than indigenous businessmen to the new opportunities as Nigeria's economy expanded (Akeredolu–Ale, 1976, pp. 107–9). A 1966 survey put foreign investment at a minimum of 70 per cent of total industrial investment and at 80 or 90 per cent in many important sectors (Nigeria, Federal Office of Statistics, 1967). Few educated Nigerians were attracted to business, but preferred politics, the civil service or the professions. Indeed, the ruling class in the immediate post-colonial period seemed more interested in reaching personally beneficial accommodations with foreign capital than in encouraging indigenous companies. Akeredolu–Ale (p. 110) explains the situation thus:

All efforts were made at the same time to ensure that the boat of the neo-colonial economy was not rocked too much. Wherever any opposition has been shown to the dominance of foreign capital in Nigeria, it seems that its foremost objective has always been to aggrandize the ruling class. Even though nationalism and pretensions to socialism were invoked by the ruling class, the 'nation' of their reference excluded the ordinary people, and their socialism was against foreign economic domination only if it was impossible to arrive at a satisfactory *modus vivendi* between themselves and foreign capital. In this, they had inverted their historic role and shirked their historic obligations – the obligations of an authentic nationalist elite.

From the late 1960s the government began to make a more determined effort to encourage Nigerian manufacturing firms. In 1972, the Indigenization Decree reserved certain sectors for Nigerians and limited foreign participation in others. The government also acquired powers in the same year to take over minority commercial banks. By such measures, the state was attempting to remove some of the barriers that had prevented Nigerians from obtaining an equal chance in business.

There were in fact very few industrial plants (as opposed to craft workshops) in Nigeria before 1945. Onyemelukwe (1978) lists only 47, divided almost equally between those processing raw materials (food processing, cotton ginning) and those serving the local market with consumer goods. There was fast growth after 1945 as Europe's demand for raw materials grew and, as a result, purchasing power in Nigeria increased to provide a market for consumer-goods industries. The limits imposed by lack of skills and technology, however, soon became evident. Despite a deliberate import substitution policy in the 1960s and a rapid growth in the number of establishments (figure 10.5), the contribution of manufacturing to GDP has remained small, rising from 4 per cent in 1959 to 6.1 per cent by 1979 (Jarmon, 1987, table 4.2).

Biersteker (1978) examined six industries in the country (tobacco, brewing, cotton, building materials, timber, sugar) to see what effects multinational penetration has had on the indigenous sector. He notes that the growth of the foreign plants has displaced many artisans, but not local firms, because there were so few in prior existence. Except in cotton textiles it also appears that the foreign plants did not cut into the markets of the Nigerian ones. The greatest effect was in what may be called 'pre-emptive displacement' – that is, the establishment of foreign plants in sectors new to Nigeria, thereby denying opportunities to indigenous firms. This was widespread in most sectors. Biersteker links it both to lack of capital amongst Nigerian entrepreneurs and to attitudes which encouraged the view that success was not possible. Most of Nigerian entrepreneurial activity has been focused on trading rather than manufacturing, not least because of the potential rewards to be gained from securing the rights to sell and distribute the products of a foreign company within Nigeria. Even those who do become involved in small-scale manufacturing generally do not possess the managerial skills required in larger enterprises. Schatz (1977, pp. 76–124) argues that the necessary technological, organizational and marketing leap has proved extremely difficult to make. Moreover, entrepreneurs have tended to rely too much on the government to solve problems. A further negative aspect is that many are considered untrustworthy, so that credit is difficult to obtain. These problems hit the manufacturing sector more than others because most modern operations are of the scale that require Schatz's leap. Moreover, very little research in the country is related to manufacturing. There is a Federal Institute of Industrial Research, established in the late 1960s, but it has failed to link adequately with indigenous manufacturers. Unlike South Korea, little has been done to adapt foreign technology to local circumstances and a study of technology transfer into Nigeria leads to pessimism about the overall economic impact to be gained from multinationals without deliberate efforts to train workers and technological entrepreneurs (Thomas, 1975). More attention is needed to 'the human element in the flow of technology in Nigeria' (Thomas, 1975, pp. 109–15).

The prospects for industrial development in Nigeria seem bleak. Modern manufacturing is almost entirely in foreign hands. There is little research and development or technological education which could lead to new products or entrepreneurs in innovative sectors. Perhaps to achieve economic independence a nation such as Nigeria has to look beyond the economic – to the cultural base which defines and supports economic activities. In this case one may argue that Nigeria's dependency on the West stems from its cultural disenfranchisement. This is what makes it almost impossible for the Nigerian elites to be true nationalists. In other words, if a people cannot define (economic) development in their own cultural terms then the chances of innovation, which is at the core of manufacturing and an independent economy, are much reduced.

International trends and national aspirations

The important role of manufacturing within the economic development process ensures that the future prospects of the sector are of concern to most governments. It is, therefore, interesting to consider the implications of current trends in manufacturing within each of the three principal economic groupings identified at the beginning of this chapter and to identify some of the policy challenges they face in managing these changes.

A further relative decline in manufacturing is likely within the developed economies as the process of deindustrialization continues in many countries (Blackaby, 1979). Policy efforts should focus on renewal and rejuvenation, encouraging product and process innovation, research and development, new firm formation and the gradual contraction of mature industrial sectors. Some basic products (steel, for example) can be expected to be retained for strategic reasons and because no country wishes to be without essential semi-finished materials, but most could be more cheaply produced elsewhere for a number of reasons: first, cheaper labour; second, exhaustion of raw materials in old industrialized countries; and third, newer plants in recently developed industrial areas.

Developed countries have tremendous advantages in the initial phases of the product cycle, where capital costs and risks are often high, but returns also very good. Much industrial policy within these countries, however, seems to be geared to the support of mature industries where developing countries have a real chance. This ranges from direct subsidies to import quotas. A policy of this type should really be temporary – a short-term welfare programme – unless special reasons can support another viewpoint. Often mature non-strategic industries (such as textiles and clothing) are supported for social, political or regional reasons as demonstrated by Canadian efforts to protect certain industries important in the French-speaking province of Quebec. However compelling the domestic political justification for such actions within developed countries, it is important to recognize that it effectively denies opportunities to developing countries which, in many cases, have little alternative to specializing in mature sectors.

Industrial policy within the developed countries needs to be set within a much broader context than in the past (Hooper and Walker, 1983). In particular, it must be co-ordinated with science, technology and education policies. These policies should aim to provide the basis for the generation of new ideas upon which future industrial progress depends. They should be directed not only at white-collar workers, but also at improving the skills and, in some cases, changing the attitudes, inherited from an era of mass production and tedious jobs, of the workforce in general. Only in an atmosphere of creativity and independence will new technologies be developed and the industries arising from them be established.

The growth in the centrally planned economies' share of world industrial production (figure 10.1) is unlikely to be maintained. This represented an expansion of well-established activities, but problems have arisen in dealing with new technologies. Cocks (1983) argues that this is primarily an organizational problem in the USSR – that the hierarchical character of the bureaucracy has made it very difficult to carry ideas into production. There is little interaction amongst researchers themselves, yet a new machine might require 25 separate approvals as it ascends through the bureaucracy, and a complex system as many as 400–500 of them (pp. 273–5). Moreover, decision-makers at the upper levels are so far removed from the innovation that they have little conception of its character. New structures have been tried since the late 1960s, particularly sectoral science–production associations which integrate research and production. Despite such attempts, however, the basic difficulties remain (pp. 273–5). Indeed Carstensen and Guroff (1983) consider that the basic problems of organizational rigidity, excessive hierarchical bureaucracy and poor financial structures are essentially Russian, and date from the imperial era. It is interesting to note that the greatest economic flexibility in the Soviet bloc is coming not from the USSR itself but from Hungary. Even small private business is now in operation there, although the changes have not had much impact on manufacturing. There does seem to be some acknowledgement of the problems at the highest level within the centrally planned economies and economic reform is central to the concept of 'perestroika' (i.e. restructuring). Nevertheless, the difficulties are formidable and major changes will be required if the Soviet bloc is to become involved in international trading on a significant scale.

Figure 10.1 emphasizes that the growth of manufacturing within the vast majority of developing countries has been disappointing and it is interesting to consider the lessons of the recent past. Individually, most countries have initially tried to follow a path of import substitution, replacing imports with domestically-produced goods. In theory, this makes good sense and can work if the country is well endowed with the necessary factors of production. In practice, however, what has often happened is the establishment of some final assembly operations, frequently under foreign control. Thus, automobiles may be produced in Nigeria or Brazil and the assembly operation may create many jobs. Analysis of backward linkages, however, reveals that virtually all the assembled components are imported, so that dependency is just put one step back in the production process. Other undesirable consequences may result from this strategy (UNIDO, 1983, pp. 109–13). There is a danger that foreign subsidiaries bring a form of production that is too capital-intensive to provide many jobs, and also that the market of a developing country may be too small for competition between these companies to operate properly – thus encouraging monopoly or oligopoly. The absence of competition may reduce the incentive to adapt technology to local conditions or to innovate in a more general sense.

All of the most successful NICs have rapidly switched to an export-oriented strategy. Foreign-owned branch plants attracted by cheap labour can provide a basis for industrial growth through the multiplier effect of wages and salaries paid to their employees. This increases the opportunities for firms producing consumer goods and services, but also works in the opposite direction to that desired by firms exploiting cheap labour. As wages increase, so the industrial structure must change to balance competition from even cheaper wage areas, and eventually closures or relocations may result. Another potentially beneficial effect of branch plants is the work experience they provide, especially if reinforced by education and training programmes. This may contribute to an improvement in skills, which may stimulate the creation of independent businesses. It has to be admitted, however, that in most cases the nature of this work experience is mind-numbing rather than stimulating.

Although the industrialization of Singapore, for example, has largely been based upon foreign investment, other countries have attempted to pursue a more independent approach as emphasized by the case-study of South Korea. This allows national governments to exercise greater control over the course of events, even if export-oriented activities are vulnerable to the vicissitudes of the global market-place. It may also offer other advantages. The export success of Hong Kong, for example, is largely based on sub-contracting carried out by innumerable, small, locally-owned businesses (Richards, 1981). Such a system does allow the large corporations which purchase from the small firm sector to dump their problems quickly on others when demand is slack. On the other hand, it does leave initiative and enterprise in Hong Kong itself, providing the entrepreneurial basis for future development.

Another important issue affecting the industrial prospects of the developing countries is the question of technology. South Korea's economic achievements reflect a recognition that industrial policy must have a technological rationale designed to pave the way for indigenous adaptation and improvement of imported technology. The high level of investment in education is, perhaps, the most distinctive feature of the South Korean experience. Other countries, such as Brazil, have been less successful in this respect and continue to import capital goods to sustain their development ambitions.

Many of the uncertainties surrounding the industrial prospects of the developing countries are connected to their relationships with the developed world. These could be reduced by a conscious effort to foster increased trade amongst the developing countries themselves. This would have the advantage of more equitable terms of trade, but there are many difficulties. Apart from primary products, these countries tend to produce similar things and the necessary complementarities between sources of supply and demand may be difficult to establish. Schemes have been proposed to co-ordinate industrial investment by public-sector corporations on a supra-national scale within trading blocs composed of many developing countries. These involve the different members of the grouping specializing in different sectors according to some agreed strategy based on calculations of comparative advantage. There was much interest in a Latin American common market during the 1960s (Carnoy, 1972), but the vested interests and political rivalries of its member states ensured that it has never been effectively implemented (Hughes and Ohlin, 1980, pp. 289–96).

The significance of political relations emphasizes the potential role of international agencies. There is a real need for some agency to counter-balance the growing internationalization of capital. Multinational and global corporations are such powerful agents of economic change that some kind of control over their activities is required to ensure that the interests of states are not secondary to those of private capital. Unfortunately there is little prospect of such regulation. Another role for international agencies is to try and promote a sense of justice in international economic relations. Various bodies, especially those under United Nations auspices, provide a forum for drawing attention to the grievances of the developing world, but their powers to change the situation are very limited. Nevertheless, attention must be given to 'the rules of the game, which regulate the economic co-operation of sovereign states in various spheres and which are sustained by the existing distribution of power' (Anell and Nygren, 1980, p. 119). Anell and Nygren argue that the current rules were essentially set up by the United States and have been influenced only by the rich countries. Discussions on a so-called new international economic order have been aimed at changing relations between these richer countries and the developing world. Such an order would focus on a reduction of tariffs and import restrictions on products from the developing countries; more aid that is free of conditions; access to technology; and a more stable world monetary system. The United Nations has been used as a forum to press for such changes, but the industrial countries have generally resisted them. Nevertheless, economic events are weakening the position of the industrial countries and the United States can no longer dominate events in the way it did after the Second World War. The danger exists, however, that economic disorder rather than a new international order may follow (Anell and Nygren, 1980, pp. 119–51). It is possible, for example, that OPEC-like attempts to control critical products may increase. In most cases too many countries are involved and substitution is possible, but such a tendency would be very disruptive. Despite recent problems, the OPEC countries have unquestionably done better than they would have done under the old system: the world as a whole, however, is worse off. Other protective moves would lead in the direction of regional free-trade areas. Apart from the European Economic Community these have not so far been very successful, but from an economic point of view their expansion would be a poor substitute for free and fair trade at the world scale.

Conclusion

Recent changes in the global distribution of manufacturing, especially the rise of the NICs, have been viewed as evidence of a transition in which 'the whole economy is moving from one equilibrium to another, according to an economic realignment between developed and developing countries' (Beenstock, 1983, p. 59). This is the second such 'transition', the first taking place when Britain faced competition from rivals in Western Europe and North America in the late nineteenth century. Although the historical analogy is interesting, we have seen that there are substantial obstacles to industrialization in the developing world and that, notwithstanding some conspicuous exceptions, the rate of progress has consistently fallen short of expectations. Nevertheless, the post-war growth of Japan followed by other South-East Asian nations suggests that independent development may be possible within the world economy, and that the developed market economies are more vulnerable than was thought twenty years ago. If this proves to be the case, a series of transitions might be expected in the future as a succession of NICs enter world markets and the previous groups move to sectors requiring high technology and better management. As the first generation of NICs gain economic strength and establish their own large corporations, it seems likely that the ability of West European and North American multinationals to control and dominate this process of change will be reduced.

Further Reading

Ballance, R. H. 1987: *International Industry and Business: Structural Change, Industrial Policy and Industry Strategies.* London: Allen and Unwin.

Beenstock, M. 1983: *The World Economy in Transition.* London: Allen and Unwin.

Dicken, P. 1986: *Global Shift: Industrial Change in a Turbulent World.* London: Harper and Row.

Norcliffe, G. B. 1985: The Industrial geography of the Third World. In M. Pacione (ed), *Progress in Industrial Geography.* London: Croom Helm, 249–83.

UNIDO 1985: *Industry in the 1980s: Structural Change and Interdependence.* New York: United Nations.

United Nations 1988: *Transnational Corporations in World Development: Trends and Prospects.* New York: United Nations.

11
Industry, Regional Development and Regional Policy

It is apparent from earlier chapters (especially 4, 8 and 9) that the various processes of economic change typically result in uneven patterns of development. At the national scale, this has stimulated, in varying degrees, intervention by governments through the medium of regional policy to try and modify the distribution of economic activity in accordance with various objectives. In practice, these objectives have generally been narrowed to a concern with raising unemployment and income levels in depressed regions to prevailing national norms. The difficulties of these regions may stem from many factors such as peripheral location relative to major markets or the decline of their traditional economic base. Given the central role of manufacturing within the economic development process, much of regional policy explicitly seeks to influence the distribution of industry. For much of the period since the Second World War, governments in most of the developed market economies have pursued some kind of regional policy, although the extent of the commitment to such intervention has varied from one country to another (Allen, 1978; Yuill et al., 1980). Regional policy in the United Kingdom, for example, has a history of more than fifty years (Law, 1980). Other West European countries have followed this example and the European Commission remains committed to regional policy in a supra-national context. Problems of uneven development have a special significance within Canada where the central government must be sensitive to real and perceived inequalities of opportunity between the provinces to limit political tensions within the federation (Walker, 1983; Savoie, 1986). Even in the United States, with its traditional antipathy towards government intervention in economic affairs, regional development has attracted the attention of policy-makers although the influence upon industrial location has been limited (Rees and Weinstein, 1983). The 1980s witnessed a significant weakening in the commitment to regional policy, especially in the United Kingdom, but also in other countries such as Canada (Cannon, 1989). Nevertheless, it is difficult, not least because of overwhelming evidence of widening regional disparities (Martin, 1988), to believe that the policy pendulum will not swing towards renewed efforts to cope with the problem. This chapter, therefore, examines some of the interrelationships between industrial location, regional development and regional policy. It is divided into three sections. The first reviews some of the more important policy instruments directed at investment at plant and firm level; the second examines strategies which have involved efforts to influence the geography of investment on a more comprehensive basis; the third evaluates some of the limitations of regional policy as it has been practised. It is important to stress that this chapter can provide only a superficial view of a complex topic and that its purpose is to demonstrate the relevance of some of the ideas discussed in previous chapters to an important policy issue.

Instruments of regional policy

Regional policy has traditionally focused on the manufacturing sector and especially upon influencing new plant location decisions. This focus has become less appropriate within developed economies as the relative importance of manufacturing has declined and the volume of potentially mobile investment (i.e. branch plants and relocations) has shrunk accordingly. Nevertheless, it is the connection between regional policy and industrial location which is of particular concern to us. The essence of regional policy is that it applies only to certain areas within a country. The definition of these areas is, therefore, a prerequisite to policy implementation. The criteria used vary between countries, but they typically involve threshold income and unemployment levels; areas with unemployment above and family income below the specified levels are eligible for assistance. These thresholds change through time *within* countries and the boundaries of the areas to which the policy relates are frequently re-drawn as the history of the British case demonstrates (figure 11.1).

Many aspects of regional policy are aimed directly at corporate balance sheets, notably at reducing the costs of capital and labour. This rests upon the belief that the corresponding reductions in investment and operating costs will influence comparative advantage between regions and induce a shift in future patterns of industrial development.

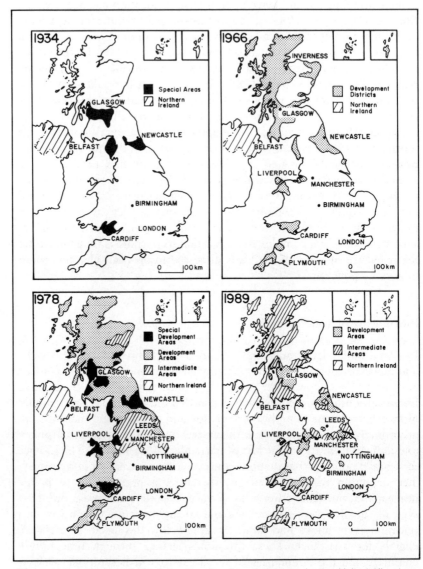

Figure 11.1 Areas qualifying for regional policy assistance in the United Kingdom, selected years

On the capital side, grants, loans and direct equity investment by public agencies have been used. Investment grants to cover part of the costs of new buildings and machinery accounted for 80 per cent of British government expenditure on regional policy in 1977–8 (Pounce, 1981,

p. 107). Huge sums of money were spent in this way during the late 1960s and the 1970s in the United Kingdom, in many cases to subsidize investment that would have been made anyway (Hudson, 1983). Furthermore, such policies tend to favour capital-intensive industries such as petrochemicals, despite the fact that employment creation is usually the priority (Woodward, 1974). If large companies such as ICI benefited disproportionately from investment grants, the provision of government-backed loans has been used to support smaller firms, especially those unable to raise capital from the usual commercial sources. Alternatively, the state may assist a venture by making a direct equity investment which, in turn, allows the firm to raise extra funds. The activities of the Scottish Development Agency and its Welsh counterpart are perhaps the best examples of this approach (Eirug, 1983; Rich, 1983). Tax allowances provide benefits which affect returns rather than initial investment by permitting firms to reduce or even eliminate their tax obligations for specified periods after start-up. Rent-free periods, often in property provided by government agencies, have a similar effect. Various schemes to subsidize labour costs represent an even more direct attempt to influence the economics of doing business. The Regional Employment Premium operated in the United Kingdom between 1967 and 1976. Under this programme, which absorbed a considerable proportion of the total regional support budget (Law, 1980, pp. 208–9; Manners et al., 1980, pp. 31–43), firms within Development Areas were entitled to subsidies depending upon the number and type of people they employed.

In addition to policies focused at plant and firm level, a whole range of more general measures have been used to improve the prospects of problem regions in attracting new investment. Infrastructure is difficult to define, but there is no doubt that it is important to industry. Clearly, serviced industrial sites, suitable properties for rent, adequate transport facilities and efficient utilities such as gas, electricity and water are all necessary for industrial development. Less obviously, an education system which produces an adaptable and enterprising workforce and an environment which provides a desirable quality of life are also important. All of these things are part of the infrastructure, something which is frequently lacking in problem regions, either because it has never been developed (in the periphery) or because it has deteriorated (in old industrial areas). Despite the difficulties of actually measuring the external economies associated with a good infrastructure, its importance is widely acknowledged. In the United States, investment in flood control schemes and new roads to encourage regional development, especially in the Appalachians, may be traced to the 'New Deal' of the 1930s (House, 1983). Although not specifically designed to influence industrial location, the British new towns have proved very attractive to certain types of manufacturing and those in Scotland, for example, were much more popular destinations for migrant firms during the 1960s than the Glasgow conurbation (Henderson, 1980; Fothergill et al., 1983). To some extent, this reflected the prevailing negative view of Glasgow, but it was also due to positive aspects of the new town environment. Indeed, the amount of time and money which regions and communities spend on polishing their 'image' is itself an indication of the importance attached to infrastructure in its broadest sense (Burgess, 1982).

Policies designed to reinforce the attractions of lagging regions are sometimes buttressed by efforts to control growth in prosperous ones. As already noted in chapter 9, powerful forces of circular and cumulative causation tend to reinforce growth in successful regions. 'Overheating' in such regions, as reflected in traffic congestion or inflated land and property values, has prompted many to argue that expansion continues long after it is socially beneficial. The classical expression of this view is found in the 1940 United Kingdom Report of the Royal Commission on the Distribution of the Industrial Population which laid the foundations for British regional policy over the next thirty years (McCrone, 1969, pp. 30–47). One aspect of this policy that was pursued with varying degrees of enthusiasm until the late 1970s was the system of Industrial Development Certificates. This required firms proposing to invest in new and expanded factories which exceeded specified floor areas to obtain certificates from a central government agency before local planning permission could be granted. The details of this scheme varied from year to year, but it allowed central government to prevent further industrial expansion in the South East and West Midlands. The hope was that such expansion would be diverted into the development areas, but there was no guarantee that this would actually happen (Law, 1980, pp. 43–56; Manners et al., 1980, pp. 74–81).

The uncertainties surrounding the response of the private sector to the sticks and carrots of regional policy may be avoided by direct state investment in industry. In centrally planned societies, the means of production are controlled by the state and may, theoretically, be used to promote broadly defined social objectives, including regional inequality (see chapter 13). This same opportunity exists, to a more limited extent, in mixed economies as the case of the Italian Mezzogiorno demonstrates. The state owns a relatively high proportion of Italian manufacturing through its holding companies (Rodgers, 1985). The Institute per la Ricostruzione Industriale, Ente Nationale Idrocarburi and Ente Participazione Manifatturiare have between them considerable activities in steel, metals, machinery, petroleum refining, petrochemicals, paper, glass and cement. Before 1957 these companies were relatively weak in the Mezzogiorno, but a law of that year changed the situation dramatically. They were subsequently required to make 40 per cent of all investments in the south and to place 60 per cent of all new industrial activities there, and in fact the proportion rose from less than 20 per cent in 1959 to around 70 per cent by the early 1970s, though it slipped back somewhat later. Employment rose from approximately 20,000 in 1953 to 136,800 in 1978 (Rodgers, 1985, pp. 60–1). The state holdings have brought not only employment but also modern sectors to the Mezzogiorno, though not without difficulties (Rodgers, 1979). India is another country where regional development considerations have influenced the location decisions of public-sector enterprises in many basic and capital goods industries. The poorest Indian states have consistently attracted a disproportionate share of investment by these enterprises since independence and this policy 'undoubtedly contributed to balancing the distribution of industry' (Udhay-Sekhar, 1983, p. (ii)). It is worth noting that just as state enterprises can act as positive influences upon regional development in times of growth, they can have the reverse effect in less favourable circumstances as Hudson (1986, p. 181) shows in the case of North East England where the policies of nationalized industries have 'been the major proximate cause of regional de-industrialization and employment decline'.

One of the principal factors in 'the demise of regional policy' in Britain has, in fact, been the radically changed macro-economic environment of the 1980s (Gibbs, 1989). Policies that have essentially been concerned with the spatial management of industrial growth obviously lose their rationale when there is no growth to be managed. In these circumstances, the emphasis has shifted towards promoting indigenous growth at the regional level rather than attracting inward investment. This shift, which finds expression in the increased interest in the dynamics of new-firm formation (chapters 3 and 9), also reflects doubts about the wisdom of dependence upon externally-owned branch plants (chapter 7). Support services to existing firms within their area are frequently provided by local government agencies in both North America and Western Europe (McFarland, 1981; Walker, 1980a, pp. 236–8) and programmes to encourage new-firm formation by helping individuals to bring their ideas to commercial fruition are becoming more widespread (Oakey, 1984). Various types of innovation centres have been set up to encourage researchers, inventors and businessmen to link up, and such centres are sometimes integrated into broader regional development thrusts (Hooper and Walker, 1983). Accompanying this change of emphasis from attracting external investment to promoting indigenous development and, by implication, from large enterprises to small firms, there has been a significant shift in the responsibility for regional policy. As central government, in the United Kingdom at least, has reduced both its financial and political commitment, local government has attempted to fill the policy vacuum (Sellgren, 1989). This may, on the one hand, be regarded as a desirable decentralizing trend, but, on the other, most local authorities lack the resources to cope with the economic problems they face.

Growth poles and growth centres

Generally speaking, regional policy is not directed at any particular manufacturing sector. However, viewed from the perspective of individual regions, it makes sense to base development strategies upon a realistic appraisal of comparative advantage so that policies may be more sharply focused on target industries. The Heckscher–Ohlin approach (chapter 10) has been used at the regional level (Moroney and Walker, 1966; Olsen, 1971; Norcliffe and Stevens, 1979). Input–output techniques (chapter 4) may be helpful in identifying local market opportunities by revealing the patterns of inter-industry flows within a region and the extent to which local demands are met by imports from outside its boundaries (Hewings, 1977). The exploitation of linkages to create growth centres of interrelated economic activities has been central to an important and influential strand of thinking in regional policy which may be traced to the work of Perroux (1950).

The term *pôles de croissance* (growth poles) was adopted by Perroux to refer to a focus of economic growth 'from which centrifugal forces emanate and to which contripetal forces are attracted' (Perroux, 1950, p. 45). He did not regard the pole as a real geographic location, but rather a position in an n-dimensional, abstract economic space. These poles are dominant and privileged points containing a group of what he called *propulsive firms or industries*. Such firms or industries are characterized by rapid growth because they are involved in activities at an early stage in the product life cycle (chapter 7) and by a tendency towards large-scale, capital-intensive production and organizational concentration. The propulsive industries or firms positively influence others which depend upon them for a high proportion of their inputs and/or outputs. This influence extends beyond direct and induced increases in production to include a change of 'atmosphere' which encourages further progress as economic and social changes set in motion the sequence of circular and cumulative causation described in chapter 9.

It was stressed earlier that the original work of Perroux was concerned with *economic space*, unrestricted by specific geographical boundaries.

However, he later applied similar ideas to geographical areas. In so doing he noted, first, that agglomeration economies (chapter 4) are another factor encouraging the development of poles and, second, that agencies operating in geographic space, such as private-sector enterprises and public institutions, affect the diffusion of growth impulses. Not surprisingly, Perroux's ideas have influenced policy in his own country where planners have used the concept of the polarized region – that is a region with development concentrated at a central point – in connection with attempts to decentralize economic activities from Paris (Boudeville, 1966, pp. 102–35; Darwent, 1969). The idea is to encourage a *metropole* in each region to act as a focus for surrounding smaller towns and to reduce their direct dependence upon Paris. This, however, bears little relation to Perroux's original concept and is closer to the growth centre notion discussed below.

The growth pole idea is closely related to the promotion of industrial complexes for regional development purposes and various efforts have been made to identify suitable candidates (Hirschmann, 1958; Hodge and Wong, 1972; Czamanski, 1976; Czamanski and Ablas, 1979; Norcliffe, 1979; Norcliffe and Kotseff, 1980; Lever 1980). Essentially, these complexes should be focused upon sectors with the characteristics of Perroux's propulsive firms or industries, including rapid rates of growth in employment and output as well as extensive backward and forward linkages to serve as the channels for the transmission of growth. The petrochemical industry met these requirements during the 1960s when it was used as an instrument of regional development policy in several different countries (Chapman, 1984). Interest in the industry was stimulated by the work of Isard et al., (1959), who used comparative cost techniques to present a case for the establishment of a fully integrated oil-based industrial complex on the Caribbean island of Puerto Rico. This was viewed as part of a wider strategy of industrialization known as 'Operation Bootstrap' initiated after the Second World War. The active promotion of oil refining and petrochemicals by the government of Puerto Rico during the 1960s was based on a belief that these capital-intensive activities would stimulate more labour-intensive downstream development such as plastics fabrication and synthetic textiles. Impressive flow-charts were produced by the island's Economic Development Administration and by private companies anxious to reinforce their arguments for financial inducements to invest in Puerto Rico. In fact, the inflated expectations were never fulfilled and, by the mid 1970s, many of the basic processing operations had shut-down. The collapse of these operations was partly due to circumstances peculiar to Puerto Rico (Chapman, 1982), but the failure of downstream developments to take place had a wider significance that was matched in other areas. The public-sector investments in the Italian Mezzogiorno described in the previous section were motivated by similar objectives, but Rodgers (1979, pp. 125–6) notes that 'There was virtually no spin-off or multiplier effect such as small- and medium-sized establishments that were linked to the basic industries.'

These examples emphasize that technical linkages do not automatically induce adjacent investment in related manufacturing activities. As already noted in chapter 4, industrial linkages are maintained over considerable distances in economies with efficient transportation systems. Furthermore, the location requirements of upstream and downstream operations in a processing chain may be very different. In the case of petrochemicals, the basic activities are drawn to their sources of raw material (natural gas supplies and oil refineries), but the plastics and textile industries which depend upon petrochemical products tend to be associated with market locations and sources of cheap labour respectively. The fact that these activities are usually carried out by different companies from those responsible for oil refining and basic petrochemical production also makes it more difficult to encourage their concentration within a single complex. Indeed, Holland (1971) has argued, with reference to the Mezzogiorno, that much greater levels of state control over the location and structure of firms is necessary to ensure that the multiplier effect of propulsive industries is retained at the regional scale. In cases where ownership is highly fragmented, the co-ordination of investment required to establish an integrated operation becomes almost impossible as illustrated by the failure of a proposed metal working complex, involving 20 separate plants, at St John, New Brunswick (Luttrell, 1972). Such problems can, in theory, be avoided in planned economies where the concept of the *territorial production complex* is analogous to the various attempts in market economies to exploit industrial linkages in accordance with regional development objectives (chapter 13).

Growth-centre policies, which seek to provide an efficient organization of public infrastructure, are yet another approach to regional development. They have generally been more successful than policies focused upon investment in regional industrial complexes. In Austria and West Germany, for example, rural development planning at provincial (Lander) level has frequently built on central place concepts to encourage the population to remain in rural areas yet be able to reach critical services in nearby towns by public transport (Blacksell, 1975, p. 185; Krumme, 1974, pp. 118–35). Such service centres (growth points) have at the same time been the recipients of special supports for job creation, including, to some degree, manufacturing jobs. Nevertheless, growth-centre policies are not without problems. The benefits tend to be focused upon the chosen centre and its immediate hinterland. Moseley (1974) suggests that there is little evidence of spread effects around growth centres and that the multiplier mechanism tends to reinforce their dominance by attracting labour and capital from their surrounding regions, a process which inevitably creates political tensions. This is not necessarily a bad thing, however, and it can be argued that concentration upon the best location is essential to maximize total regional income. Thinking back to our New England example of chapter 9, it will be recalled that regional renewal there has been accompanied by a significant concentration of new developments around the Boston area.

The history of growth poles, growth centres and industrial complexes illustrates the whole problem of spatial planning in free-market economies. There has always been strong resistance to one area being favoured over another, and a democratic system gives political focus to any discontent. Feelings run particularly high at any attempt to direct private firms to specific locations, which is exactly what is required to guarantee the success of growth-pole strategies. Selective support for infrastructure as found under growth-centre policy, however, has been more acceptable. Countries with strong central planning agencies are in a much better position to impose particular spatial arrangements – with the accompanying risk, however, of being insensitive to regional aspirations (chapter 13).

Policy problems

It is very difficult to evaluate the achievements of regional policy, not least because of the uncertainty of knowing what would have happened in its absence (Diamond and Spence, 1983). The time-lag between the introduction of a specific policy measure, investment decisions and, for example, the actual construction of a new factory is often so long that there can be no certainty of a simple cause-and-effect relationship. The fact that both policies and the areas to which they relate frequently change is a further difficulty. Despite these and other problems, there has been no shortage of attempts to assess the effectiveness of regional policy, especially in the United Kingdom (Frost, 1975; Keeble, 1976; Schofield 1979; Regional Studies Association (UK), 1983). Various studies have estimated the net gains in manufacturing employment attributable to policy effects within the assisted areas during the 1960s and 1970s (Moore and Rhodes, 1973; 1976; Keeble, 1976; McKay and Thomson, 1979; Fothergill and Gudgin, 1982). These all agree that the combination of positive inducements and restrictions did have significant employment effects, although they vary in their assessments of the magnitude of these effects. On the other hand, Massey (1979b) argues that the policy effects in the United Kingdom have been exaggerated, because the shift in manufacturing to the peripheral regions during the 1960s would have occurred anyway as a result of the spatial division of labour practised by large firms seeking to reduce their wage costs by establishing branch plants in such regions (see chapter 7).

Whatever the precise effect of regional policy, it cannot be regarded as an unqualified success. The recession of the 1980s emphasized that, with the exception of the West Midlands, the regions in the United Kingdom with the highest levels of unemployment and the lowest per capita incomes were the same ones that had been the focus of policy concern fifty years earlier. The persistence of these problems is reflected in figure 11.2 which illustrates the cumulative incidence of assisted status between 1934 and 1984 in terms of the number of years the different parts of the United Kingdom have qualified for prevailing inducements to investment. The actual 'score' for certain areas has been modified by distinguishing between levels of assistance. Thus distinctions were made for many years between Development Areas, Special Development Areas and Intermediate Areas. In figure 11.2 Special Development Areas are given a score of 1.5 for each year they were accorded this status and Intermediate Areas a score of 0.5 to reflect greater and lesser degrees of support respectively relative to the Development Areas. Despite this somewhat arbitrary procedure, the map does give a reasonable indication of the overall geographical pattern of support and it shows that most of the 'problem' areas that stimulated the introduction of regional policy in the early 1930s including Clydeside, West Cumberland, North-East England and South Wales, have remained areas of concern throughout the fifty-year period.

Chapter 9 emphasized the gradual nature of economic change and the persistence of regional problems partly reflects this reality. Governments frequently have unreasonable expectations which are encouraged by their political need for quick results. Furthermore, they often fail to recognize that many policies have geographical effects which directly contradict their declared regional development objectives. Nowhere is this more apparent than in defence expenditure (Law, 1983; Breheny, 1988). The Ministry of Defence is the largest single customer (by value) of British industry. Table 11.1 indicates the geographical distribution of its procurement expenditure in 1983-4 compared with the corresponding distribution of regional aid. It emphasizes the huge disparity in the absolute levels of expenditure and the inverse relationship in the regional incidence of the two types of expenditure. The relatively prosperous South East receives the lion's share of defence contracts and there is evidence that this geographical concentration is increasing (Breheny, 1988). The implications of this extend beyond the direct

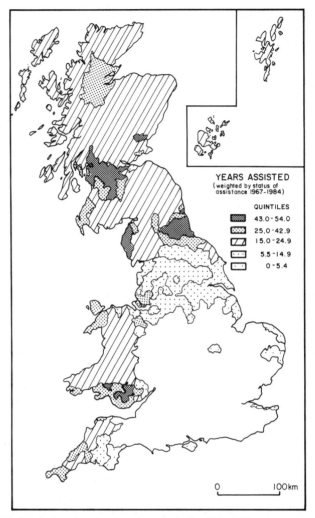

Figure 11.2 Continuity of regional assistance in the United Kingdom, 1934–1984
Source: Townsend in Lever, 1987

economic impact of the expenditures, as measured by job creation, to include their indirect influence upon future development. The military's requirements for increasingly sophisticated equipment has meant that defence expenditure has promoted high-technology sectors such as electronics and aerospace. In the United States, the rise of Silicon Valley and the economic revival of New England have, for example, been boosted by military contracts. These contracts tend to sustain research

Table 11.1 A comparison of defence expenditure and regional aid in the United Kingdom

Region	Procurement expenditure 1983–1984 absolute (£ million)	%	Regional aid 1983–1984 absolute (£ million)	%
South East	3,747.1	54.0	–	–
South West	763.3	11.0	–	–
East Anglia	208.2	3.0	–	–
East Midlands	346.9	5.0	18	2.5
West Midlands	277.6	4.0	–	–
North West	763.3	11.0	137	18.8
Yorks/Humber	138.8	2.0	36	5.0
Northern	138.8	2.0	92	12.6
Scotland	416.3	6.0	222	30.5
Wales	69.4	1.0	114	15.7
Northern Ireland	69.4	1.0	108	14.8
Totals	6,939.0	100.0	727	100.0

Source: Breheny, 1988

and development in already prosperous regions, thereby underpinning their future prosperity. This polarizing effect obviously runs counter to and, by virtue of the disparity in the sums of money involved, almost certainly overwhelms any tendency towards dispersal resulting from the operation of regional policy.

The contradictions apparent in geographical patterns of defence expenditure and regional policy are symptomatic of a much wider problem – the failure of policy makers to appreciate that a national economy is composed of a system of regions and that *national* policies will have differential regional effects. Industrial, science, and technology policies all have a geographical dimension, partly because of existing differences in the economic structure of regions. Despite variations in levels of intervention, virtually all governments in developed economies support basic and applied research in the hope of accelerating the development of new industries to provide the basis for future economic growth. Maintaining national competitiveness is the principal objective of such policies. However, the uneven regional distribution of both private-sector and government research establishments has already been noted in chapter 7 and it is likely that these establishments will attract a major share of future research funding. Bearing in mind the connections between innovation, the origin and location of new industries outlined in earlier chapters, the tendency for science and technology policies to increase the gap between rich and poor regions is clear (Malecki, 1981). One response to the potentially divisive influence of 'top–down' science and technology policies has been an increasing awareness of the need to promote indigenous innovation at the regional level. This is closely related to the already-noted interest in encouraging new firms and worries about the negative implications of external control. Creating the kind of environment conducive to the formation not only of new firms, but, more especially, firms associated with 'young' products and industries is the essence of 'an innovation-oriented regional policy' (Ewers and Wettmann, 1980). Such a policy must necessarily be regarded as a long-term commitment involving, for example, fundamental changes in education. It is widely recognized that vocational education has close links to the success of development programmes, but much more rarely acknowledged that it is general education which most profoundly influences the nature of any society. Vocational education is geared to existing business practices and is, therefore, essentially conservative. It is general education which, by encouraging creativity, should provide the stimulus to change.

Although education is important in encouraging initiative, often it is not just attitudes, but business conditions themselves, which inhibit entrepreneurship in general and innovation in particular. The progressive concentration of economic power in the hands of fewer, larger corporations throughout much of the twentieth century (chapter 5) has been based upon the assumption that big is better. This assumption, which was challenged by Schumacher (1974), has created many difficulties for small firms including, for example, the higher cost of borrowing as compared with large enterprises (Taylor and Thrift, 1983b). Most governments in developed economies have accepted the need to provide special support for small firms. This support may complement regional policy to the extent that smaller units have greater flexibility than the large specialized establishments operated by multiplant companies which, as a result of contraction or closure, have frequently had devastating impacts upon local economies. Glasgow has had more than its fair share of such blows and considerable efforts have been made to promote the small-firm sector within the city during the 1980s (Lever and Moore, 1986). In some cases, these efforts have involved unorthodox approaches including worker-managed enterprises and community businesses. Such efforts are not necessarily geared towards high technology and Glasgow's enterprise workshops, for example, are intended to provide space, simple machinery and advice for anyone wishing to experiment with an idea.

A very different kind of small-firm support is that associated with the promotion of new technologies in which innovation centres provide a link between business and pure research. These were first introduced in the 1970s at such US universities as Massachusetts Institute of Technology and Carnegie–Mellon, but have since been adopted much more widely throughout the developed world. Figure 11.3 indicates that more than 70 such centres were established, under construction or planned throughout West Germany in 1985. The concept of innovation centres reinforces the argument regarding the importance of education in regional development since they are usually associated with academic institutions which serve both as sources of ideas and also provide more general support such as courses in entrepreneurship and financial management. The provision of incubator facilities and other infrastructure in the form of science or research parks frequently represent the physical expressions of the innovation centre idea (Buck et al., 1980; Walker, 1984b). Many so-called science parks are merely up-market industrial property developments which fail because they are not

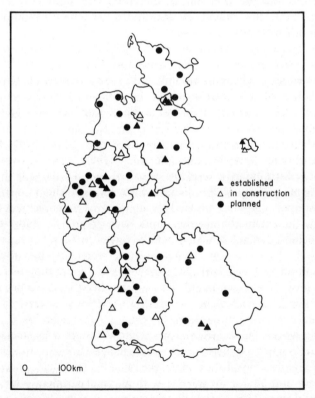

Figure 11.3 Incubator and innovation centres in West Germany, 1985
Source: Meyer-Krahmer, 1985

effectively linked to the sources of research (Christy and Ironside, 1987). Nevertheless, some, such as Research Triangle Park in North Carolina, which provides approximately 52,000 jobs, and the one associated with Cambridge University, have been conspicuously successful by whatever criteria they are judged (Peltz and Weiss, 1984; Segal, Quince and Partners, 1985). In the case of Cambridge, however, this success is reinforcing regional disparities within the United Kingdom because of its location on the prosperous side of the north–south divide, once again emphasizing the need to take account of the regional consequences of national policies such as the funding of further education.

Conclusion

Although regional policy is ostensibly concerned with economic issues, the underlying justification is often political. Disparities in economic opportunity between one part of a country and another are potentially divisive, especially when superimposed upon ethnic or cultural distributions which themselves create tensions between regional interests and central government. Economic inequalities are often exploited by separatist movements to further their political objectives. Federal political systems are generally more responsive to regional interests, but they face the problem of co-ordinating provincial policies into a coherent national strategy. One approach that has worked well for Austria and West Germany is to set up a conference of representatives of provinces, relevant federal ministries, municipalities and labour (OECD, 1977; Österreichische Raumplanungskonferenz, 1978). This operates at the level of politicians, civil servants and advisers, and has been a means of bringing people together for discussions of problems and policies as well as a way of initiating and implementing research. A system which depends upon regular meetings is more difficult to operate in a large country such as Canada which has attempted to maintain links between Ottawa and the provinces since the early 1970s by decentralizing a high proportion of federal staff concerned with regional policy.

The process of economic development will always create differences between places and there will always be pressures to limit these differences by policy intervention. Although the forces responsible for unbalanced economic growth, many of which have been identified in earlier chapters, are very powerful, it is worth noting that there are certain incipient trends in industrial organization – which may increase the opportunities for greater local or regional autonomy in economic matters. Internal pressures towards more decentralized management structures within some large corporations were described in chapter 7.

These pressures, combined with a revival of small business, may improve the economic prospects of peripheral regions.

Further reading

Friedmann, J. and Weaver C. 1979: *Territory and Function: the Evolution of Regional Planning*. London: Edward Arnold.

Lo, Fu Chen and Salih, K. 1978: *Growth Pole Strategy and Regional Development: Asian Experiences and Alternative Approaches*. Oxford, Pergamon.

Moriarty, B. M. 1980: *Industrial Location and Community Development*. Chapel Hill, NC: University of North Carolina Press.

Regional Studies Association (UK) 1983: *Report of an Inquiry into Regional Problems in the United Kingdom*. Norwich: Geo Books.

Walker, D. F. 1983: Canadian regional development policy. In A. Hecht, (ed.), *Regional Development in the Peripheries of Canada and Europe*, Winnipeg: University of Manitoba, Department of Geography, 116–36.

12
Industry in the City

Whatever attempts have been made by governments to influence the location of industry have mainly been focused at the regional scale. By the late 1970s, however, there was growing concern in many developed countries about the rate of manufacturing job losses within urban areas and especially within the older, inner cities. In the United Kingdom, for example, there was a sharp contrast between the generally prosperous image of the Greater London area and the very high unemployment levels within specific London boroughs such as Southwark and Wandsworth. Indeed these levels were often higher than in parts of the Development Areas – a situation which led many to suggest that the inner city had become the most important regional problem (Massey, 1979; Elias and Keogh, 1982). Unemployment itself reflects imbalance in the labour market and there is abundant evidence of both absolute industrial job losses in the inner cities and certainly an overall relative decline in the share of total manufacturing employment accounted for by metropolitan areas within developed economies. Several studies have described these trends within British cities since the 1950s (see Bull, 1978; Dennis, 1978; Lloyd and Mason, 1978; 1984; Lever and Moore, 1986) and it has been estimated that the inner cities alone experienced a net loss of more than one million manufacturing jobs between 1951 and 1981 (Audit Commission, 1989, p. 9). The problem is not unique to the United Kingdom. Many of the largest US cities such as Chicago and New York have experienced similar sharp falls in manufacturing employment and there has also been a simultaneous tendency for industry to grow more rapidly beyond the boundaries of the metropolitan regions in smaller towns and rural settlements (see Hamer, 1973; Lonsdale and Seyler, 1979; Scott, 1982a; Soja et al., 1983). Indeed, this so-called urban–rural shift of manufacturing seems to have been a feature of virtually all developed economies (Keeble et al., 1983) and 'is clearly the geographical manifestation of an almost universal process' (Norcliffe, 1984b, p. 27).

This chapter examines the impact of this process upon urban areas. It is divided into four sections. The first explores the features of the urban core which have traditionally attracted manufacturing industry; the second examines the later trend favouring the dispersal of manufacturing to the suburbs and beyond; the third combines these opposing influences into an integrated view of recent industrial location change as it has affected metropolitan areas; the fourth focuses upon the implications of these events for the inner cities and upon the prospects for their economic regeneration.

Industry in the urban core

Theories of urban land-use have traditionally emphasized the key role of accessibility and transport costs, as reflected in land values, in determining the distribution of land uses within the city (see Haig, 1926; Alonso, 1964). The argument is based upon the proposition that the centre of an urban area is the most desirable location because it offers the greatest accessibility to the entire urban market. This central point, therefore, becomes the focus around which urban land-use patterns are formulated. The cost of land is highest at this point and declines with increasing distance from it. Competition between different land uses is resolved by their willingness to pay rents, with the central locations being reserved for those retail and commercial activities most dependent upon accessibility relative to the urban market. The implication of this argument is the generation of a concentric or zonal land use pattern with successive activity rings arranged around the city centre (figure 12.1). Whilst accessibility to markets is important to manufacturing, it is less critical than for retailing or some other activities serving the general public. Indeed only a small proportion of modern manufacturing (measured by value added) is geared towards specific local or urban markets and, in these circumstances, high land prices at the core of the city may be expected to repel industry.

Accessibility in a more general sense has, however, been vital in shaping the intra-urban location of industry. Transport systems are typically focused upon the urban core and access to railway lines and waterfront sites was particularly important for heavy, large-scale, raw material-based industries during the nineteenth and early twentieth centuries. Figure 12.2 indicates the distribution of manufacturing employment in Chicago in 1873 in terms of distance zones around a core location at the intersection of Madison and State Streets. The steady

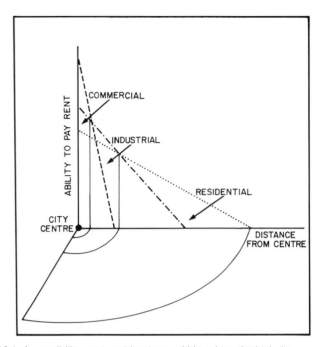

Figure 12.1 Accessibility, rent and land-use within a hypothetical city

decline of industrial activity away from this point suggests that high
land costs at the urban core were not a deterrent to industry. This
reflects the considerable expense of moving heavy and bulky commodities
with prevailing transport technology. Fales and Moses (1972, p. 67)
observe that such commodities cost 25 to 30 times more per ton mile
to transport by horse and cart than by rail and water in the Chicago
of the 1870s. It is not surprising, therefore, that operations such as
brick-making, blast furnaces and iron foundries should cluster around
sites with access to rail and water transport in the nineteenth-century
city. Furthermore, these sites were often close to the historic core of the
city, thereby creating the kind of employment distribution indicated in
figure 12.2.

Accessibility to labour also played a part in influencing the location
of industry within the nineteenth-century city. The cost of moving people
was low relative to the cost of moving goods. With the advent of mass
public transportation such as horse-drawn and then electric trams, it
became possible to extend the range of the daily journey to work.
Nevertheless, these transport systems, like those geared to the movement
of commodities were oriented towards the city centre so that 'industry

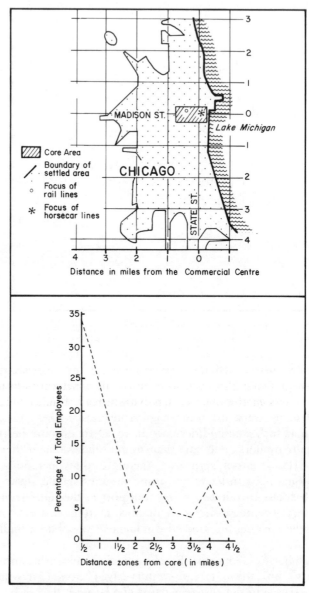

Figure 12.2 Manufacturing employment in Chicago, 1873
Source: Fales and Moses, 1972

of all kinds occupied central locations, where it was at once accessible to major transport terminals and to the total urban labour force' (Scott, 1982b, p. 188).

Labour factors, which have their origins in conditions established during the last century continue to have some residual influence in attracting, or at least holding, certain types of industry within the inner city. Skills required in craft industries such as jewellery-making have been passed on from one generation to another through apprenticeship schemes, creating relatively localized 'pools' of labour. Changes in methods of production, however, have tended to reduce the importance of such considerations and it is cheap, unskilled labour which is the more significant attraction in contemporary inner cities. These areas often include deprived, ethnic and working-class neighbourhoods with high unemployment rates. Such neighbourhoods are a source of low wage labour and various analyses have suggested a growing divergence since the 1950s between lower inner-city and higher suburban wage rates within many metropolitan areas (see Scott, 1981; Randall, 1983). This differential has encouraged firms in labour-intensive industries such as clothing to remain in the inner city (Scott, 1984).

The various forces encouraging firms to gravitate towards central locations have been reinforced by a closely related, but logically distinct, tendency towards clustering. This arises where activities are organized into functional complexes bound together by extensive linkages between interdependent plants and firms. The various urbanization and localization economies described in chapter 4 are important in such complexes which were a more distinctive feature of the nineteenth-century city than the modern metropolis (see Wise, 1949; Hall, 1962; Bater, 1975). Nevertheless, there are still some manufacturing activities for which the advantages of an inner-city location outweigh the disadvantages. Most of these can be described as 'communication-oriented' industries. In the late 1950s, Hoover and Vernon (1962, pp. 258–69) noted about two dozen of these in New York, if various branches of women's clothing are included. The other major sector was printing and publishing. They are characterized by non-standard products, frequently also by non-standard materials, by the need for contact with people for ideas and information and often by the need for personal contact with customers. Downtown offices, for example, generate a considerable amount of custom work for some printing and advertising firms. This work often needs checking before going into final production, and may well be required urgently. For custom and fashion clothing as well, links to the retail outlets and salesrooms are important. Small firms often get their start on the basis of sub-contracts from larger ones and such arrangements are becoming a favoured strategy of large enterprises in many sectors.

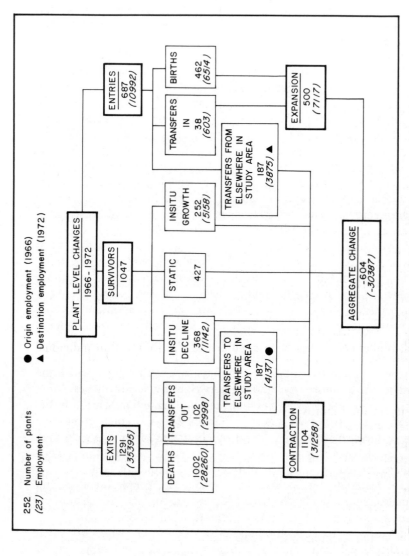

Figure 12.3 Components of industrial change in Inner Manchester, 1966–1972
Source: Lloyd and Mason, 1978

Scott (1983a) suggests that this encourages clustering because of the importance both of physical linkages and, especially, communication linkages when sub-contractors are required to respond quickly to frequent changes in the specifications demanded by their clients. These constellations of firms do not have to be in the older parts of cities, but many are because they have evolved from an earlier period and have remained close to their roots. Scott (1984) notes the influence of such considerations upon the location of the women's dress industry in Greater Los Angeles, emphasizing the high degree of clustering of small firms around the downtown area.

Despite these examples, there is no doubt that the relative significance of the inner city as a location for industry has declined. This is partly due to improvements in transport technology since the nineteenth century which have reduced the real costs of intra-urban movement. These costs have, therefore, become a less constraining influence upon the relative location of linked activities. It is also due to the increasing scale both of business organization and of industrial production which have diminished the importance of localized inter-firm linkages and small production units. In these circumstances, the decentralization of industry from the core of metropolitan areas to the suburbs seems to have started during the first quarter of the twentieth century. Writing in 1926 with reference to New York, Haig (p. 183) noted that 'the peak of manufacturing in the center of the city was reached about ten years ago and that a process of decentralization is already under way'. This process seems to have accelerated since the Second World War and, as already noted, numerous studies have documented the shift within individual cities.

Industry in the suburbs

The process of decentralization is a relative locational shift from the core to the suburbs involving various components of industrial change. These components, which affect both the number of establishments (plants) and the level of employment within an area, may be disaggregated into the negative effects of contraction, out-migration and closure (i.e. death) of individual plants and the positive effects of expansions, in-migration and openings (i.e. births). Figure 12.3 applies this accounting framework to an analysis of industrial change within the inner core of Manchester between 1966 and 1972. Despite the short time period, it reveals a net loss of 604 plants and over 30,000 jobs. It is evident that a relatively small proportion (17 per cent of plants and 10 per cent of jobs) of these losses were due to transfers or relocations out of the study area and that contractions and closures had by far the biggest effects. This is typical of other cities and it emphasizes the comprehensive nature of the apparent shift in comparative advantage to the suburbs and, more recently, to locations outside the cities. Focusing upon the intra-urban scale, this shift may be explained partly in terms of external changes in the urban core and the suburbs as environments for industry, and partly in terms of internal changes in the technology and organization of production.

Shortage of space has often been identified as an obstacle to industrial growth within the inner city (see Keeble, 1968; Dennis, 1978). The problem has been aggravated by the changing physical requirements of modern industrial production. The multi-storey factories that were once favoured are unsuited to contemporary methods and Hoover and Vernon (1962, p. 27) note a more than fourfold increase in average site space per worker (from 1040 sq. ft to 4550 sq. ft) from before 1922 to 1945 in plants outside the old cities of the New York metropolitan region. This trend has meant that it is not only difficult for a new business to find a suitable site within the inner city, but, more importantly, existing businesses also have problems in re-equipping with the latest technology. Such constraints to adaptation and expansion have been viewed by some writers as a major influence upon the decentralization of industry from the inner city (Fothergill and Gudgin, 1982).

Land-use planning restrictions may be regarded as a special case of constrained location. The redevelopment of inner cities has, for example, reduced the supply of cheap, rented property which is often used as a first home by new businesses (Lloyd and Mason, 1978; Bull, 1979). In a more general sense, the policies of planning authorities strongly influence the spatial arrangement of activities within urban areas. Admittedly, the extent of intervention is greater in some places than others, but it is often difficult to secure permission for industrial development outside officially approved zones. Even in a city such as Houston, where land-use planning is widely regarded as an infringement of personal liberties, the policies of the public sector, especially with regard to road construction, have had a major impact upon the distribution of economic activity within the metropolitan area (Feagin, 1988). Very often, these policies have been instrumental in promoting decentralization both in Houston and in other cities.

The concept of deglomerative factors or diseconomies of scale with respect of agglomeration was introduced in chapter 4. These include the impact of such variables as traffic congestion and high rents on land and property. In some cases, the 'push' factors are couched in more general terms to embrace the various dimensions of urban blight such as the condition of buildings and socio-economic indicators relating to, for example, poverty and crime. Focusing upon the relocation of industrial and commercial establishments from central Milwaukee between 1964 and 1974, Erickson (1980b) attempted to test systematically the relationship between negative environmental conditions and the rate of out-migration. He found little evidence that the rate was significantly higher from the most blighted inner areas and concluded that such 'push' factors were probably less important than 'pull' factors drawing industry to the suburbs from *anywhere* within the core, regardless of conditions in the immediate vicinity of the original location.

'Pull' factors favouring the suburbs are, in many respects, mirror-images of the 'push' factors affecting the core. Thus peripheral industrial estates, which have often been sited in accordance with the requirements of land-use planning policy, offer modern facilities with opportunities for more extensive factory layouts on cheaper land, pleasanter working environments and better access to intra- and inter-urban motorways. The interaction of 'push' and 'pull' factors provides only a partial explanation for the suburbanization of industry. These factors, associated with changes in the physical (i.e. external) environment of industry are subsidiary to more fundamental causes arising from changes in the nature and organization of the industrial production process. Various analyses of spatial variations in the profitability of industries and firms have suggested that these changes have made non-metropolitan locations more attractive. There are many technical difficulties in making such estimates, but most studies point in the same direction – that profit rates are lower in large cities than in smaller settlements and rural locations (see Miller, 1981; Fothergill et al., 1984). Thus the relative shift of manufacturing away from the conurbations may be interpreted as a rational business response to changing comparative advantage. In order to understand industrial location change *within* the city, it is necessary to consider the wider context responsible for this shift in comparative advantage relative to areas *beyond* the city.

Metropolitan industrial location change in context

The growing significance of large companies within the modern economy was emphasized in chapter 5 and the impact of their business strategies upon the economic fortunes of places was demonstrated in chapters 7 and 9. These impacts have often been considerable at the urban scale where large, multi-plant companies may account for a substantial proportion of total employment. Over 90 per cent of manufacturing employment in the Merseyside conurbation in 1975 was, for example, provided by such companies and most of these jobs were controlled from head-offices outside the city (Lloyd and Dicken, 1983). In these circumstances, it is not surprising that the actions of large companies have been responsible for many of the changes affecting the level and distribution of manufacturing employment within cities (see Massey and Meegan, 1978; Danson, 1982). This in turn 'creates a number of problems for an understanding of industrial change within cities' because individual plants are elements of wider corporate systems and 'the reasons for spatial change become increasingly less local in origin' (Bull, 1985, p. 99). Furthermore, the rate of such change is often accelerated by the operational flexibility implicit in such systems which allow investment to be switched from one location to another.

The trend towards larger units of business organization is closely related to changes in the technology of production. The desire to internalize linkages within the framework of a single company, rather than rely upon external suppliers and markets has been a powerful motive encouraging corporate growth (see chapter 5). This, together with the reduced real costs of movement resulting from improvement in transportation, has contributed to the dissolution of many of the labour-intensive complexes drawn to the urban core by linkages between interdependent firms and by other agglomeration economies. Thus many of these complexes have 'become gradually reconstituted within large capital-intensive and vertically integrated plants which . . . have a propensity to disperse outwards across the economic landscape' (Scott, 1983b, p. 367). This propensity is itself linked to various aspects of the spatial division of labour within large companies (see chapter 7) which have worked to the disadvantage of metropolitan areas in general and inner cities in particular.

Labour costs tend to be lower in non-metropolitan areas and this has encouraged large companies to establish plants in smaller towns (Lonsdale and Seyler, 1979). This trend has been linked to the product-cycle concept in the sense that labour costs rather than skills become more important in the mature stage. Thus the 'filter-down' theory of industrial development rests upon the proposition that industrial activities will successively shift from larger to smaller settlements as the nature of the products, and the processes used to manufacture them, evolve into standardized specifications and routine tasks (see Leinbach, 1978; Park and Wheeler, 1983). This trend is not only driven by spatial variations in direct wage costs, but also by the power relationships between capital and labour. The relative absence of trade union activity in smaller communities is often in sharp contrast to the traditions of militancy in old-established, metropolitan industrial regions (see Massey, 1979b; Walker and Storper, 1981; Peet, 1983; Storper and Walker, 1989). Furthermore, branch plants established in small towns and rural areas are often so large in relation to other employers that they are able to dominate and control the labour market. This is a further attraction from the point of view of the firm.

An important corollary of the 'filter-down' theory is the question of the geographical origins of job creation. This was touched upon in chapters 8 and 9 which suggested that innovation is more likely in established centres of economic activity than in peripheral locations. More specifically, it has been argued that, by providing an attractive and supportive economic environment through the availability of low-cost accommodation and various other *urbanization economies* (see chapter 4), the older inner cities act as 'incubators' or 'seedbeds' for new firms. This idea, if not the metaphor, is generally attributed to Hoover and Vernon's (1962) work on New York, but there have been several attempts to test its validity in other cities (see Goldberg, 1969; Leone and Struyk, 1976; Steed, 1976c; Fagg, 1980). The results are generally negative or inconclusive. With reference to the clothing industry, Steed (1976c) found no evidence in support of the incubator role in the inner cities of Toronto and Montreal, whilst Leone and Struyk (1976) were unable to demonstrate a systematic relocation of successful new firms to the suburbs in an analysis of five US cities. It seems likely that despite the frequent provision of cheap or free 'nursery units' for small firms by local authorities, the incubator function of inner cities is declining. Certainly the net loss of manufacturing employment experienced by many metropolitan regions over the last twenty years or so suggests that whatever jobs are 'filtering down', first to the suburbs and then beyond, are not being replaced by the creation of an equivalent number of new jobs at a dynamic core.

This situation is explained by Scott (1982a; 1982b; 1983a) as a consequence of a systemic shift within the modern industrial economy towards capital-intensive methods of production. Thus technical change is important not only in the context of the life cycle of individual products, but also on a much more comprehensive macro-economic level. Applying the Heckscher–Ohlin model, which is normally associated with the analysis of international trade (see chapter 10), Scott suggests that the core areas of metropolitan regions have tended to have a comparative advantage for labour-intensive industrial activities whilst the peripheral areas have tended to have a comparative advantage for capital-intensive operations. To the extent that the latter have become the dominant method of production in many sectors, this argument accounts for the net loss of manufacturing jobs experienced by so many major cities.

Figure 12.4 explores the spatial and temporal dimensions of comparative advantage at the metropolitan scale with reference to the relative

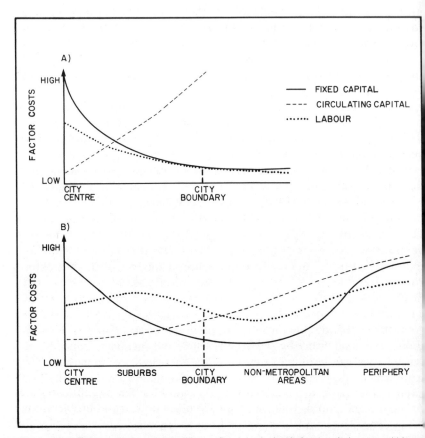

Figure 12.4 Temporal changes in labour, fixed and circulating capital costs within a space economy
Source: Norcliffe, 1984b, and Bull, 1985

costs of capital and labour. A distinction is made between two types of capital costs – fixed and circulating. The former includes buildings, machinery and vehicles; the latter is represented by the various inputs, such as raw materials or semi-manufactured goods, that are needed to produce further commodities or are held as inventory. The cost of these inputs includes the cost of assembling them on a c.i.f. (cost, insurance, freight) pricing basis. Figure 12.4a represents the situation prevailing in the nineteenth-century industrial city and is consistent with the pattern observed in 1873 Chicago (figure 12.2). The limitations of prevailing transport technology ensured that the cost of circulating capital rose steeply from the centre of urban areas for most industrial activities.

Land for industry at or near the core was therefore at a premium and labour demand was concentrated in these areas, resulting in high labour costs as emphasized by Hoover and Vernon's (1962) demonstration of the steady decline in industrial wage rates in the New York metropolitan region with increasing distance from Manhattan, a pattern which persisted into the 1930s.

Figure 12.4b represents the situation towards the end of the twentieth century. The distance axis is extended well beyond the city boundary to reflect the increasing scale of economic organization and the greater integration of the modern economy. Little change is evident in the fixed capital cost curve within the city as demand for central urban space (for commercial rather than industrial purposes) has remained buoyant. The circulating capital cost curve is, however, much flatter as a result of improvements in transportation which have reduced the real costs of movement and the degree to which transport networks are focused upon the city centre. Within the city, the labour cost curve is reversed as compared with figure 12.4a, being lowest at the city centre and highest in the suburbs. Some of the empirical evidence for this spatial variation in intra-urban labour costs was reviewed earlier in the chapter, but the phenomenon is difficult to explain. Certainly improvements in transport technology suggest that any distinction between inner-city and suburban labour markets may be eroded by commuting patterns. On the other hand, levels of car ownership in inner-city neighbourhoods tend to be low and public transport is often poorly developed, especially for 'inside-out' commuting from the urban core to suburban industrial estates (Hughes and James, 1975). In these circumstances, travel problems may be sufficient to ensure a disequilibrium between labour supply and demand, creating upward pressure on wage rates in expanding suburban industrial estates. Beyond the suburban peak, labour costs typically fall in the non-metropolitan areas which, as already emphasized, have recently experienced more favourable trends in manufacturing employment than the cities. The attractions of these areas have been reinforced by the generally low cost of fixed capital in smaller urban centres, whilst the rise in circulating capital costs away from the city is fairly gradual if these centres are well-served by transportation links to the metropolitan core. Ultimately, the gradients for all three types of factor costs begin to rise sharply in the more remote peripheral regions which tend to be unattractive to most forms of manufacturing other than those based upon the processing of local raw materials.

The factor cost relationships indicated in figure 12.4b, together with the variables identified in figure 12.5, suggest that the inner cities, suburbs and non-metropolitan areas will each be associated with different general types of industry. The non-metropolitan areas are suitable for

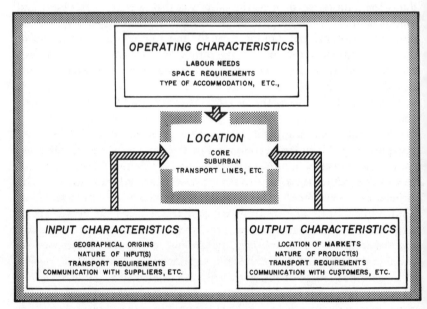

Figure 12.5 Determinants of intra-urban industrial location

operations with substantial space and labour requirements such as major assembly and fabrication plants. Within the city, these relationships imply that labour- and communication-intensive activities, often characterized by cramped premises and primitive working conditions, will be found near the core and that more modern capital-intensive operations, such as automated assembly plants and warehouses and distribution facilities, requiring more extensive sites, will be found in the suburbs. The contrasting attributes of inner-city, suburban and non-metropolitan manufacturing suggested by this scheme raise important policy issues. In particular, they suggest that the inner cities are inheriting a legacy of residual industrial activities at the wrong end of any spectrum of desired characteristics. This is one important aspect of the widely recognized 'inner-city problem'.

The inner-city problem

Our concept of the 'central city' or 'inner city' is not very precise, but roughly corresponds to the area built-up before the First World War. Nevertheless, since the problems are essentially those associated with ageing (see chapter 9), the concept is dynamic and it may be expected that other, more recently established, areas of the city will ultimately inherit similar problems. These problems are not only related to the decline of manufacturing and it is usually the poor quality of the housing stock which is the most obvious symptom. These conditions ensure that the inner cities are the home of the most deprived sections of society, including immigrant groups and ethnic minorities. Decaying buildings, neglected infrastructure and limited economic opportunities combine to encourage a wide range of social problems reflected in such indicators as crime rates and health statistics. These difficulties are often compounded by political structures which allow wealthy suburban municipalities to abdicate any responsibility for the inner cities. This is certainly true of the United States where administrative boundaries in cities such as New York do not reflect the realities of the metropolitan system. Thus residents of Tarrytown may travel to work in downtown Manhattan, but pay local taxes in Westchester County, which does nothing to solve the massive social and economic problems of Harlem and The Bronx.

Having emphasized the comprehensive nature of the inner-city problem, we will now focus attention upon its industrial aspects. Many of these have already been discussed and they include: dated facilities and infrastructure; competition for limited available space from other land-uses such as offices and roads; an ill-educated and poorly-trained labour force unsuited for employment in new or sophisticated sectors; and a failure of new business start-ups to match the rate of job losses. These problems have, to a considerable extent, been made worse by various strands of public policy which have, almost incidentally, undermined the attractiveness of the inner city as a location for industry. Public investment in urban motorways, for example, may shift the balance of economic advantage in favour of the suburbs. More directly, such motorways may be responsible for the destruction of former inner-city industrial areas, whilst the direct intervention of local authorities in the industrial property market through the provision of serviced sites has often been targetted upon the suburbs. Furthermore, well-intentioned comprehensive re-development schemes designed to improve housing conditions have displaced population from the inner city to peripheral estates in places such as Birmingham and Glasgow, thereby reducing the potential local labour supply for the businesses that remain.

In the case of the United Kingdom, there has been a growing realization since the mid-1970s that the traditional regional focus of economic development policy (see chapter 11) was not addressing the problems of many metropolitan areas and, especially, the inner cities. Parts of inner London, for example, had higher unemployment rates than Development Areas in northern England and Scotland. This situation stimulated a series of research and policy initiatives targetted on the inner cities. Employment creation has been a key objective of these initiatives and, to the extent that the inner-city problem has been recognized to be, at least partially, an economic one, there are similarities between conventional regional policy measures directed at industry and the corresponding urban-based policies introduced during the 1980s.

The similarities are demonstrated by the enterprise zone concept. This was first promoted during the 1970s and is based upon the proposition that red-tape and planning restrictions inhibit entrepreneurship – a view which was consistent with the free-market, private-sector sympathies of the Conservative government elected in Britain in 1979. The essence of the idea is that governments should simplify paperwork and relax planning regulations as they affect small businesses in particular zones. Eleven of these zones were created in 1980 and many more were added to the list during the decade. They are not confined to the inner cities, but a substantial proportion have been established in such locations. Enterprise zones have also been tried as an approach to urban regeneration in the United States (Jones and Manson, 1982). The concept does, however, create a number of problems (see Norcliffe and Hoare, 1982; Lloyd and Botham, 1985). It tends to create a static view of the urban economy and the need for continuous monitoring is even more pressing than in the case of designated regions (chapter 11). Furthermore, by defining relatively small areas as enterprise zones, businesses which lie outside their boundaries are inevitably disadvantaged. Within the inner city, these boundaries involve arbitrary, bureaucratic decisions which can make all the difference to firms situated on opposite sides of a street.

Enterprise zones are not specific to the inner cities, but in Britain a series of programmes have been targetted upon the problems of these areas during the 1980s. These reflect a recognition by central government that these problems are a matter of national concern. Many of the policies are similar to the measures which have been associated with attempts to promote economic development at the regional scale, the only difference being the more restricted geographical focus upon the inner city. Thus under the terms of the Urban Programme introduced in 1977, central government funds have been made available to local authorities for approved expenditure within specified inner-city areas. By 1989, 57 such areas (Inner Area Programme districts) qualified for assistance and there has been a gradual shift in the balance of total expenditure away from social, housing and environmental improvements towards projects classified as 'economic' (Audit Commission, 1989, p. 20). This implies expenditure upon facilities or support for schemes directly intended to assist industry and commerce. Urban Development Corporations have been another important strand of inner-city policy

in the United Kingdom. These are independent private-sector organizations in which property development interests are usually prominent.
They have comprehensive powers of land assembly and servicing,
superseding many of the traditional functions of local authorities within
their areas. Eleven such corporations were operating within different
British cities by 1989 and were associated with such schemes as the
redevelopment of London Docklands. The general objective of these
corporations is to attract private- as well as public-sector capital into
the inner cities.

Local authorities not only act as the agents of central government in
inner-city regeneration and many have become involved on their own
account. Of course their traditional functions, such as the provision of
housing, planning, education, social services and infrastructure, are all
relevant to the overall objective of creating an environment that is
attractive to people and industry. Nevertheless, there has been a
clear tendency for local authorities in the United Kingdom, especially
metropolitan authorities, to take a more active role in promoting
economic development (see Lawless, 1981; Sellgren, 1989). Table 12.1,
which is based upon the results of a survey in which metropolitan
district councils were asked if they were directly operating the identified
policies at some time during the period 1984-6, provides some indication
of the range and relative importance of the various initiatives. Not
surprisingly, the commitment to direct intervention tends to reflect
political circumstances and Labour-controlled authorities have been the
most active (Mawson and Miller, 1986). Nevertheless, it is important
to place such activities in perspective and less than 1 per cent of total
local authority expenditure in the United Kingdom is specifically
committed to economic development programmes (Audit Commission,
1989, p. 34).

The policies of both central and local government in the United
Kingdom and, to a lesser extent, other countries (see Chinitz, 1979;
Peterson, 1979; Christie, 1980; Lever 1989), reveal a belated awareness
of the importance of economic development as the ultimate solution to
the inner-city problem. These policies should be realistic. It has already
been argued that there are many basic and long-established forces which
are making the inner cities less attractive as locations for industry. These
forces are unlikely to be reversed and it follows that efforts should be
concentrated upon encouraging local entrepreneurship and retaining
existing businesses rather than attracting mobile industrial investment.

Although the historic role of the inner cities as 'incubators' or
'seedbeds' for new firms seems to have diminished, there seems to be
some scope for a revival of this function. Many of the traditional
attractions of the inner city for small, innovative firms remain

Table 12.1 UK metropolitan district councils operating specific industrial development initiatives, 1984–1986

Type of policy	% of respondents directly operating policy
1 Grants to firms	67
2 Loans to firms	61
3 Rates/rent free periods	61
4 Rates/rent guarantees	14
5 Other guarantees	26
6 Provision of sites	82
7 Provision of premises	78
8 Promotion/information	
(a) national advertising	39
(b) local advertising	59
(c) technical press advertising	37
(d) business directory	47
(e) guide to sources of finance	59
(f) register of premises	92
(g) competitions, good ideas, schemes, etc.	14
9 Business advice	80
10 Promotion of enterprise agencies	57
11 Support for co-operatives	51
12 Joint ventures:	
(a) with private sector	63
(b) with public sector	43
13 Training	55
14 Information technology centres	53

Source: Audit Commission, 1989

intact – good access to skilled workers, research institutions and a wide range of services and suppliers. It is, therefore, not surprising that several urban economic development policies are specifically orientated towards the support of small firms and prospective entrepreneurs including financial packages, business advice and the provision of accommodation (table 12.1). Unfortunately, whatever successes have been achieved with small firms have tended to be more than offset by job losses in large ones.

As far as established businesses are concerned, steps should be taken to prevent their displacement through redevelopment, especially those in sectors which can benefit from a central location. Such steps include planning policies which are more sensitive to the needs of industry, including the provision of both land and property for industrial purposes. There are opportunities even within the congested inner cities to redevelop substantial areas of derelict land into modern industrial estates. In central Birmingham, for example, various schemes are under consideration to convert canal-side land and sites formerly occupied by power stations and gas works into new industrial and commercial property. Such schemes are just one manifestation of a more positive approach towards industry within the inner city. This is also reflected in the increased importance attached to promotion and marketing by local authorities (table 12.1). Most major cities and many smaller towns have economic development units responsible for ensuring that businessmen know what they have to offer (Hunker, 1980). In the United States, this responsibility is often taken on by the chamber of commerce. Once established, links between the public and private sector can be maintained and in the United Kingdom there is evidence of a more harmonious relationship emerging as local authorities and business interests have begun to recognize an identity of purpose in the future of the inner cities (Audit Commission, 1989).

Conclusion

The importance of continuity of policy was stressed in the last chapter with respect to regional development. This point applies equally at the urban scale and uncertainty about policy direction has aggravated the problems of the inner cities. This uncertainty has often been increased by political tensions between central and local government which have been an obstacle to effective policy implementation in the United Kingdom (Audit Commission, 1989). It is even more true of inner cities than of regions that they cannot be considered in isolation from broader industrial and geographical trends. It is also true that the scale and extent of the problem will change as areas age. Policy must therefore strike a delicate balance between the continuity required to establish confidence and the flexibility needed to respond to a dynamic situation. There is no doubt, however, that economic, and specifically industrial, matters will remain important elements within any comprehensive policy focused upon the problems of the inner city.

Further Reading

Lawless, P. 1981: *Britain's Inner Cities: Problems and Policies*. London: Harper and Row.

Scott, A. J. 1982a: Locational patterns and dynamics of industrial activity in the modern metropolis. *Urban Studies*, 19, 111–42.

Scott, A. J. 1988: *Metropolis: from the Division of Labor to Urban Form*. Berkeley and Los Angeles: University of California Press.

13
Industrial Location and Human Welfare

This concluding chapter draws together and further develops some of the wider issues concerning the place of manufacturing in society which have been implicit in the material included in the final section of the book. We have seen that decisions affecting the location, status and function of individual factories, taken by private enterprise on the basis of commercial judgements, can have important consequences for places. Studies of industrial location have traditionally approached the problem from the viewpoint of the entrepreneur or firm, but it is evident that what is best for the corporate balance sheet is not necessarily best for society in general. One way of ensuring that industry acknowledges its wider obligations is through the creation of appropriate public agencies to monitor and control its activities as they affect, for example, the quality of the environment. The ultimate objective must, however, be to define the goals of, and create the mechanisms capable of implementing, a planning strategy which not only takes account of the pollution problem, but also all other aspects of industrial location which have a bearing upon human welfare.

Impacts of industrial development

The impacts of any factory extend beyond its boundary fence. These impacts may be beneficial or harmful to the surrounding community. On the positive side, income generated by employment in the factory will have a multiplier effect upon the local area as money circulates through the economic system boosting the trade of shops and other businesses. Such impacts have already been discussed in earlier chapters and we will now focus our attention upon the negative effects which are often of greater concern from a welfare point of view because they are frequently neglected in evaluating the costs and benefits of industrial development. Air and water pollution fall into this category as do the various economic and social problems associated with the introduction of large-scale industrial facilities into relatively remote rural areas (see Sewel, 1979). Several previously isolated communities in the Highlands and Islands of Scotland, for example, have become sites for major industrial facilities such as gas terminals and oil platform fabrication yards as a result of the rapid development of North Sea oil and gas during the 1970s. It requires little imagination to appreciate some of the disruptive consequences for these communities resulting from the location on their doorstep of construction labour camps with populations many times their own size.

The wider impacts of industrial development are embraced within the concept of *externalities*. An externality is a side-effect of an activity which is not reflected in costs and prices. Thus a factory which discharges large quantities of unpleasant fumes to the atmosphere, despite the availability of technology capable of controlling the problem, is reducing its own costs of production and, presumably, the price of its product to its customers, at the expense of the health and welfare of others. In this situation, the costs of pollution are not borne by those responsible for it. The costs are not necessarily limited in their geographical extent to the immediate vicinity of a factory. The problem of acid rain, for example, which is damaging forests and polluting lakes in Canada and Scandinavia, has been partially attributed to the effects of emissions from coal-burning power stations in other countries. Similarly, effluent discharges into, for example, the Ohio River at Pittsburgh contribute, because it is part of the same river system, to the state of the Mississippi at New Orleans. Nevertheless, many externalities are much more local and their effects are attenuated by distance from their source, making it meaningful to think in terms of an externality gradient relating impacts (expressed in terms of utility) to distance (figure 13.1) (see Smith, 1977, pp. 88–93; Bale, 1978). Several of the less desirable impacts of industrial activity such as noise, smell, certain types of atmospheric pollution and traffic congestion are relatively localized. Such effects as job creation and income generation represent the reverse side of the coin and it is theoretically possible to visualize separate gradients reflecting positive and negative effects. The slope of these gradients may vary and figure 13.1 illustrates the not unusual situation in which the adverse effects of a development are most strongly felt in the immediate neighbourhood, whilst its beneficial effects extend over a wider area. The rapid exploitation of the oil and gas resources of the North Sea, for

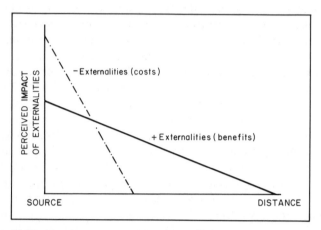

Figure 13.1 Hypothetical externality gradients

example, has been dictated in the United Kingdom by national policy considerations. However, the local and regional consequences of this policy have not always been favourable and the environmental and social costs of rapid development have been experienced most acutely in places such as Drumbuie – a community of less than 30 on the west coast of Scotland which became the site of a massive oil platform fabrication yard in 1978.

It is one thing to acknowledge the existence of spatially variable externalities, quite another to resolve the balance of advantages and disadvantages. On a technical level, it is often difficult to actually measure the various impacts. The prediction of economic multipliers is notoriously uncertain and effects upon air and water quality, for example, cannot be accurately assessed when, as frequently happens, a development is proposed for a location where no baseline environmental monitoring has previously been carried out. Even where the necessary data are available, the ability to make accurate predictions is constrained by our inadequate understanding of the operation of environmental systems. Nevertheless, there is a growing realization, especially within developed economies, that such efforts should be made and there has been a trend since the 1960s to make the formal assessment of potential externalities a statutory requirement prior to the approval by various public agencies of a major industrial development. This trend has been accompanied by the introduction of techniques and procedures such as cost–benefit analysis and environmental-impact assessment explicitly designed to identify the various dimensions of externality associated with industrial and other developments and to improve the quality of decision making. However sophisticated and scientific in appearance, technical evaluations in the form of environmental-impact statements do not remove decisions on controversial development proposals from the political arena (Sandbach, 1980; Chapman, 1981). Ultimately, value judgements, which may involve, for example, setting the anticipated loss of wildfowl breeding grounds against the new jobs created by the establishment of an oil refinery, must be made.

Although such judgements are difficult, the introduction of environmental-impact assessment procedures ensures that, in many countries at least, they enter the public domain. The same cannot be said of most decisions regarding the future of existing factories. The kind of locational adjustments described in chapter 7 reflect judgements which are internal to the firm, but such decisions obviously have adverse consequences for communities directly affected by them. The prospects of regions such as Upper Steiermark in Austria (see chapter 9) are inextricably linked to their industrial base. Just as the establishment of a new factory creates employment opportunities and optimism within a community, so the closure of an existing plant may have the reverse effects. Despite the fact that the frequency of such events has increased during the recession of the 1980s, these effects are rarely taken into account when major factory closures are under consideration. There is a powerful case for suggesting that such decisions should be subject to public scrutiny in just the same way as those relating to new plants (see Harrison and Bluestone, 1982) and several countries have introduced legislation requiring companies to provide advance notice of proposed closures. Such a requirement amounts to little more than a public statement of a decision already taken. Nevertheless, it does represent a move towards greater accountability and increases pressure upon management to explain, and possibly reconsider, closure decisions prior to implementation. The nature and extent of plant closure legislation varies widely between countries and is, for example, poorly developed in the United States by comparison with Western Europe (Stafford, 1989). One area in which the need to regulate the external effects of industrial activity has been almost universally accepted, albeit with differing degrees of official enthusiasm, is that associated with the problem of pollution.

Industry and the pollution problem

Industry has traditionally regarded the environment as a source of raw materials, but has also used it as a waste-sink for dumping unwanted by-products. This attitude was firmly established during the nineteenth century and its consequences were reflected in the slag heaps, chemical tips and dead rivers which blighted the landscapes of such centres of the Industrial Revolution as North-West England and the Ruhr. These legacies were classic examples of externalities in the sense that not only were the various consequences of pollution ignored by the nineteenth-century industrialists who usually lived a discreet distance away from the factories which created their wealth, but also the costs of cleaning up the mess were passed on to subsequent generations. Such irresponsible behaviour may seem inconceivable today, but there are several reasons why the problem of industrial pollution is of even greater contemporary concern. The potential for environmental damage is related to the scale of operation and modern industrial facilities tend to be very much larger than their predecessors. This is especially true of industries such as chemicals, iron and steel and pulp and paper manufacture which are responsible for the bulk of discharges to the environment from manufacturing operations. A large petrochemical complex may release millions of gallons a day of cooling and process water and the cumulative impact upon the environment of the massive agglomerations of such activities near Houston and Rotterdam, for example, is considerable (Chapman, 1983). It is not only size which is important. New technologies create new problems. Nuclear power is perhaps the most obvious case, but the use of toxic chemicals, radioactive materials and biologically active substances is a feature of many of the more dynamic industrial sectors. Although these do not usually discharge residuals to the environment on anything like the same scale as basic, raw material processing industries, the consequences of accidents may be profound as the Bhopal tragedy demonstrated.

Public awareness of the problem of industrial pollution is part of a wider concern regarding the ecological implications of economic growth. This concern, which has been enhanced by specific incidents as at Seveso in Italy, Three Mile Island in the United States and Chernobyl in the Soviet Union, has been reflected in the growth of various pressure groups which have advanced the environmental cause (see O'Riordan, 1976, pp. 228–63). Governments have also responded to the prevailing mood and the machinery of environmental regulation has been overhauled and strengthened in many countries since the 1960s. The Environmental Protection Agency and the Department of Environment were created in the US and the UK respectively at the beginning of the 1970s and similar agencies exist in most other developed countries. Their precise role and function varies considerably, but, in general terms, they are responsible for the development, co-ordination and enforcement of environmental policy.

It is difficult to provide any comprehensive definition of the scope of environmental policy, but it is possible to identify various strands which contribute towards the achievement of the ultimate goal of protecting and maintaining the quality of the environment in its broadest sense. Land-use planning, pollution control legislation and environmental-impact assessment all have a bearing upon this objective and all impinge upon the activities of manufacturing industry. Figure 13.2 is a simple portrayal of a complex situation, but it demonstrates the way in which the observed impact of industry upon environmental quality has provoked a policy response which has in turn changed the political framework within which industry operates. These external pressures seek to force industry to limit at least some of the negative externalities associated with its existing activities and to take account of such considerations when planning new investment.

Capital expenditure on pollution control in industry relative to total investment in plant and equipment reached a peak in most developed countries in the latter half of the 1970s. Figure 13.3 indicates that 1975 was the peak year in the United States where the legislature was initially more responsive to the environmental movement than in most other countries. Despite a significant decline in the political commitment to 'green' issues during the Reagan years, the downward trend in figure 13.3 is mainly due to the impact of retrospective legislation introduced in the early 1970s which forced major improvements in existing factories. Many of these investments were once-and-for-all outlays, after which the capital costs of pollution control could be expected to fall even if operating expenditures represented a continuing commitment. Figure

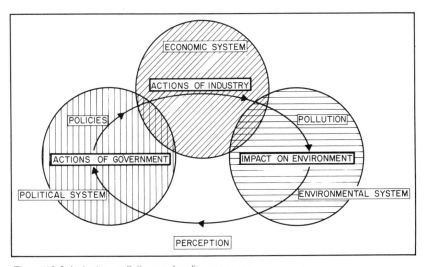

Figure 13.2 Industry, pollution and policy response

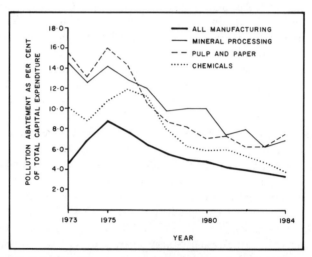

Figure 13.3 Pollution abatement expenditures in selected US industries 1973–1984
Source: Leonard, 1988

13.3 also emphasizes that aggregate data obscure wide differences between industries. It is evident that for sectors such as mineral processing, pulp and paper and chemicals, pollution control expenditures are substantial by any standards, whilst many others obviously lie below the industry average indicated in the graph. Furthermore, the significance of these expenditures for the operations of individual firms within the same industry also varies widely (Leone, 1976). Age and size of plant are significant influences. Economies of scale in pollution control ensure that treatment costs per unit of production to attain a specified standard are generally lower for large operations. Similarly, different raw materials and processes may be used to manufacture the same end-product. This is true of pulp and paper manufacture, for example, in which the sulphate and sulphite processes raise quite different pollution problems and hence involve different outlays on control equipment.

Environmental policy and industrial location

Despite the complexity of influences upon the expenditures faced by industries and their constituent firms, there is a remarkable consistency in the relationship between costs and efficiency of pollution control measured in terms of the percentage reduction in discharges to the environment. Figure 13.4, which is based upon the results of empirical

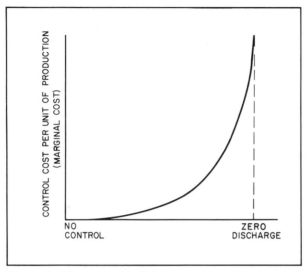

Figure 13.4 The costs of pollution control

studies of residuals management in many industries (see Kneese and Bower, 1979), indicates the rapidly increasing marginal costs of pollution control. The technical problems and, therefore, the costs involved in approaching the ultimate theoretical goal of zero discharge increase exponentially. This relationship has important policy implications. First, it emphasizes that very low levels of pollution can only be achieved at high cost against which the wider benefits must be set. Second, it follows that pollution control regulations which require a company to operate at a significantly different position on the residuals output control cost curve in one location rather than another may influence the spatial distribution of future investment. This possibility is clearly most relevant for those industries in which it can be demonstrated that 'as zero discharge is approached, residuals management costs become a substantial proportion of total costs' (Bower, 1975, p. 317). Speculation regarding the possible influence of environmental policy upon industrial location has therefore focused upon the major polluting industries such as pulp and paper, chemicals and iron and steel (see Walter, 1976; Stafford, 1977; Chapman, 1980a).

It has frequently been alleged that, by exerting little or no control over some of the more unpleasant and hazardous manufacturing operations, Third World 'pollution havens' have provoked 'industrial flight' by attracting investment by multinational corporations seeking to avoid stricter regulations in the developed countries (see Castleman, 1979; Goldman, 1980; Davis, 1984). The balance of evidence suggests that international shifts inspired by such considerations have been few and far between (Gladwin and Welles, 1976; Leonard, 1984, 1988). The diversion of investment from one country to another on environmental policy grounds assumes an unreasonable degree of locational flexibility. Any temptation to transfer investment is often reduced by an awareness that significant differences in required levels of pollution control may disappear as developing countries adopt similar standards to those applied in the developed world. This is emphasized by Leonard (1988) in a series of case-studies which explore the politics of the relationship between host governments and foreign companies as they affect environmental matters. These studies show how the relationship changes through time. In particular, there is evidence of a trend towards more demanding standards as the multinationals' room for manoeuvre is limited by their increased capital commitment to a specific site. This conclusion is important because it suggests that ultimate convergence of environmental standards is more likely than divergence at the international scale, thus undermining the basic premise upon which the twin hypotheses of 'pollution havens' and 'industrial flight' rest.

Despite this conclusion, the fact remains that, whatever their effect upon location decisions at the global scale, significant differences in environmental standards continue to exist between countries and there is little doubt that the externalities associated with industrial activity are more acutely felt in certain parts of the developing world. Cubatao in Brazil, for example, is one of Latin America's largest petrochemical centres, but it has also been described as 'one of the most polluted places on earth' (Davis, 1984, p. 221). It is reminiscent of the alkali towns of Victorian England with smoking chimneys, boiling rivers and toxic dumps (Golstein and Carvalhaes, 1986). In a different country, the Bhopal tragedy reinforced suspicions that the kind of precautions taken for granted in 'the north' are less rigidly enforced in 'the south'. Thus, both in their capacities as employees and as neighbours, industrial workers in the Third World often have good reason to reflect on the high price of a factory job.

By comparison with the differences in standards apparent at the international scale, spatial variations in pollution control requirements within countries are slight. However, the locational flexibility of firms is much greater at this scale and it has been suggested that such variations may influence industrial location decisions, especially within the United States (see Stafford, 1977; Chapman, 1982a). There is no doubt that certain states are widely perceived by industry as having a more favourable 'business climate' and that the nature and extent of regulatory control, including environmental and land-use policies, has a bearing upon executive images of place. Thus California and Maine tend to lie at the 'strict' end of a subjective spectrum of environmental regulation whilst Alabama and Mississippi are at the opposite extreme. Inspired by well-publicized individual cases in which such distinctions were alleged to have influenced location decisions, the Conservation Foundation made a systematic attempt to relate industrial employment trends between 1970 and 1980, especially in pollution-intensive sectors, to inter-state variations in environmental policy (reported in Duerksen, 1983). It was hypothesized that states at the 'lax' end of the regulatory spectrum would have obtained a higher-than-average competitive shift in manufacturing employment. The results revealed some support for the hypothesis, but were not robust enough to isolate environmental regulation from other potential influences upon the observed pattern, such as labour costs or levels of unionization.

This conclusion is not surprising since one of the major reasons for the growing intervention of the federal government in United States environmental policy since the late 1960s was a desire to impose national standards to prevent 'environmental blackmail' in which firms could play one state against another in an attempt to minimize their pollution-control costs. Nevertheless, federal legislation itself created situations in which environmental policy has influenced the location of industry. The 1970 Clean Air Amendments established national ambient standards of air quality measured in terms of specific pollutants such as sulphur dioxide. In certain parts of the United States the prevailing level of air quality was better than the prescribed standards whilst in others it fell below these levels. Thus similar industrial plants could face very different pollution control regulations depending upon whether they were located in a 'clean' or a 'dirty' area. In the case of new plants, this issue did not arise because such facilities were required to meet certain minimum standards of air pollution control regardless of their location, but regulatory authorities in most states anticipated a gradual shift of economic activity away from the 'dirty' metropolitan centres as a direct consequence of the 1970 legislation. Further legislation in 1977 created a more complicated system which defined different categories of area in terms of the importance attached to air-quality considerations as constraints upon industrial development. The concept of air-quality zones has effectively introduced a kind of land-use planning which, by defining areas of greater or lesser restrictiveness of air pollution control, has implications for the location of industry. The full extent of these implications has not been systematically explored, but there are many situations in which the location of individual facilities has been influenced by the complex requirements of the Clean Air Amendments (see Manners and Rudzitis, 1981; Thornton and Koepke, 1981).

The locational effects of US clean-air policies are probably the exception rather than the rule and Stafford (1985) has suggested that environmental legislation is a relatively minor influence upon the spatial distribution of manufacturing investment in the United States. A more subtle influence may be the anticipation of controversy as a deterrent to investment. For example, it has been suggested that such fears discouraged several companies from even attempting to expand oil refining capacity on the East Coast of the United States during the early 1970s (Healy, 1979). Once a site has been selected and a proposal becomes public knowledge, it enters the political arena and companies may face organized opposition, frequently motivated by environmental concerns (Gladwin, 1980). The ensuing conflicts occasionally result in the re-location or abandonment of a project. Plans for a major petrochemical complex in Solano County, 55 kms north east of San Francisco, were eventually dropped in 1977 by Dow Chemical, ostensibly as a response to public opposition and bureaucratic delays (Storper, Walker and Widess, 1981). This case is probably typical of the way in which environmental regulations affect location in the sense that the influence is negative rather than positive; pushing facilities away from controversial sites rather than pulling them towards places with less demanding standards.

The significance of environmental policy as an influence upon the location of specific projects is, in many respects, less important than the general issue of the impact of such external legislative pressures upon corporate attitudes to their wider responsibilities. The obligation to defend and justify siting decisions, enshrined in environmental-impact assessment and related procedures, has forced industry to acknowledge that the consequences of its actions should be assessed in broader terms than corporate balance sheets. Nevertheless, the sincerity of this acknowledgement varies widely. Studies of the oil refining (Kerlin and Rabovsky, 1975) and petrochemical (Chapman, 1980b) industries in the United States indicate that certain companies view pollution control legislation as a form of unwelcome government interference to be challenged and resisted as far as possible and accepted only at the eleventh hour. Others take a more positive view and frequently anticipate legislative requirements. Generally speaking, however, industry responds rather than initiates and Gladwin (1975, p. 256) observes that 'natural processes are often disregarded and full consideration of environmental values is typically absent in the project planning behaviour of multi-national corporations'. On the other hand, most large enterprises now formally recognize the necessity, if not always the legitimacy, of environmental considerations in their decision making. This recognition is usually based more upon self-interest than altruism since anticipation of objections may help to avoid costly delays. Indeed, South (1986) believes that the creation of procedures which force companies to make this connection between self-interest and environmental responsibility is one of the principal achievements of US legislation.

The challenge of industrial-development planning

The limitation of adverse impacts upon the quality of the physical environment obviously represents only one aspect of any overall strategy which attempts to ensure that manufacturing best serves the interests of the greatest number of people (see Walker, 1980c). Expressed in these terms, the scope of industrial-development planning extends beyond questions of location to include such matters as the terms and conditions of employment. Indeed, policies relating to manufacturing should, in an ideal world, be regarded as one element in a comprehensive development strategy which seeks to maximize human welfare. Such a general objective involves establishing a set of more specific goals against which the success or failure of policies may be judged (Walker, 1984a). One such goal is to ensure that economic development is based upon ecological principles which acknowledge the limitations imposed by the physical environment and the obligation to preserve and protect it for posterity (see Francis, 1976; Cumberland, 1978). What has been called eco-development is not only concerned with the allocation of resources between generations, but also with inequalities in contemporary patterns of resource use. Sachs (1977, p. 8) convincingly argues that 'social inequality leads to a twofold degradation of the environment at the two extremes of the social scale. The wealthy waste resources in ostentatious consumption, while the poor overuse the few resources to which they have access'.

For anybody struggling to find a job, concern for the environment seems a less pressing priority than the need to provide adequate employment opportunities, especially if environmental policies are perceived to be hindering economic development. Although full employment is a policy goal within all developed countries, it seems to have become a more and more remote objective as the dole queues have, almost without exception, lengthened during the present recession. Even if welfare payments ensure that the basic requirements for life are provided, unemployment is, for most people, a psychological as well as a financial disaster. Work, or lack of it, has a close relationship to self-esteem and the creation of a society in which everybody at least has the opportunity for employment appropriate to their capabilities is, therefore, a desirable goal.

The nature of these opportunities is, however, also important. Many of the changes described in earlier chapters, such as the spatial division of labour within large corporations, are linked to developments in the technology of production which have progressively reduced job satisfaction for the majority of people. By fragmenting the production process in many branches of industry into specialized and simple tasks, higher rates of productivity have been achieved at the expense of increasingly boring and repetitive occupations for those on the shop floor. This trend has devalued or entirely replaced many craft-based operations and has enabled large enterprises to substitute relatively expensive skilled labour in traditional industrial centres with cheap, unskilled, often female, labour in peripheral regions (see Massey and Meegan, 1978). There is some evidence of a reaction against this 'de-skilling' process as large firms have come to recognize that boredom has contributed to worker-alienation which has in turn led to frequent labour disputes in industries such as motor-vehicle manufacture (Holmes, 1987). On a more general level, the reorganization of shop-floor working practices is paralleled by calls for the creation of smaller units of economic organization (see Schumacher, 1974; Roux, 1980) which imply a reversal of the trends, based on concepts of technical and economic efficiency, of the last one hundred years.

Despite its intuitive appeal and its theoretical simplicity, the maximization of human welfare provides an elusive and intangible basis for policy-making. The problem is exemplified in microcosm by disputes over particular projects. An unemployed school-leaver is likely to have a very different attitude towards a major industrial development than an old-age pensioner who has retired to the same community because of the attractiveness of its surroundings. The existence of a multitude of such contrasting perspectives epitomizes the much more general problem of deriving a consensus within society at large. The differing priorities of individuals are paralleled by similar differences between places. Thus the importance attached to environmental and amenity considerations is likely to be greater where job security is guaranteed and standards of living are high. In the United States, for example, it is no surprise that relatively prosperous states such as California and Oregon generally appear at the top of any subjective league table of environmental awareness, whilst states such as Alabama and Mississippi, which face more acute problems of poverty, lie at the opposite end. A corollary of this argument is the fact that priorities change through time. Cobb (1982, pp. 229–53), for example, discusses the environmental price paid by these and other southern states in their attempts to attract industry since the 1930s and notes the shifting balance in the trade-off between their economic-development objectives and their desire to limit the environmental damage associated with achieving these objectives.

Industrial location under socialism

Notwithstanding recent economic and political changes in the USSR and Eastern Europe, the existing distribution of industry within these countries largely reflects decisions taken under a very different system. In theory, a centrally planned socialist economy offers the best opportunity to carry through the changes in the organization of industrial production necessary to achieve the kind of welfare objectives we have discussed. Planning in capitalist and mixed economies, especially relating to the location of industry, is essentially reactive as public agencies respond to the initiatives of private enterprise. In socialist systems the wealth created by industrial activity accrues to the state and not to the owners of capital. Organs of the state are also responsible for making location decisions and they may be expected to approach the problem in a radically different manner to a private corporation motivated by profit or growth and, in particular, to take account of welfare criteria at the earliest stage in planning new investment.

The 'maximization of the social productivity of labour' has traditionally been the overriding economic objective of Soviet planners (Ye Probst, 1974). The precise meaning of this phrase is not always clear, but it implies an attempt to reconcile, on the one hand, a commitment to economic growth, with, on the other, a commitment to social equality. A similar duality is apparent in the so-called 'Socialist principles of industrial location'. Otherwise referred to as 'laws' and 'regularities', these 'principles' identify various criteria for evaluating the relative merits of alternative locations (Huzinec, 1977). Some of these criteria are primarily economic in character whilst others tend to be of an ideological nature. The minimization of transport costs, the encouragement of regional specialization to take advantage of differences in the availability of the various factors of production and the promotion of an international division of labour between the various member countries of the Council for Mutual Economic Assistance (COMECON), all indicate the importance attached to economic efficiency. By contrast, the declared need to take account of national security, and to minimize spatial variations in standards of living between urban and rural areas and between regions reflect a commitment to broader criteria which would not, for example, enter into the deliberations of a private corporation operating within the capitalist system.

It is often easier to establish a set of principles, than to abide by them and it seems that Soviet decision-makers have found no simple formula for resolving the contradictions inherent in the juxtaposition of efficiency and equity criteria. Reference was made in chapter 11 to the Soviet concept of the *territorial production complex*. This involves the creation of an integrated system of linked economic activities which are theoretically planned to ensure the co-ordination of productive and infrastructure investment. These complexes are conceived on a massive scale. For example, several such complexes have been established in Siberia, involving the simultaneous construction of electricity-generating facilities, the exploitation and processing of diverse raw materials and the development of new towns to accommodate the associated influx of population (see Warren, 1978). The various elements which constitute these systems are frequently dispersed over vast areas, but are linked together by transport and communication networks including pipelines and electricity cables as well as roads and railways. Economic criteria, related to the internal efficiency of territorial production complexes and their external relationships with and contributions to the national economy, appear to be the principal yardsticks against which their success or failure is judged. Although Soviet planners emphasize the comprehensive scope of their activities (see Aganbegyan and Bandman, 1984), priority in the development of these complexes is accorded to productive rather than social investment. Thus delays in the construction of adequate housing, education and health facilities to serve the labour force required by major industrial projects seem to occur in the USSR just as in capitalist economies, despite the existence of a centralized planning machinery ostensibly designed to eliminate these problems (see Linge, Karaska and Hamilton, 1978; Rutt 1986).

The difficulties involved in reconciling economic and welfare objectives in the planning of territorial production complexes are reflected, on a broader scale, in the persistence of the kind of problems which socialist principles of industrial location explicitly attempt to solve. It has already been argued that the unfettered capitalism epitomized by the activities of nineteenth-century industrialists in places such as the Ruhr character-istically displayed a total disregard for the environmental consequences of economic activity and that such externalities are only reluctantly controlled by the giant enterprises which dominate contemporary Western society. To the extent that socialism indicates a greater awareness of social costs, it may be expected that pollution from industrial sources would be better controlled in Eastern Europe and the USSR. In practice, there is abundant evidence that this problem is much more serious behind the Iron Curtain (see Volgyes, 1974; Singleton, 1976; Carter, 1985). Indeed, 'glasnost' is exposing the full extent of environmental disasters in the Soviet Union ranging from the draining of the Aral Sea to levels of atmospheric pollution in the great iron and steel centre of Magnitogorsk that probably exceed by a considerable margin those prevailing in any comparable industrial city in the West. Such situations emphasize that environmental considerations have consistently been subordinated to the achievement of economic growth targets. The declared concern for equity of living standards at various geographical scales has been similarly relegated and numerous observers have stressed that the spatial imbalances which are such a feature of industrial development in the West are also evident in the East (see Berentsen, 1979; Fuchs and Demko, 1979; Zimon, 1979; Sillince, 1987).

The parallels extend beyond the symptoms of the problem to the underlying causal mechanisms. Not only are these related to the basic influence of uneven resource distributions upon the location of economic activity and the universal nature of, for example, agglomeration economies, but also the way in which decisions are actually made. At first sight, the organizational structures associated with multinational corporations, the agencies of democratically elected governments and the institutions of socialist states have little in common. However, all are, to a greater or lesser extent, centralized systems of economic management in which outcomes are determined as much by internal power struggles as by rational debate. This seems to be especially true of the Soviet planning system in which the influence of Moscow relative to the rest of the union has always been paramount, a situation which has recently provoked a political reaction in many of the republics constituting the USSR. Traditionally, however, pork-barrel politics, with its implications of self-interest and greed, seems to be as much a fact of life in the USSR where '[industrial] sites have often been chosen on the principle of who shouted the louder' (Hutchings, 1982, p. 215) as in any 'democratic' society.

Industrial location and inequality

The problems of Soviet planners in reconciling the conflicting interests and objectives implicit in 'maximizing the social productivity of labour' are, of course, familiar to policy-makers in the West where the influence of welfare considerations upon industrial location has also been limited. However, one area of concern has been the relationship between industrial development and inequalities of economic opportunity arising from the fact that 'industrialization . . . seems to be inextricably bound up with an increase in spatial disparity' (Walker, 1980b, p. 1). Although some have argued that this problem is a particular characteristic of capitalism (see Browett, 1984), similar experiences in socialist states suggest that it is more appropriate to regard it as a feature of the industrial mode of production regardless of the political system within which it is set. Thus the mechanisms of cumulative causation that we have already discussed in chapter 9 seem to have a universal validity. Consequently, policies designed to influence the location of industry within diverse political and economic environments display a common overriding concern with the reduction of spatial disparities in economic opportunity expressed in terms of such indicators as income and, especially, unemployment levels.

Events have demonstrated that the achievement of this goal by attempting to influence the location of industry has, to say the least, proved difficult. Public policies in this area have generally been characterized by pragmatism inspired by short-term political expediency rather than the kind of long-term view required to bring about significant changes in the spatial structure of national economies. As noted in chapter 11, considerable efforts have been made in the United Kingdom, for example, to influence the location decisions of industry in accordance with the overall goal of reducing regional variations in unemployment levels, but these efforts have been described as 'empiricism run mad, a game of hit-and-miss, played with more enthusiasm than success' (Expenditure Committee, 1973). Most criticisms of state intervention in industrial location in capitalist and mixed economies has focused upon the cost-effectiveness of various policy instruments such as investment grants, labour subsidies and tax incentives. However, a much more fundamental problem is the lack of appropriate models to test the outcomes of different policies. Such models are widely used in the management of national economies to predict the consequences of, for example, different levels of central-bank control over the amount of money circulating within an economy. The construction of such models must be based upon a clear understanding of the operation of economic systems, and the value of the results they generate is also determined by the availability and quality of input data. These conceptual and practical requirements are not always fulfilled at the national scale, but the problems are multiplied when attempts are made to incorporate the spatial dimension. Thus it is difficult enough to forecast the impact of a particular course of action upon the performance of a national economy, but infinitely more difficult to say how it may affect the different regions within that economy. In these circumstances, it is hardly surprising that the development of policies designed to influence the location of industry in order to achieve greater inter-regional equity in the various dimensions of economic well-being frequently owes more to trial and error than to advances in economic theory.

Attempts to establish optimal distributions of industry are not restricted to the allocation of investment between regions, and public agencies are frequently involved in planning at the intra-regional and local scales. Policies applied at these different levels are not always compatible and what is good for a nation is not necessarily in the best interests of all of its constituent parts. These difficulties are most clearly seen in federal states because an extra tier of government is placed between local and national authorities (see Walker, 1980d). Nevertheless, similar problems exist in more centralized political systems such as the United Kingdom even if they do not receive the same kind of exposure associated with the often public and acrimonious disputes over economic policies between federal and provincial authorities, in, for example, Canada. Various public bodies, including planning authorities, development agencies and chambers of commerce, have frequently over-lapping interests in the distribution of industry at the local level. A broad distinction may be made between those policies which seek to promote new industrial development and those which are concerned with regulating the activities of existing industry. Both dimensions of policy are consistent with broadly conceived concepts of optimality. The attraction of new jobs and the diversification of employment opportunities are obviously in the economic interests of communities, whilst the kind of controls upon industry associated with land-use planning are designed to limit the various negative externalities such as traffic congestion and pollution. Not surprisingly, the relative importance attached to promotion and regulation tends to change through time and inner-city authorities faced with problems of unemployment and manufacturing decline are becoming more actively involved in encouraging local economic initiatives.

The industrial-development policy goals of provincial, regional and metropolitan authorities are similar to their local counterparts, although their powers to influence location are generally greater. In pursuing these goals at the broader scale, however, it is often impossible to satisfy the aspirations of all of the individual elements which make up the larger unit. For example, both the individual boroughs which operate at the community level, and the Greater London Council, which was responsible for planning at the metropolitan scale until its abolition in 1986, were actively involved in attempting to stem the decline of manufacturing within the conurbation which first became apparent in the late 1960s. North and Leigh (1984) emphasize the confusions and contradictions arising from the existence of a bewildering array of elected authorities, often of very different political complexions, all attempting to secure a greater share of the available cake of manufacturing employment and effectively competing with one another through their various incentives. In advocating the need to plan at the metropolitan scale (ironically made more difficult since the abolition of the Greater London Council), they also recognize that concentrating efforts upon the most deprived parts of the city such as the docklands implies the diversion of resources from other areas. The welfare case for such a strategy may be overwhelming, but, by definition, redistribution benefits some at the expense of others and the losers, however well-off they may be, will always object. Exactly the same issues arise in resolving regional and national interests. Thus national economic policy goals aimed at maximizing the growth of GNP, for example, may not be consistent with a regional policy which seeks to minimize spatial variations in unemployment levels.

Closely related to the problem of reconciling policies at different spatial scales is the desire of political units to control their own economic destiny. Ultimately the only way to ensure this is a return to the more spatially restricted scales of economic organization which preceded the Industrial Revolution (see Roux, 1980). Such an apocalyptic transformation of contemporary economic structures is inconceivable. Despite evidence of the emergence of more decentralized systems of management within some major corporations (see chapter 7), it would surely be premature to predict the collapse of the giant corporations which, as we have seen, exert such a powerful influence upon the distribution of manufacturing. While the idea that the accountability of business organizations extends beyond obligations to their shareholders has at least filtered into the boardrooms of the largest enterprises (see McKie, 1974; Walter, 1975), the extent to which this notion is incorporated within strategic decisions, such as the location of a new factory, probably lies, in most cases, somewhere on a scale ranging from non-existent to minimal. Thus the fortunes of countries, regions and communities seem likely to remain, to a large extent, hostages to the decisions of large industrial organizations which, ultimately, are guided by the principle of corporate self-interest rather than any concept of collective human welfare.

Conclusion

Even more fundamental than the continuing importance of giant enterprises in economic life, is the future role of manufacturing itself. Despite its recent stagnation and decline in countries such as the United Kingdom and United States (see chapter 1), this trend is by no means universal so that, viewed at a global scale, output and employment have both continued to increase. Manufacturing will, therefore, always play a critical role in human welfare. This role is inextricably linked to broader questions of social justice. The majority of the world's population have had little opportunity to enjoy the undoubted material benefits resulting from the consumption of manufactured goods. The implications for industry of a few hundred dollars increase in per capita annual incomes in countries such as India and China are enormous. It is in the long-term interests of the developed countries and the multinational corporations based in them to facilitate the expansion of global demand by reversing the widening disparity between the rich and poor members of the international community.

Further reading

Leonard, H. J. 1988: *Pollution and the Struggle for the World Product.* Cambridge: Cambridge University Press.
Pallot, J. and Shaw, D. J. B. 1981: *Planning in the Soviet Union.* London: Croom Helm.
Walker, D. F. (ed.) 1980c: *Planning Industrial Development.* Chichester: Wiley.

References

Aaronovitch, S. and Sawyer, M. C. 1975: Mergers, growth and concentration. *Oxford Economic Papers*, 27, 136–55.

Acheson, T. W. 1972: The national policy and the industrialization of the Maritimes, 1880–1910. *Acadiensis*, 3–38.

Aganbegyan, A. G. and Bandman, M. K. 1984: Territorial production complexes as integrated systems: theory and practice. *Geoforum*, 15, 25–32.

Agarwal, J. P. 1980: Determinants of foreign direct investment: a survey. *Weltwirtschaftliches Archivs*, 116, 739–73.

Akeredolu-Ale, E. O. 1976: Private foreign investment and the underdevelopment of indigenous entrepreneurship in Nigeria. In G. Williams (ed.), *Nigeria: Economy and Society*, London: Rex Collings, 106–22.

Alchian, A. A. 1950: Uncertainty, evolution and economic theory. *Journal of Political Economy*, 58, 211–21.

Alderfer, E. B. and Michl, H. E. 1942: *Economics of American Industry*. New York: McGraw-Hill.

Alexander, J. W., Brown, S. E. and Dahlberg, R. E. 1958: Freight rates: selected aspects of uniform and nodal regions. *Economic Geography*, 34, 1–18.

Allen, K. (ed.) 1978: *Regional Problems and Policies in the European Community: A Bibliography*, 2 vols, London: Saxon House.

Alonso, W. 1964: *Location and Land Use*. Cambridge, Mass.: Harvard University Press.

Amin, S. 1976: *Unequal Development*. Hassocks, Sussex: Harvester Press.

Anastassopoulos, J. P., Blanc, G. and Dussauge, P. 1987: *State-owned Multinationals*. Chichester: Wiley.

Anell, L. and Nygren, B. 1980: *The Developing Countries and the World Economic Order*. London: Methuen.

Ashcroft, B. and Love J. H. 1989: Evaluating the effects of external takeover on the performance of regional companies: the case of Scotland 1965 to 1980. *Environment and Planning A*, 21, 197–220.

Audit Commission 1989: *Urban Regeneration and Economic Development*. London: HMSO.

Auty, R. M. 1975: Scale economies and plant vintage: toward a factor classification. *Economic Geography*, 51, 150–62.

——1984: The product life-cycle and the location of the global petrochemical industry after the second oil shock. *Economic Geography*, 60, 325–38.

——1988: Oil exporters' disappointing diversification into resource-based industry. *Energy Policy*, 16, 230–42.

Averitt, R. T. 1968: *The Dual Economy: the Dynamics of American Industry Structure*. New York: Norton.

Aydalot, P. 1984: The reversal of industrial trends in French regions since 1974. Presented at symposium on Regional Development Process/Policies and the Changing International Division of Labour, Vienna, 20–24 August.

——1985: The location of new firm creation: the French case. Presented at conference on New Firms and Area Development in the European Community, Utrecht, 21–22 March.

Bacchetta, M. 1978: The crisis of oil refining in the European Community. *Journal of Common Market Studies*, 17, 87–119.

Bacon, R. and Eltis, W. 1976: *Britain's Economic Problems: Too Few Producers*. London: Macmillan.

Bale, J. 1978: Externality gradients. *Area*, 10, 334–6.

Ballance, R. H. 1987: *International Industry and Business: Structural Change, Industrial Policy and Industry Strategies*. London: Allen and Unwin.

Bannock, G. 1971: *The Juggernauts: the Age of the Big Corporation*. Harmondsworth: Penguin.

Barr, B. M. and Waters, N. M. (eds) 1984: *Regional Diversification and Structural Change*. Vancouver: Tantalus.

Bassett, K. 1984: Corporate structure and corporate change in a local economy: the case of Bristol. *Environment and Planning A*, 16, 879–900.

Bater, J. H. and Walker, D. F. 1970: Further comments on location and linkage. *Area*, 4, 59–63.

——1971: The linkage study of Hamilton metal industries. Hamilton: Hamilton Planning Dept, Chamber of Commerce and Economic Development Commission.

——1974: Aspects of industrial linkage: the example of the Hamilton metalworking complex, Ontario. *Révue de Géographie de Montréal*, 28, 233–43.

——1975: Industrialization in nineteenth-century St Petersburg: the role of linkages in shaping location patterns. In L. Collins and D. F. Walker (eds), *Locational Dynamics of Manufacturing Activity*, London: Wiley, 255–78.

——1977: Industrial services: literature and research prospects. In D. F. Walker (ed.), *Industrial Services*, Waterloo: University of Waterloo, Department of Geography, 1–25.

Beattie, D. L. 1980: Conglomerate diversification and performance: a survey and time series analysis. *Applied Economics*, 12, 251–73.

Beattie, E. W. F. and Watts, H. D. 1983: Some relationships between manufacturing activity and the urban system: an exploratory study. *Geoforum*, 14, 125–32.

Beckmann, M. 1968: *Location Theory*. New York: Random House.

Beenstock, M. 1983: *The World Economy in Transition*: Allen and Unwin.

Bell, D. 1973: *The Coming of Post-industrial Society*. London: Heinemann.

Berentsen, W. H. 1979: Regional planning in the German Democratic Republic: its evolution and goals. *International Regional Science Review*, 4, 137–54.

Beyers, W. B. 1974: On geographical properties of growth centre linkage systems. *Economic Geography*, 50, 203–18.

Bhaskar, K. 1980: *The Future of the World Motor Industry*. London: Kogan Page.

Biersteker, T. J. 1978: *Distortion or Development? Contending Perspectives on the Multinational Corporation*. Cambridge, Mass.: MIT Press.

Birch, D. L. 1979: *The Job Generation Process*. Cambridge, Mass.: MIT Program of Neighborhood and Regional Change.

Blaas, W., Rusch, G. and Schonback, W. 1984: *Regionalökonomische Analysen für österreich*. Vienna: Wirtschaftsverlag Orac.

Blackaby, F. (ed.) 1979: *De-industrialization*. London: Heinemann.

Blackbourn, A. 1974: The spatial behaviour of American firms in Western Europe. In F. E. I. Hamilton (ed.), *Spatial Perspectives on Industrial Organisation and Decision Making*, London: Wiley, 245–64.

Blacksell, M. 1975: West Germany. In H. Clout (ed.), *Regional Development in Western Europe*, London: Wiley.

Bloomfield, G. 1978: *The World Automotive Industry*. Newton Abbott: David and Charles.

——1981: The changing spatial organization of multinational corporations in the world automative industry. In F. E. I. Hamilton and G. J. R. Linge (eds), *Spatial Analysis, Industry and the Industrial Environment. Volume II: International Industrial Systems*, Chichester: Wiley.

Bluestone, B. 1984: Coping with labor and community: capitalist strategies in the 1980s. Presented at symposium on Regional Development Processes/ Policies and the Changing International Division of Labour, Vienna, 20–24 August.

Bluestone, B. and Harrison, B. 1982a: *The Deindustrialization of America*. New York: Basic Books.

——1982b: The incidence and regulation of plant closings. In F. S. Redburn and T. F. Buss (eds), *Public Policies for Distressed Communities*. Lexington, Mass.: Lexington Books.

Boas, C. 1961: Locational patterns of American automobile assembly plants. *Economic Geography*, 37, 218–30.

Bolton, R. 1978: The outlook for the northeast: New England. In B. Chinitz (ed.), *The Declining Northeast*, New York: Praeger, 164–74.

Borchert, J. R. 1978: Major control points in American economic geography. *Annals, Association of American Geographers*, 68, 214–32.

Boudeville, J. R. 1966: *Problems of Regional Economic Planning*. Edinburgh: Edinburgh University.

Bower, B. T. 1975: Studies of residuals management in industry. In E. S. Mills (ed.), *Economic Analysis of Environmental Problems*, New York: National Bureau of Economic Research, 275–320.

Bower, J. L. 1986: *When Markets Quake: the Management Challenge of Restructuring Industry*. Boston, Mass.: Harvard Business School.

Bradley, K. and Gelb, A. 1983: *Co-operation at Work: the Mondragon Experience*. London: Heinemann.

Breheny, M. J. 1988: Contracts and contacts: defence procurement and local economic development in Britain. In M. J. Breheny (ed.), *Defence Expenditure and Regional Development*, London: Mansell, 188–211.

Britton, J. N. H. 1969: A geographical approach to the examination of industrial linkages. *Canadian Geographer*, 13, 185–98.

——1974: Environmental adaptation of industrial plants: service linkages, locational environment and organizations. In F. E. I. Hamilton (ed.), *Spatial Perspectives on Industrial Organization and Decision Making*, Chichester: Wiley.

——1976: The influence of corporate organization and ownership on the linkages of industrial plants: a Canadian enquiry. *Economic Geography*, 52, 311–24.

——1980: Industrial dependence and technological under-development: Canadian consequences of foreign direct investment. *Regional Studies*, 14, 181–99.

——1981: Industrial impacts of foreign enterprise: a Canadian technological perspective. *Professional Geographer*, 33, 36–47.

Brocard, M. 1981: Aménagement du territoire et développement régional: le cas de la recherche scientifique. *L'Espace Géographique*, 6, 61–73.

Brooke, M. Z. 1979: Multinational corporate structures: the next stage. *Futures*, 11, 1–21.

Browett, J. 1984: On the necessity and inevitability of uneven spatial development under capitalism. *International Journal of Urban and Regional Research*, 8, 155–77.

Brown, D. M. 1979: The location decision of the firm: an overview of theory and evidence. *Papers of the Regional Science Association*, 43, 23–40.

Brusco, S. 1985: Small firms and industrial districts: the experience of Italy. Presented at conference on New Firms and Area Development in the European Community. Utrecht, 21–22 March.

Bryant, C. R. 1985: *Waterloo Lectures in Geography. Volume 1: Regional Economic Development*. Waterloo: University of Waterloo, Department of Geography.

Buck, W. P., Middleton, D. J. and Walker, D. F. 1980: Encouraging innovative entrepreneurship: a neglected aspect of development policy. In D. F. Walker (ed.), *The Human Dimension in Industrial Development*, Waterloo: University of Waterloo, Department of Geography.

Bull, P. J. 1978: The spatial component of intra-urban manufacturing change: suburbanization in Clydeside, 1958 to 1968. *Transactions of Institute of British Geographers*, (*New Series*), 3, 91–100.

——1979: The effects of central redevelopment schemes on inner-city manufacturing industry, with special reference to Glasgow. *Environment and Planning A*, 11, 455–62.

——1985: Intra-urban industrial geography. In M. Pacione (ed.), *Progress in Industrial Geography*, London: Croom Helm, 82–110.

Burgess, J. 1982: Selling places: environmental images for the executive. *Regional Studies*, 16, 1–17.

Burns, A. F. 1934: *Production Trends in the United States*. New York: National Bureau of Economic Research.

Cameron, G. C. and Clark, B. D. 1966: Industrial movement and the regional problem. University of Glasgow Social and Economic Studies, occasional paper 5.

Canada, Government of 1972: *Foreign Direct Investment in Canada*. Ottawa: Supply and Services.

Canada, Royal Commission on Corporate Concentration 1978: *Report*. Ottawa: Supply and Services.

Cannon, J. B. 1989: Directions in Canadian regional policy. *Canadian Geographer*, 33, 230–9.

Carnoy, M. 1972: *Industrialization in a Latin American Common Market*. Washington DC: Brookings Institution.

Carstensen, F. W. and Guroff, G. (eds) 1983: *Entrepreneurship in Imperial Russia and the Soviet Union*. Princeton: Princeton University.

Carter, F. W. 1985: Pollution problems in post-war Czechoslovakia. *Transactions, Institute of British Geographers*, (New Series), 10, 17–44.

Castleman, B. I. 1979: The export of hazardous factories to developing nations. *International Journal of Health Services*, 9, 569–606.

Caves, R. E. and Porter, M. E. 1980: The dynamics of changing seller concentration. *Journal of Industrial Economics*, 29, 1–15.

Chandler, A. D. 1962: *Strategy and Structure: Chapters in the History of the Industrial Enterprise*. Cambridge, Mass.: MIT.

——1977: *The Visible Hand: the Managerial Revolution in American Business*. Cambridge, Mass.: Harvard University Press.

——1986: The evolution of modern global competition. In M. E. Porter (ed.), *Competition in Global Industries*, Boston, Mass.: Harvard Business School Press, 405–48.

Channon, D. F. 1973: *The Strategy and Structure of British Enterprise*. London: Macmillan.

Channon, D. F. and Jalland, M. 1978: *Multinational Strategic Planning*. New York: AMACOM.

Chapman, K. 1973: Agglomeration and linkage in the United Kingdom petrochemical industry. *Institute of British Geographers, Transactions*, 60, 33–68.

——1974: Corporate systems in the United Kingdom petrochemical industry. *Annals, Association of American Geographers*, 64, 126–37.

——1980a: Environmental policy and industrial location. *Area*, 12, 209–16.

——1980b: *Petrochemicals and Pollution in Texas and Louisiana: a Study of Trends in Pollution Control and Environmental Quality*. Aberdeen: Department of Geography, University of Aberdeen.

——1981: Issues in environmental impact assessment. *Progress in Human Geography*, 5, 190–210.

——1982a: Environmental policy and industrial location in the United States. In R. Flowerdew (ed.), *Institutions and Geographical Patterns*, London: Croom Helm, 141–68.

——1982b: Petrochemicals and economic development: the implications of the Puerto Rican experience. *Professional Geographer*, 34, 405–16.

——1983: The incorporation of environmental considerations into the analysis of industrial agglomeration: examples from the petrochemical industry in Texas and Louisiana. *Geoforum*, 14, 37–44.

—— 1984: The petrochemical industry and regional development: a review of expectations and experiences. In B. M. Barr and N. M. Waters (eds), *Regional Diversification and Structural Change*, Vancouver: Tantalus, 87–98.

Chenery, H. B. 1960: Patterns of industrial growth. *American Economic Review*, 50, 624–54.

Child, J. 1973: Parkinson's progress: accounting for the number of specialists in organizations. *Administrative Science Quarterly*, 18, 328–48.

Chinitz, B. 1961: Contrasts in agglomeration: New York and Pittsburgh. *American Economic Review*, 51, 279–89.

——(ed.) 1979: *Central City Economic Development*. Cambridge, Mass.: Abt Books.

Chisholm, M. 1971: Freight transport costs, industrial location and regional development. In M. Chisholm and G. Manners (eds), *Spatial Policy Problems of the British Economy*. Cambridge: Cambridge University Press, 213–44.

Christie, R. C. 1980: Developing an industrial policy for a central city: a case study of Toronto, Canada. In D. F. Walker (ed.), *Planning Industrial Development*, Chichester: Wiley.

Christy, C. V. and Ironside, R. G. 1987: Promoting 'high technology' industry: location factors and public policy. In K. Chapman and G. Humphrey (eds), *Technical Change and Industrial Policy*, Oxford: Blackwell, 233–52.

Clarke, I. M. 1985: *The Spatial Organization of Multinational Corporations*. London: Croom Helm.

Clarke, R. and Davies, S. W. 1983: Aggregate concentration, market concentration and diversification. *Economic Journal*, 93, 182–92.

Clement, W. 1975: *The Canadian Corporate Elite*. Toronto: McLelland and Stewart.

Cobb, J. C. 1982: *The Selling of the South: the Southern Crusade for Industrial Development 1936-1980*. Baton Rouge, La: Louisiana University Press.

Cocks, P. 1983: Organizing for technological innovation in the 1980s. In F. W. Carstensen and G. Guroff (eds), *Entrepreneurship in Imperial Russia and the Soviet Union*, Princeton: Princeton University Press.

Collins, L. and Walker, D. F. (eds) 1975: *Locational Dynamics of Manufacturing Industry*. Chichester: Wiley.

Commission of the European Communities 1981: Steel: agreement in the Council. *Bulletin*, 14(6), 17–19.

Cooke, P. 1985: Regional innovation policy: problems and strategies in Britain and France. *Environment and Planning C*, 3, 253–68.

Cooke, P., Morgan, K. and Jackson, D. 1984: New technology and regional development in austerity Britain: the case of the semiconductor industry. *Regional Studies*, 18, 277–89.

Cooper, M. J. M. 1975: *The Industrial Location Decision Making Process*.

Birmingham: Centre for Urban and Regional Studies, occasional paper 34.

Cortes, M. and Bocock, P. 1984: *North–South Technology Transfer: a Case Study of Petrochemicals in Latin America*. Baltimore: Johns Hopkins University Press.

Court, W. H. B. 1938: *The Rise of Midland Industries, 1600–1838*. London: Oxford University.

Cross, M. 1981: *New Firm Formation and Regional Development*. Westmead: Gower.

Crum, R. and Gudgin, G. 1978: *Non-production Activities in UK Manufacturing Industry*. Brussels: European Economic Commission.

Cumberland, J. H. 1978: Planning future industrial development in response to energy and environmental constraints. In F. E. I. Hamilton (ed.), *Industrial Change*, London: Longman, 1–10.

Curry, B. and George, K. D. 1983: Industrial concentration: a survey. *Journal of Industrial Economics*, 31, 203–52.

Cyert, R. M. and March, J. G. 1963: *A Behavioural Theory of the Firm*. Englewood Cliffs, NJ: Prentice-Hall.

Czamanski, S. 1976: *Study of Spatial Industrial Complexes*. Halifax, Nova Scotia: Inst. of Public Affairs, Dalhousie University.

Czamanski, S. and Ablas, L. A. de Q. 1979: Identification of industrial clusters and complexes: comparison of methods and findings. *Urban Studies*, 16, 61–80.

Danson, M. W. 1982: The industrial structure and labour market segmentation: urban and regional implications. *Regional Studies*, 16, 255–65.

Darwent, D. F. 1969: Growth poles and growth centres in regional planning: a review. *Environment and Planning*, 1, 5–32.

Davis, L. N. 1984: *The Corporate Alchemists*. London: Temple Smith.

Dean, R. D. 1972: Plant location decision processes. *Review of Regional Studies*, 3, 1–14.

Dennis, R. D. 1978: The decline of manufacturing employment in Greater London: 1966–1974. *Urban Studies*, 15, 63–73.

Devine, P. J., Jones, R. M., Lee, N. and Tyson, W. J. 1976: *An Introduction to Industrial Economics*, London: Allen and Unwin.

Diamond, D. R. and Spence, N. A. 1983: *Regional Policy Evaluation*. Farnborough, Hants: Gower.

Dicken, P. 1971: Some aspects of the decision-making behaviour of business organizations. *Economic Geography*, 47, 426–37.

——1977: A note on location theory and the large business enterprise. *Area*, 9, 138–45.

——1986: *Global Shift: Industrial Change in a Turbulent World*. London: Harper and Row.

Dicken, P. (no date): Overseas investment by UK manufacturing firms: some trends and issues. North West Industry Research Unit Working Paper 12, Manchester: University of Manchester, Department of Geography.

Dicken, P. and Lloyd, P. E. 1978: Inner metropolitan industrial change, enterprise structures and policy issues: case studies of Manchester and Merseyside. *Regional Studies*, 12, 181–97.

Donges, J. B. 1976: A comparative study of industrialization policies in fifteen semi-industrial countries. *Weltwirtschaftliches Archiv*, 112, 626–57.

Dorfman, N. S. 1983: Route 128: the development of a regional high technology economy. *Research Policy*, 12, 299–316.

Dorward, N. M. M. 1979: Market area analysis and product differentiation: a case study of the West German truck industry. In F. E. I. Hamilton and G. J. R. Linge (eds), *Spatial Analysis and the Industrial Environment, Volume 1: Industrial Systems*. Chichester: Wiley, 213–60.

Duerksen, C. J. 1983: *Environmental Regulation of Industrial Plant Siting: How to Make it Work Better*. Washington DC: Conservation Foundation.

Downie, J. 1958: *The Competitive Process*. London: Duckworth.

Dunford, M. P. 1979: Capital accumulation and regional development in France. *Geoforum*, 10, 81–108.

Dunning, J. H. 1973: The determinants of international production. *Oxford Economic Papers*, 25, 289–336.

——1974: The future of the multinational enterprise. *Lloyds Bank Review*, 11(3), 15–32.

——1988: *Explaining International Production*. London: Unwin Hyman.

Dunning, J. H. and Pearce, R. D. 1981: *The World's Largest Industrial Enterprises*. Westmead, Farnborough: Gower.

——1985: *The World's Largest Industrial Enterprises 1962–1983*. New York: St Martins Press.

Economist 1985: Into intrapreneurial Britain. 16 February, 19–26.

Eirug, A. 1983: The Welsh Development Agency. *Geoforum*, 14, 375–88.

Elias, P. and Keogh, G. 1982: Industrial decline and unemployment in the inner city area of Great Britain: a review of the evidence. *Urban Studies*, 19, 1–15.

Enos, J. L. and Park, W. H. 1988: *The Adoption and Diffusion of Imported Technology: the Case of Korea*. London: Croom Helm.

Erickson, R. A. 1974: The regional impact of growth firms: the case of Boeing 1963–1968. *Land Economics*, 50, 127–36.

——1980a: Corporate organization and manufacturing branch plant closures in non-metropolitan areas. *Regional Studies*, 14, 491–501.

——1980b: Environment as 'push factor' in the suburbanization of business establishments. *Urban Geography*, 1, 167–78.

Estall, R. C. 1966: *New England: a Study in Industrial Adjustment*. London: Bell.

Estall, R. C. and Buchanan, R. O. 1980: *Industrial Activity and Economic Geography*, 4th edn, London: Hutchinson.

Ettlinger, N. 1984: Comments on the concept of linkages from the perspective of corporate organization in the modern capitalist system. *Tijdschrift voor Economische en Sociale Geografie*, 75, 285–91.

Evely, R. and Little, I. M. D. 1960: *Concentration in British Industry*. Cambridge: Cambridge University Press.

Eversley, D. E. C. 1965: Social and psychological factors in the determination of industrial location. In T. Wilson (ed.), *Papers on Regional Development* (supplement to *Journal of Industrial Economics*), Oxford: Blackwell.

Ewers, H. J. and Wettmann, R. W. 1980: Innovation-oriented regional policy.

Regional Studies, 14, 161–79.

Expenditure Committee (UK) 1973: *Regional Development Incentives. Minutes of Evidence, Appendices and Index*. Session 1973–4. HC85-1. London: HMSO.

Fagg, J. 1980: A re-examination of the incubator hypothesis: a case study of Greater Leicester. *Urban Studies*, 17, 35–44.

Fales, R. L. and Moses, L. N. 1972: Land use theory and spatial structure. *Paper, Regional Science Association*, 28, 49–82.

Fayad, M. and Motamen, H. 1986: *Economics of the Petrochemical Industry*. London: Frances Pinter.

Feagin, J. R. 1988: *Free Enterprise City: Houston in Political and Economic Perspective*. New Brunswick, NJ: Rutgers University Press.

Feller, I. 1975: Invention, diffusion and industrial location. In L. Collins and D. F. Walker (eds), *Locational Dynamics of Manufacturing Industry*. Chichester: Wiley, 83–108.

Ferrier, R. W. 1982: *The History of the British Petroleum Company* (vol. 1). Cambridge: Cambridge University Press.

Fetter, F. 1924: The economic law of market areas. *Quarterly Journal of Economics*, 39, 520–9.

Financial Times 1987: Supplement on Puerto Rico. Friday 27 March.

Fishwick, F. 1982: *Multinational Companies and Economic Concentration in Europe*. Aldershot: Gower.

Fleming, D. K. and Krumme, G. 1968: The Royal Hoesch Union: case analysis of adjustment patterns in the European steel industry. *Tijdschrift voor Economische en Sociale Geografie*, 58, 177–99.

Foltman, F. F. 1976: *Business Climate in New York State: Perceptions of Management Officials*. Ithaca, NY: Cornell University Press.

Forbes, D. 1982: Energy imperialism and a new international division of resources: the case of Indonesia. *Tijdschrift voor Economische en Sociale Geografie*, 73, 94–108.

Forsyth, D. J. C. 1972: *US Investment in Scotland*. New York: Praeger.

Foster, R. 1977: Economic and quality of life factors in industrial location decisions. *Social Indicators Research*, 4, 247–65.

Fothergill, S. and Gudgin, G. 1982: *Unequal Growth: Urban and Regional Employment Growth in the United Kingdom*. London: Heinemann.

Fothergill, S., Gudgin, G., Kitson, M. and Monk, S. 1984: Differences in the profitability of the UK manufacturing sector between conurbations and other areas. *Scottish Journal of Political Economy*, 31, 72–91.

Fothergill, S., Kitson, M. and Monk, S. 1983: The Impact of new and expanded towns on industrial location in Britain, 1960–78. *Regional Studies*, 17, 251–60.

Foust, J. B. 1975: Ubiquitous manufacturing. *Annals, Association of American Geographers*, 65, 13–17.

Francis, G. 1976: *Eco-development, National Development and International Co-operation Policies*. Ottawa: Environment Canada and Canadian International Development Agency.

Frank, A. G. 1966: The development of underdevelopment. *Monthly Review*, 18, 17–31.
——1975: *On Capitalist Underdevelopment*. Bombay: Oxford University.
Frankel, P. H. and Newton, W. L. 1968: Economics of petroleum refining: present state and future prospects. *Journal of the Institute of Petroleum*, 54, 23–32.
Franko, L. G. 1976: *The European Multinationals*. London: Harper and Row.
Fredriksson, C. G. and Lindmark, L. G. 1979: From firms to systems of firms. In F. E. I. Hamilton and G. J. R. Linge (eds), *Spatial Analysis, Industry and the Industrial Environment. Volume 1: Industrial Systems*. Chichester: Wiley, 155–86.
Freeman, C. 1982: *The Economics of Industrial Innovation*, 2nd edn, London: Frances Pinter.
——1987: Technical innovation, long cycles and regional policy. In K. Chapman and G. Humphrys (eds), *Technical Change and Industrial Policy*, Oxford: Blackwell, 10–25.
Freeman, C., Clark, J. and Soete, L. 1982: *Unemployment and Technical Innovation*. London: Frances Pinter.
Friedman, A. L. 1977: *Industry and Labour: Class Struggle at Work and Monopoly Capitalism*. London: Macmillan.
Friedmann, J. 1972: A general theory of polarized development. In N. M. Hansen (ed.), *Growth Centres in Regional Economic Development*, New York: Free Press, 82–107.
Friedmann, J. and Weaver, C. 1979: *Territory and Function: the Evolution of Regional Planning*. London: Edward Arnold.
Fröbel, F., Heinrichs, J. and Kreye, O. 1980: *The New International Division of Labour*. Cambridge: Cambridge University.
Frost, M. E. 1975: The impact of regional policy. *Progress in Planning*, 4, 3.
Fuchs, R. J. and Demko, G. J. 1979: Geographic inequality under socialism. *Annals, Association of American Geographers*, 69, 304–18.
Galbraith, J. K. 1967: *The New Industrial State*. London: Hamish Hamilton.
Galbraith, J. R. and Nathanson, D. A. 1978: *Strategy Implementation: the Role of Structure and Process*. St. Paul, Minn.: West.
George, K. D. and Ward, T. 1975: *The Structure of Industry in the EEC*. Cambridge: Cambridge University Press.
Gershuny, J. I. and Miles 1983: *The New Service Economy*. London: Frances Pinter.
Gertler, M. S. 1988: The limits of flexibility: comments on the post-Fordist vision of production and its geography. *Transactions, Institute of British Geographers (New Series)*, 13, 419–432.
——1989: Resurrecting flexibility? A reply. *Transactions, Institute of British Geographers (New Series)*, 14, 109–112.
Gibbs, D. 1989: Government policy and industrial change: an overview. In D. Gibbs (ed.), *Government Policy and Industrial Change*. London: Routledge, 1–22.
Giddy, I. H. and Young, S. 1982: Conventional theory and unconventional

multinationals: do new forms of multinational enterprise require new theories? In A. M. Rugman (ed.), *New Theories of the Multinational Enterprise*. London: Croom Helm, 55–78.

Gilmour, J. M. 1972: *Spatial Evolution of Manufacturing: Southern Ontario 1851–1881*. Toronto: University of Toronto, Department of Geography.

——1974: External economies of scale, inter-industrial linkages and decision making in manufacturing. In F. E. I. Hamilton (ed.), *Spatial Perspectives on Industrial Organization and Decision Making*, London: Wiley, 335–62.

Ginzberg, N. 1982: The mechanization of work. *Scientific American*, 247(3), 39–47.

Gladwin, T. N. 1975: *Environment, Planning and the Multinational Corporation*. Greenwich, Conn.: JAI Press.

——1980: Patterns of environmental conflict over industrial facilities in the United States 1970–1978. *Natural Resources Journal*, 20, 243–74.

Gladwin, T. N. and Welles, J. G. 1976: Environmental policy and multinational corporate strategy. In I. Walter (ed.), *Studies in International Environmental Economics*, New York: Wiley, 177–224.

Gleave, M. B. 1965: Some contrasts in the English brick making industry. *Tijdschrift voor Economische en Sociale Geografie*, 56, 54–62.

Goddard, J. B. 1973: Office linkages and location. *Progress in Planning*, 1.

——1978: The location of non-manufacturing activities within manufacturing industries. In F. E. I. Hamilton (ed.), *Contemporary Industrialization*, London: Longman, 62–85.

Goddard, J. B., Gillespie, A. E., Robinson, J. F. and Thwaites, A. T. 1985: The impact of new information technology on urban and regional structure in Europe. In A. T. Thwaites and R. P. Oakey (eds). *The Regional Economic Impact of Technological Change*. London: Frances Pinter, 215–241.

Goddard, J. B. and Smith, I. J. 1978: Changes in corporate control in the British urban system, 1972–1977. *Environment and Planning A*, 10, 1073–84.

Golbe, D. C. and White, L. J. 1988: Mergers and acquisitions in the US economy: an aggregate and historical overview. In A. J. Auerbach (ed.), *Mergers and Acquisitions*. Chicago: University of Chicago Press, 25–48.

Gold, B. 1964: Industry growth patterns: theory and empirical results. *Journal of Industrial Economics*, 13, 53–73.

Goldberg, B. 1969: Industry growth patterns: theory and empirical results. *Journal of Industrial Economics*, 13, 53–73.

Goldman, A. 1980: The export of hazardous industries to developing countries. *Antipode*, 12, 40–6.

Golstein, L. and Carvalhaes, S. G. 1986: Industry and the human and ecological tragedy of Cubatao, Brazil. In F. E. I. Hamilton (ed.), *Industrialization in Developing and Peripheral Regions*. London: Croom Helm, 266–82.

Goodman, E., Bamford, J., Kumar, K. and Saynor, P. (eds), 1989: *Small Firms and Industrial Districts in Italy*. London: Routledge.

Goudie, A. W. and Meeks, G. 1982: Diversification by merger. *Economica*, 49, 447–59.

Gough, P. 1984: Location theory and the multiplant firm: a framework for empirical studies. *Canadian Geographer*, 28, 127–41.

Grant, R. M. 1977: The determinants of the inter-industry pattern of diversification by UK manufacturing enterprises. *Bulletin of Economic Research*, 29, 84–95.

Grass, E. and Hayter, R. 1989: Employment change during recession: the experience of forest product manufacturing plants in British Columbia 1981–5. *Canadian Geographer*, 33, 240–52.

Green, M. B. 1990: *Mergers and Acquisitions: Geographical and Spatial Perspectives*. London: Routledge.

Green, M. B. and Cromley, R. G. 1982: The horizontal merger: its motives and spatial employment impacts. *Economic Geography*, 58, 358–70.

——1984: Merger and acquisition fields for large United States cities 1955–1970. *Regional Studies*, 291–301.

Green, M. B. and McNaughton, R. B. 1989: Canadian interurban merger activity 1962–1984. *Canadian Geographer*, 33, 253–64.

Greenhut, M. C. 1981: Spatial pricing in the US, West Germany and Japan. *Economica*, 48, 79–86.

Greenhut, M. L. 1956: *Plant Location in Theory and Practice*. Chapel Hill, NC: University of North Carolina Press.

——1963: *Microeconomics and the Space Economy*. Chicago: Scott Foresman.

——1964: *A Theory of the Firm in Economic Space*. Austin, Texas: Austin Press.

——1974: *A Theory of the Firm in Economic Space*. Austin, Tx.: University of Texas Press.

Greenhut, M. L. and Colberg, M. R. 1962: *Factors in the Location of Florida Industry*. Tallahassee, Florida: Florida State University.

Gribbin, J. D. 1976: The conglomerate merger. *Applied Economics*, 8, 19–36.

Grice, K. and Drakakis-Smith, D. 1985: The role of the state in shaping development: two decades of growth in Singapore. *Transactions, Institute of British Geographers*, (New Series), 10, 347–59.

Groo, E. S. 1971: Choosing foreign locations: one company's experience. *Columbia Journal of World Business*, 6, 71–8.

Grunberg, L. 1981: *Failed Multinational Ventures*. Lexington, Mass.: Lexington Books.

Grunwald, J. and Flamm, K. 1985: *The Global Factory: Foreign Assembly in International Trade*. Washington DC: Brookings Institution.

Gudgin, G. 1978: *Industrial Location Processes and Regional Employment Growth*. Farnborough: Saxon House.

Gudgin, G., Crum, R. and Bailey, S. 1979: White-collar employment in UK manufacturing industry. In P. W. Daniels (ed.), *Spatial Patterns of Office Growth and Location*, Chichester: Wiley, 127–58.

Gwynne, R. N. 1979: Oligopolistic reaction. *Area*, 11, 315–19.

Haig, R. M. 1926: Towards an understanding of the metropolis. Reprinted in R. H. T. Smith et al., 1968, *Readings in Economic Geography*, Chicago: Rand McNally, 44–57.

Håkanson, L. 1979: Towards a theory of location and corporate growth. In F. E. I. Hamilton and G. J. R. Linge (eds), *Spatial Analysis, Industry and the Industrial Environment. Volume 1: Industrial Systems*. Chichester: Wiley,

115–38.

Hall, M. (ed.) 1959: *Made in New York*. Cambridge, Mass.: Harvard University.

Hall, P. G. 1962: *The Industries of London since 1861*. London: Hutchinson.

——1985a: The geography of the fifth Kondratieff. In P. Hall and A. Markusen (eds), *Silicon Landscapes*, Boston: Allen and Unwin, 1–19.

——1985b: The new geography of innovation. In C. R. Bryant (ed.), *Waterloo Lectures in Geography. Volume 1: Regional Economic Development*, Waterloo: University of Waterloo, Department of Geography, 29–38.

Hall, P. G. and Markusen, A. (eds) 1985: *Silicon Landscapes*. Boston: Allen and Unwin.

Hamer, A. M. 1973: *Industrial Exodus from Central City*. Lexington, Mass.: Lexington Books.

Hamilton, F. E. I. 1973: Spatial dimensions of Soviet economic decision making. In V. N. Bandera and Z. L. Melnyk (eds), *The Soviet Economy in Regional Perspective*, New York: Praeger, 235–60.

——(ed.) 1974a: *Spatial Perspectives on Industrial Organization and Decision Making*. London: Wiley.

——1974b: A view of spatial behaviour, industrial organization and decision making. In F. E. I. Hamilton (ed.), *Spatial Perspectives on Industrial Organisation and Decision Making*, London: Wiley, 3–46.

——1981: Industrial systems: a dynamic force behind international trade. *Professional Geographer*, 33, 26–35.

Hamilton, F. E. I. and Linge, G. J. R. (eds) 1979: *Spatial Analysis, Industry and the Industrial Environment. Volume 1: Industrial Systems*, Chichester: Wiley.

——1981: *Spatial Analysis, Industry and the Industrial Environment. Volume II: International Industrial Systems*. Chichester: Wiley.

——1983: *Spatial Analysis, Industry and the Industrial Environment. Volume III: Regional Economies and Industrial Systems*. Chichester: Wiley.

Hannah, L. 1983: *The Rise of the Corporate Economy*, 2nd edn, London: Methuen.

Hansen, N. M. 1979: The new international division of labour and manufacturing decentralization in the United States. *Review of Regional Studies*, 9, 1–11.

——1988: Regional consequences of structural changes in the national and international division of labour. *International Regional Science Review*, 11, 121–36.

Harris, C. D. 1954: The market as a factor in the location of industry in the United States. *Annals, Association of American Geographers*, 44, 315–48.

Harris, C. S. 1983: Plant closing: the magnitude of the problem. Working paper 13, Business Microdata Project, Washington DC: Brookings Institute.

Harrison B. 1982: The tendency toward instability and inequality underlying the 'revival' of New England. *Papers, Regional Science Association*, 50, 41–65.

Harrison, B. and Bluestone, B. 1982: The incidence and regulation of plant closings. In F. S. Redburn and T. F. Buss (eds), *Public Policies for Distressed Communities*, Lexington, Mass.: Lexington.

Harrison, R. T., Bull P. J. and Hart, M. 1979: Space and time in industrial linkage studies. *Area*, 11, 333–8.

Hart, P. E. and Clarke, R. 1980: *Concentration in British Industry*. Cambridge: NIESR.

Hayter, R. 1976: Corporate strategies and industrial change in the Canadian forest product industries. *Geographical Review*, 66, 209–28.

——1981: Patterns of entry and the role of foreign-controlled investments in the forest product sector of British Columbia. *Tijdschrift voor Economische en Sociale Geografie*, 72, 99–113.

——1982: Truncation, the international firm and regional policy. *Area*, 14, 277–82.

Hayter, R. and Watts, H. D. 1983: The geography of enterprise: a reappraisal. *Progress in Human Geography*, 7, 157–81.

Healey, M. 1981: Product changes in multi-plant enterprises. *Geoforum*, 12, 359–70.

——1983: Components of locational change in multi-plant enterprises. *Urban Studies*, 20, 327–41.

Healey, M. and Clark, D. 1984: Industrial decline and government response in the west midlands: the case of Coventry. *Regional Studies*, 18, 303–18.

Healy, R. G. 1979: Environmental regulations and the location of industry in the US: a search for evidence. Presented at conference on Role of Environmental and Land-use Regulation in Industrial Siting. Washington DC: Conservation Foundation.

Hekman, J. S. 1978: An analysis of the changing location of iron and steel production in the twentieth century. *American Economic Review*, 68, 123–33.

——1980a: The future of high technology industry in New England: a case study of computers. *New England Economic Review*, January–February, 5–17.

——1980b: The product cycle and New England textiles. *Quarterly Journal of Economics*, 94, 699–717.

Henderson, A. and Schlaifer, R. 1954: Mathematical programming: better information for better decision making. *Harvard Business Review*, 32, 73–100.

Henderson, R. A. 1980: The location of immigrant industry within a UK assisted area: the Scottish experience. *Progress in Planning*, 14, 105–226.

Hepworth, M. E. 1986: The geography of technology change in the information economy. *Regional Studies*, 20, 407–424.

Heron, F. 1975: *Labour Markets in Crisis: Redundancy at Upper Clyde Shipbuilders*. London: Macmillan.

Herron, F. 1981: *Post-Industry Act (1972): industrial movement into and expansion in the assisted areas of Great Britain: some survey findings*. London: Government Economic Service Working paper 46, Department of Trade and Industry.

Hewings, G. J. D. 1977: *Regional Industrial Analysis and Development*. London: Methuen.

Hill, C. 1953: Some aspects of industrial location. *Journal of Industrial*

Economics, 2, 184–92.

Hill, C. W. L. 1983: Conglomerate performance over the economic cycle. *Journal of Industrial Economics*, 32, 197–212.

Hirsch, S. 1967: *Location of Industry and International Competitiveness*. Oxford: Clarendon.

Hirschmann, A. O. 1958: *The Strategy of Economic Development*. New Haven: Yale University.

——1977: A generalized linkage approach to development with special reference to staples. *Economic Development and Cultural Change* (Supplement), 25, 67–98.

Hoare, A. G. 1985: Industrial linkage studies. In M. Pacione (ed.), *Progress in Industrial Geography*, London: Croom Helm, 40–81.

Hodge, G. and Wong, C. C. 1972: Adapting industrial complex analysis to the realities of regional data. *Papers, Regional Science Association*, 28, 145–66.

Holland, S. 1971: Regional underdevelopment in a developed economy: the Italian case. *Regional Studies*, 5, 71–90.

Holmes, J. 1983: Industrial re-organization, capital restructuring and locational change: an analysis of the Canadian automobile industry in the 1960s. *Economic Geography*, 59, 251–71.

——1987: Technical change and restructuring in the North American automobile industry. In K. Chapman and G. Humphrys (eds), *Technical Change and Industrial Policy*, Oxford: Blackwell, 121–56.

Hood, N. and Young, S. 1980: *European Development Strategies of US-owned Manufacturing Companies Located in Scotland*. Edinburgh: HMSO.

Hooper, D. J. and Walker, D. F. 1983: Innovative and co-operative entrepreneurship (towards a new thrust in industrial development policy). In F. E. I. Hamilton and G. J. R. Linge (eds), *Spatial Analysis, Industry and the Industrial Environment. Volume III: Regional Economies and Industrial Systems*. Chichester: Wiley, 217–32.

Hoover, E. M. 1937: *Location Theory and the Shoe and Leather Industries*. Cambridge, Mass.: Harvard University.

——1948: *The Location of Economic Activity*. New York: McGraw-Hill.

Hoover, E. M. and Vernon, R. 1962: *Anatomy of a Metropolis*, New York: Anchor Books.

Hotelling, H. 1929: Stability in competition. *Economic Journal*, 39, 41–57.

House, J. W. 1982: *Frontier on the Rio Grande*. Oxford: Oxford University Press.

——1983: Regional and area development. In J. W. House (ed.), *United States Public Policy: a Geographical View*, Oxford: Clarendon, 34–79.

Houston, C. 1969: Market potential and potential transportation costs: an evaluation of the concepts and their surface patterns in the USSR. *Canadian Geographer*, 13, 216–35.

Howells, J. R. L. 1984: The location of research and development: some observations and evidence from Britain, *Regional Studies*, 18, 13–29.

Hoyle, B. S. and Pinder, D. A. 1981: Seaports, cities and transport systems. In B. S. Hoyle and D. A. Pinder (eds), *Cityport Industrialization and Regional Development*, Oxford: Pergamon, 1–10.

Hudson, R. 1983: Capital accumulation and chemical production in Western Europe in the postwar period. *Environment and Planning A*, 15, 105–22.

——1986: Producing an industrial wasteland: capital, labour and the state in North East England. In R. Martin and B. Rowthorn (eds), *The Geography of De-industrialisation*, London: Macmillan, 169–213.

——1988: Uneven development in capitalist societies: changing spatial division of labour, forms of spatial organization of production and service provision, and their impacts on localities. *Transactions, Institute of British Geographers (New Series)*, 13, 484–96.

Hughes, A. and Kumar, M. S. 1984: Recent trends in aggregate concentration in the United Kingdom economy. *Cambridge Journal of Economics*, 8, 235–50.

Hughes, H. and Ohlin, G. 1980: The international environment. In J. Coy, H. Hughes and D. Wall (eds), *Policies for Industrial Progress in Developing Countries*, New York: Oxford University for the World Bank.

Hughes, J. W. and James, F. J. 1975: Changing spatial distribution of jobs and residences. *Growth and Change*, 6, 20–5.

Hunker, H. L. 1980: The evolution of industrial development planning in North America. In D. F. Walker (ed.), *Planning Industrial Development*. Chichester: Wiley, 15–46.

Hutchings, R. 1982: *Soviet Economic Development*. 2nd edn, Oxford: Blackwell.

Huzinec, G. A. 1976: Some initial comparisons of Soviet and Western regional development models. *Soviet Geography, Review and Translation*, 17, 552–65.

——1977: A re-examination of Soviet industrial location theory. *Professional Geographer*, 29, 529–65.

Hymer, S. 1972: The multinational corporation and the law of uneven development. In J. N. Bhagwati (ed.), *Economics and World Order*, London: Collier–Macmillan, 113–40.

Isard, N. 1956: *Location and Space-Economy*. Cambridge, Mass.: MIT Press.

——1960: *Methods of Regional Analysis*, Cambridge, Mass.: MIT Press.

——1969: *General Theory: Social, Political, Economic and Regional*. Cambridge, Mass.: MIT Press.

——1977: Location theory, agglomeration and the pattern of world trade. In B. Ohlin, P. O. Hesselborn and P. M. Wijkman (eds), *The International Allocation of Economic Activity*. London: Macmillan, 159–77.

Isard, W., Schooler, E. W. and Vietorisz, T. 1959: *Industrial Complex Analysis and Regional Development*. Cambridge, Mass.: MIT Press.

Isard, W. and Smith, T. E. 1966: On the resolutions of conflicts among regions of a system. *Papers, Regional Science Association*, 17, 19–46.

——1967: Location games: with applications to classic location problems. *Papers, Regional Science Association*, 19, 45–80.

——1968: Coalition location games, Paper 3. *Papers, Regional Science Association*, 20, 95–107.

Jarmon, C. J. 1987: *Nigeria: Reorganization and Development Since the Mid-Twentieth Century*. Monographs and Theoretical Studies in Sociology and Anthropology in Honour of Nels Anderson, 23, Leiden: E. J. Brill.

Johnson, M. L. 1985: Post-war industrial development in the South East and the pioneer role of labour intensive industries. *Economic Geography*, 61, 45–65.

Johnson, P. S. and Cathcart, D. G. 1979: New manufacturing firms and regional development: some evidence from the northern region. *Regional Studies*, 13, 269–80.

Jones, B. G. and Manson, D. M. 1982: The geography of enterprise zones: a critical analysis. *Economic Geography*, 58, 329–42.

Karaska, G. J. 1969: Manufacturing linkages in the Philadelphia economy: some evidence of external agglomeration forces. *Geographical Analysis*, 1, 354–69.

Katona, G. and Morgan, J. N. 1952: The quantitative study of factors determining business decisions. *Quarterly Journal of Economics*, 66, 67–90.

Keeble, D. 1967: Models of economic development. In R. Chorley and P. Haggett (eds), *Models in Geography*, London: Methuen.

——1968: Industrial decentralization and the metropolis: the north-west London case. *Transactions, Institute of British Geographers*, 44, 1–54.

——1969: Local industrial linkage and manufacturing growth in outer London. *Town Planning Review*, 40, 163–187.

——1976: *Industrial Location and Planning in the United Kingdom*. London: Methuen.

——1978: Industrial decline in the inner city and conurbation. *Transactions, Institute of British Geographers*, (*New Series*), 3, 101–14.

——1980: Industrial decline, regional policy and the urban–rural manufacturing shift in the United Kingdom. *Environment and Planning A*, 12, 945–62.

Keeble, D. and McDermott, P. 1978: Organisation and industrial location in the United Kingdom: preface. *Regional Studies*, 12, 139–41.

Keeble, D., Owens, P. and Thompson, C. 1983: The urban–rural manufacturing shift in the European Community. *Urban Studies*, 20, 405–18.

Kellerman, A. 1985: The evolution of service economies: a geographical perspective. *Professional Geographer*, 37, 133–43.

Kenyon, J. 1967: Manufacturing and Sprawl. In J. Gottman and R. A. Harper (eds), *Metropolis on the Move*. New York: Wiley, 102–21.

Kerlin, G. and Rabovsky, D. 1975: *Cracking Down: Oil Refining and Pollution Control*. New York: Council on Economic Priorities.

Kerr, D. and Spelt, J. 1960: Some aspects of industrial location in Southern Ontario. *Canadian Geographer*, 15, 12–25.

Kilby, P. 1969: *Industrialization in an Open Economy: Nigeria 1945–1966*. Cambridge: Cambridge University Press.

Kim, An–jae 1978: Industrialization and growth-pole development in Korea: a case study of Ulsan industrial complex. In Fu-chen Lo and Kamal Salih (eds), *Growth-pole Strategy and Regional Development Policy*, Oxford: Pergamon, 53–77.

Kneese, A. V. and Bower, B. T. 1979: *Environmental Quality and Residuals Management*. Baltimore: Resources for the Future.

Knickerbocker, F. T. 1973: *Oligopolistic Reaction and Multinational Enterprise*. Cambridge, Mass.: Harvard University.

Köstler, H. J. 1984: Das steirische Eisenhüttenwesen von den Anfängen des Flossofenbetriebes in 16 Jahrhundert bis zür Gegenwart. In P. W. Roth (ed.),

Erz und Eisen in der Grünen Mark. Beiträge zum Steirischen Eisenwesen, Graz: Styria Verlag, 109–55.

Kravis, I. B. and Lipsey, R. E. 1982: The location of overseas production and production for export by US multinational firms. *Journal of International Economics,* 12, 201–23.

Krumme, G. 1969a: Notes on locational adjustment patterns in industrial geography. *Geografiska Annaler,* 51B, 15–19.

——1969b: Towards a geography of enterprise. *Economic Geography,* 45, 30–40.

——1970: The inter-regional corporation and the region, *Tijdschrift voor Economische en Sociale Geografie,* 61, 18–33.

——1974: Regional policies in West Germany. In N. M. Hansen (ed.), *Public Policy and Regional Economic Development: the Experience of Nine Western Countries.* Cambridge, Mass.: Ballinger, 103–35.

Kuznets, S. 1930: *Secular Movements in Production and Prices.* Boston: Houghton Mifflin.

Lall, S. 1983: *The New Multinationals: the spread of Third World Enterprises.* Chichester: Wiley.

Lampe, D. (ed.) 1988: *The Massachusetts Miracle: High Technology and Economic Revitalization.* Cambridge, Mass.: MIT Press.

Landes, D. S. 1969: *The Unbound Prometheus: Technological Changes and Industrial Development in Western Europe from 1750 to the Present.* Cambridge: Cambridge University Press.

Lasuen, J. R. 1971: Venezuela: an industrial shift-share analysis, 1941–1961. *Regional and Urban Economics,* 1, 153–220.

Laulajainen, R. 1981: Three tests on locational matching. *Geografiska Annaler,* 63B, 35–45.

Law, C. M. 1980: *British Regional Development Since World War I,* Newton Abbott: David and Charles.

——1983: The defence sector in British regional development. *Geoforum,* 14, 169–84.

Lawless, P. 1981: *Britain's Inner Cities: Problems and Policies.* London: Harper and Row.

Leblanc, R. G. 1969: *Location of Manufacturing in New England in the 19th Century.* Dartmouth, N. H.: Dartmouth College, Department of Geography.

Leechor, C., Kohli, H. S. and Hur, S. 1983: *Structural Changes in World Industry: a Quantitative Analysis of Recent Development.* Washington, DC: World Bank.

Le Heron, R. B. 1977: Patterns of company control and regional development in New Zealand. *Pacific Viewpoint,* 18, 58–78.

Le Heron, R. B. and Schmidt, C. G. 1976: An exploratory analysis of linkage change within two regional industries. *Regional Studies,* 10, 465–78.

Le Heron, R. B. and Warr, E. C. W. 1976: Corporate organization, corporate strategy and agribusiness development in New Zealand. *New Zealand Geographer,* 32, 1–16.

Leigh, R. and North, D. J. 1978a: Acquisitions in British industries: implications for regional development. In F. E. I. Hamilton (ed.), *Contemporary Industrial-*

ization, London: Longman, 158–81.
——1978b: Regional aspects of acquisition activity in British manufacturing industry. *Regional Studies*, 14, 227–45.
Leinbach, T. R. 1978: Locational trends in non-metropolitan industrial growth: some evidence from Vermont. *Professional Geographer*, 30, 30–6.
Leonard, H. J. 1984: *Are Environmental Regulations Driving US Industry Overseas*. Washington DC: Conservation Foundation.
——1988: *Pollution and the Struggle for the World Product*. Cambridge: Cambridge University Press.
Leone, R. A. 1976: *Environmental Controls: a Study of the Impact on Industries*. Lexington, Mass.: Lexington.
Leone A. and Struyk, R. 1976: The incubator hypothesis: evidence from five SMSAs. *Urban Studies*, 13, 325–31.
Leontief, W. W. 1951: *The Structure of the American Economy, 1919–1939*. New York: Oxford University.
Lerner, A. P. and Singer, H. W. 1937: Some notes on duopoly and spatial competition. *Journal of Political Economy*, 45, 145–86.
Lever, W. F. 1975: Manufacturing decentralization and shifts in factor costs and external economies. In L. Collins and D. F. Walker (eds), *Locational Dynamics of Manufacturing Industry*, Chichester: Wiley, 295–324.
——1980: Manufacturing linkages, industrial dynamics and the transmission of growth. *Regional Science and Urban Economics*, 10, 491–502.
——1989: International comparative aspects of government intervention in local economic policy. In D. Gibbs (ed.) *Government Policy and Industrial Change*. London: Routledge, 209–31.
——(ed.) 1987: *Industrial Change in the United Kingdom*. Harlow: Longman.
Lever, W. F. and Moore, C. (eds) 1986: *The City in Transition: Policies and Agencies for the Economic Regeneration of Clydeside*. Oxford: Clarendon.
Linge, G. J. R., Karaska, G. J. H. and Hamilton, F. E. I. 1978: Appraisal of the Soviet TPC concept. *Soviet Geography Review and Translation*, 19, 681–97.
Lipietz, A. 1980: The structuration of space, the problem of land and spatial policy. In J. Carney, R. Hudson and J. R. Lewis (eds), *Regions in Crisis*, London: Croom Helm, 60–75.
Lloyd, M. G. and Botham, R. W. 1985: The ideology and implementation of enterprise zones in Britain. *Urban Law and Policy*, 7, 33–55.
Lloyd, P. E. and Dicken, P. 1977: *Location in Space: a Theoretical Approach to Economic Geography*. New York: Harper and Row.
——1983: The components of change in metropolitan areas: events in their corporate context. In J. B. Goddard and A. G. Champion (eds), *The Urban and Regional Transformation of Britain*, London: Methuen.
Lloyd, P. E. and Mason, C. M. 1978: Manufacturing in the inner city: a case study of Greater Manchester. *Institute of British Geographers Transactions (New Series)*, 3, 66–90.
——1984: Spatial variations in new firm formation in the United Kingdom: comparative evidence from Merseyside, Greater Manchester and South Hampshire. *Regional Studies*, 18, 207–220.

Lloyd, P. E. and Reeve, D. E. 1982: North west England 1971–1977: a study in industrial decline and economic restructuring. *Regional Studies*, 16, 345–59.

Lo, Fu Chen and Salih, K. 1978: *Growth Pole Strategy and Regional Development: Asian Experiences and Alternative Approaches*. Oxford: Pergamon.

Locksley, G. and Ward, T. 1979: Concentration in manufacturing in the EEC. *Cambridge Journal of Economics*, 3, 91–7.

Logan, M. I. 1970: Location decisions in industrial plants in Wisconsin. *Land Economics*, 46, 325–8.

Lonsdale, R. E. and Seyler, H. L. (eds) 1979: *Nonmetropolitan Industrialization*. Washington DC: Winston.

Lösch, A. 1954: *The Economics of Location*. New Haven: Yale University Press.

Lowe, J. C. and Moryadas, S. 1975: *The Geography of Movement*. Boston: Houghton Mifflin.

Lund, L. 1986: *Locating Corporate R and D Facilities*. New York: The Conference Board Inc.

Luttrell, W. F. 1962: *Factory Location and Industrial Movement: a Study of Recent Experiences in Great Britain*. London: National Institute of Economic and Social Research.

——1972: Industrial complexes and regional economic development in Canada. In A. Kuklinski (ed.), *Growth Poles and Growth Centres in Regional Planning*, Paris: Mouton, 243–62.

Lyons, B. R. 1980: A new measure of minimum efficient plant size in UK manufacturing industry. *Economica*, 47, 19–34.

Magee, S. P. 1977: Multinational corporations, the industry technology cycle and development. *Journal of World Trade Law*, 11, 297–321.

Malecki, E. J. 1979: Locational trends in R & D by large US corporations, 1965–1977. *Economic Geography*, 55, 309–23.

——1980: Corporate organization of R & D and the location of technological activities. *Regional Studies*, 14, 219–34.

——1981: Science, technology and regional economic development: review and prospects. *Research Policy*, 10, 312–34.

——1982: Federal R and D spending in the United States of America: some impacts on metropolitan economies. *Regional Studies*, 16, 19–35.

——1983: Technology and regional development: a survey. *International Regional Science Review*, 8, 89–126.

——1984: High technology and local economic development. *APA Journal*, 262–9.

——1988: Industrial location and corporate organization in high technology industries. *Economic Geography*, 61, 345–69.

Manners, G., Keeble, D., Rodgers, H. B. and Warren, K. (eds), 1980: *Regional Development in Britain*, 2nd edn, Chichester: Wiley.

Manners, I. and Rudzitis, G. 1981: Federal air quality legislation: implications for land-use. In G. Hoffman (ed.), *Federalism and Regional Development*, Austin, Tx.: University of Texas, 429–527.

Mansfield, E. 1968: *Technological Change*. New York: Norton.

Mansfield, E., Rappoport, J., Romeo, A., Villano, E., Wagner, S. and Husic, F. 1977: *The Production and Application of New Industrial Technology*. New York: Norton.

March, J. G. and Simon, H. A. 1958: *Organizations*. New York: Wiley.

Marquand, J. 1983: The changing distribution of service employment. In J. B. Goddard and A. G. Champion (eds), *The Urban and Regional Transformation of Britain*, London: Methuen, 99–134.

Marshall, J. N. 1979: Ownership, organization and industrial linkage: a case study of the northern region of England. *Regional Studies*, 13, 531–57.

——1982: Organizational theory and industrial location. *Environment and Planning A*, 14, 1667–83.

Martin, R. 1988: The political economy of Britain's North–South divide. *Transactions, Institute of British Geographers, (New Series)*, 13, 389–418.

Martin, R. and Rowthorn, B. (eds) 1986: *The Geography of Deindustrialisation*. London: Macmillan.

Mason, C. M. 1981: Manufacturing decentralization: some evidence from Greater Manchester. *Environment and Planning A*, 13, 869–84.

——1987: The small firm sector. In E. F. Lever (ed.), *Industrial Change in the United Kingdom*. Harlow: Longman, 125–48.

Mason, C. M. and Harrison, R. T. 1985: The geography of small firms in the United Kingdom: towards a research agenda. *Progress in Human Geography*, 9, 1–37.

Massey, D. 1977: *Industrial Location Theory Reconsidered*. Course D204, Unit 26. Milton Keynes: Open University.

——1979a: A critical evaluation of industrial location theory. In F. E. I. Hamilton and G. J. R. Linge (eds), *Spatial Analysis, Industry and the Industrial Environment. Volume I: Industrial Systems*, Chichester: Wiley, 57–72.

——1979b: In what sense a regional problem? *Regional Studies*, 13, 233–43.

——1984: *Spatial Divisions of Labour*. London: Macmillan.

Massey, D. and Meegan, R. 1978: Industrial restructuring versus the cities. *Urban Studies*, 15, 273–88.

——1979: The geography of industrial reorganisation: the spatial effects of the restructuring of the electrical engineering sector under the Industrial Reorganisation Corporation. *Progress in Planning*, 10, 155–237.

——1982: *The Anatomy of Job Loss*. London: Methuen.

Mawson, J. and Miller, D. 1986: Interventionist approaches in local employment and economic development: the experience of Labour local authorities. In V. Hausner (ed.), *Critical Issues in Urban Economic Development (Vol. 1)*, Oxford: Clarendon.

McCrone, G. 1969: *Regional Policy in Britain*. London: Allen and Unwin.

McDermott, P. J. 1973: Spatial margins and industrial location in New Zealand. *New Zealand Geographer*, 29, 64–74.

McFarland, G. M. Jr. 1981: Survey of existing industry strategies used in Mississippi. *AEDC Journal*, 14, 48–61.

McKay, R. R. and Thomson, L. 1979: Important trends in regional policy and regional employment: a modified interpretation. *Scottish Journal of Political Economy*, 26, 233–60.

McKie, J. W. (ed.) 1974: *Social Responsibility and the Business Predicament.* Washington DC: Brookings Institution.

McKinnon, A. C. 1983: The development of warehousing in England. *Geoforum,* 14, 389–99.

——1989: *Physical Distribution Systems.* London: Routledge.

McMillan, T. E. Jr. 1965: Why manufacturers choose plant location vs determinants of plant locations. *Land Economics,* 43, 239–46.

McNee, R. B. 1960: Towards a more humanistic geography: the geography of enterprise. *Tijdschrift voor Economische en Sociale Geografie,* 51, 201–6.

——1974: A systems approach to understanding the geographic behaviour of organizations, especially large corporations. In F. E. I. Hamilton (ed.), *Spatial Perspectives on Industrial Organization and Decision Making,* London: Wiley, 47–76.

McRobie, G. 1982: *Small is Possible.* Aylesbury: Abacus.

Meeks, G. and Whittington, G. 1975: Giant companies in the UK 1948–1969. *Economic Journal,* 85, 824–43.

Meyer-Krahmer, F. 1985: Innovation behaviour and regional indigenous potential. *Regional Studies,* 19, 523–34.

Miernyk, W. H. 1965: *The Elements of Input–Output Analysis.* New York: Random House.

Miller, D. W. and Starr, M. K. 1967: *The Structure of Human Decisions.* Englewood Cliffs, NJ: Prentice-Hall.

Miller, E. W. 1981: Variation of productivity, wages and profitability with location. *Review of Regional Studies,* 11, 27–41.

Mock, D. 1976: *Economic Linkages of the Communication-oriented Industries in Metropolitan Toronto.* Toronto: City of Toronto Planning Board.

Moore, B. and Rhodes, J. 1973: Evaluating the effects of British regional economic policy. *Economic Journal,* 83, 87–110.

——1976: Regional economic policy and the movement of manufacturing firms to the development areas. *Economica,* 43, 17–31.

Moore, C. W. 1973: Industrial linkage development paths: a case study of the development of two industrial complexes in the Puget Sound region. *Tijdschrift voor Economische en Sociale Geografie,* 64, 93–107.

Moran, T. H. 1979: Foreign expansion as an institutional necessity for US corporate capitalism. In A. Mack, D. Plant and U. Doyle (eds), *Imperialism, Intervention and Economic Development,* London: Croom Helm.

Moriarty, B. M. 1980: *Industrial Location and Community Development.* Chapel Hill, NC: University of North Carolina Press.

——1983: Hierarchies of cities and the spatial filtering of industrial development. *Papers of the Regional Science Association,* 53, 59–82.

Moroney, J. H. and Walker, J. M. 1966: A regional test of the Heckscher–Ohlin hypothesis. *Journal of Political Economy,* 74, 573–86.

Morrison, J. L., Scripter, M. W. and Smith, R. H. T. 1968: Basic measures of manufacturing in the United States 1958. *Economic Geography,* 44, 296–311.

Moseley, M. 1974: *Growth Centres in Spatial Planning.* Oxford: Pergamon.

Mueller, E. and Morgan, J. N. 1962: Location decisions of manufacturers. *American Economic Review, Papers and Proceedings,* 502, 204–17.

Muller, E. K. and Groves, P. A. 1979: The emergence of industrial districts in mid-nineteenth-century Baltimore. *Geographical Review*, 69, 159–78.

Müller, R. 1973: The multinational corporation and the underdevelopment of the Third World. In C. K. Wilber (ed.), *The Political Economy of Development and Underdevelopment*. New York: Random House, 124–51.

Mulligan, G. J. 1984: Agglomeration and central place theory: a review of the literature. *International Regional Science Review*, 9, 1–42.

Myrdal, G. 1956: *Economic Theory and Underdeveloped Regions*. London: Methuen.

National Science Foundation 1988: *Geographic Distribution of Industrial R and D Performance*. Washington DC: NSF 88–317.

NEDC 1985: *British Industrial Performance*. London: National Economic Development Office.

Nelson, J. R. 1973: Transportation pricing and costs. In M. L. Fair and J. R. Nelson (eds), *Criteria for Transport Pricing*. Cambridge, Mass.: Cornell Maritime Press.

Nevins, A. and Hill, F. E. 1954: *Ford: The Times, The Man, The Company*. New York: Scribner.

——1957: *Ford: Expansion and Challenge, 1915–1933*. New York: Scribner.

——1963: *Ford: Decline and Rebirth, 1933–1962*. New York: Scribner.

Newbould, G. 1970: *Management and Merger Activity*. Liverpool: Guthstead.

Nicholas, J. C. 1974: Industrial location: the special case of Florida. *Review of Regional Studies*, 4, 27–33.

Nigeria, Federal Office of Statistics 1967: *Industrial Survey of Nigeria, 1966*. Lagos.

Nishioka, H. and Krumme, G. 1973: Location conditions, factors and decisions: an evaluation of selected location surveys. *Land Economics*, 49, 195–205.

Norcliffe, G. B. 1975: A theory of manufacturing places. In L. Collins and D. F. Walker (eds), *Locational Dynamics of Manufacturing Industry*, Chichester: Wiley, 19–57.

——1979: Identifying local industrial complexes. *Canadian Journal of Regional Science*, 2, 25–36.

——1984a: Industrial specialization versus industrial diversification: an assessment of policy alternatives. In B. M. Barr and N. G. Waters (eds), *Regional Diversification and Structural Change*, Vancouver: Tantalus, 7–24.

——1984b: Nonmetropolitan industrialization and the theory of production. *Urban Geography*, 5, 25–42.

——1985: The industrial geography of the Third World. In M. Pacione (ed.), *Progress in Industrial Geography*, London: Croom Helm, 249–83.

Norcliffe, G. B. and Hoare, A. G. 1982: Enterprise zone policy for the inner city: a review and preliminary assessment. *Area*, 14, 265–74.

Norcliffe, G. B. and Kotseff, L. E. 1980: Local industrial complexes in Ontario. *Annals Association of American Geographers*, 70, 68–79.

Norcliffe, G. B. and Stevens, J. H. 1979: The Hekscher–Ohlin hypothesis and structural divergence in Quebec and Ontario, 1961–1964. *Canadian Geographer*, 23, 239–54.

Norman, G. 1981: Uniform pricing as an optimal spatial pricing policy. *Economica*, 48, 87–91.

North, D. and Leigh, R. 1984: Alternative approaches to urban economic policy: the case of London. In B. M. Barr and N. M. Waters (eds), *Regional Diversification and Structural Change*, Vancouver: Tantalus, 185–207.

North, D. C. 1981: *Structure and Change in Economic History*. New York: Norton.

North, D. J. 1974: The process of locational change in different manufacturing organizations. In F. E. I. Hamilton (ed.), *Spatial Perspectives in Industrial Organization and Decision Making*. London: Wiley, 213–44.

Norton, R. D. and Rees, J. 1979: The product cycle and the spatial decentralization of American manufacturing. *Regional Studies*, 13, 141–51.

Noyelle, T. J. and Stanback, T. M. 1984: *The Economic Transformation of American Cities*, Totowa, NJ: Rowman and Allanheld.

Oakey, R. P. 1984: *High Technology and Small Firms: Regional Development in Britain and the US*. London: Frances Pinter.

Oakey, R. P., Thwaites, A. T. and Nash, P. A. 1980: The regional distribution of innovative manufacturing establishments in Britain. *Regional Studies*, 14, 235–54.

OECD 1977: *Regional Problems and Policies in OECD Countries* (vol. 2) Paris: OECD.

——1981: *North–South Technology Transfer: the Way Ahead*. Paris: OECD.

——1983a: *Industry in Transition*. Paris: OECD.

——1983b: *Long Term Outlook for the World Automobile Industry*. Paris: OECD.

——1983c: *Textile and Clothing Industries: Structural Problems and Policies in OECD Countries*. Paris: OECD.

——1983d: *Telecommunications: Pressures and Policies for Change*. Paris: OECD.

——1985: *Petrochemical Industry: Energy Aspects of Structural Change*. Paris: OECD.

——1988: *The Newly Industrialising Countries*. Paris: OECD.

Olsen, E. 1971: *International Trade Theory and Regional Income Differences*. Amsterdam: North–Holland.

Onyemelukwe, J. O. C. 1978: Structural and locational characteristics of manufacturing. In J. S. Oguntoyinbo (ed.), *A Geography of Nigerian Development*, Ibadan: Heinemann, 261–75.

O'Riordan, T. 1976: *Environmentalism*. London: Pion.

Osleeb, J. and Cromley, R. G. 1978: The location of plants of the uniform delivered price manufacturer: a case study of Coca Cola Ltd. *Economic Geography*, 54, 40–52.

Österreichische Raumplanungskonferenz 1978: *Regional Planning in Austria*. Vienna.

Owens, P. R. 1980: Direct foreign investment and some spatial implications for the source economy. *Tijdschrift voor Economische en Sociale Geografie*, 71, 50–62.

Pacione, M. (ed.) 1985: *Progress in Industrial Geography*. London: Croom Helm.

Pallot, J. and Shaw, D. J. B. 1981: *Planning in the Soviet Union*. London:

Croom Helm.

Palme, G. 1984: Standortanforderungen und regionalwirtschaftliche Wirkungen industrieller Betriebsgründungen am. Beispiel der Obersteiermark. In W. Blaas, G. Rusch and W. Schonback (eds) *Regionalökonomische Analysen für österreich*, Vienna: Wirtschaftsverlag Orac.

Park, S. O. and Wheeler, J. O. 1983: The filtering down process in Georgia: the third stage in the product life cycle. *Professional Geographer*, 35, 18–31.

Pavitt, K. (ed.) 1980: *Technical Innovation and British Economic Performance*. London: Macmillan.

Peck, F. 1988: *Manufacturing Linkages in Tyne and Wear*. Tyne and Wear Countrywide Research and Intelligence Unit.

Peck, F. and Townsend, A. 1984: Contrasting experience of recession and restructuring: British Shipbuilders, Plessey and Metal Box. *Regional Studies*, 18, 319–38.

Peet, R. 1983: Relations of production and the relocation of United States manufacturing industry since 1960. *Economic Geography*, 59, 112–43.

Peltz, M. and Weiss, M. A. 1984: State and local government roles in industrial innovation. *American Planning Association Journal*. summer, 270–9.

Penrose, E. 1959: *The Theory of the Growth of the Firm*. Oxford: Blackwell.

Perrons, D. C. 1981: The role of Ireland in the new international division of labour: a proposed framework for regional analysis. *Regional Studies*, 15, 81–100.

Perroux, F. 1950: Economic space: theory and applications. *Quarterly Journal of Economics*, 64, 89–104.

——1961: *L'économie de XXee siècle*. Paris: Presses Universitaires de France.

Peterson, J. E. 1979: The role of the city in the region's economy. In B. Chinitz (ed.), *Central City Economic Development*, Cambridge, Mass.: Abt Books, 150–60.

Peterson, R. 1977: *Small Business: Building a Balanced Economy*. Erin, Ontario: Press Porcepic.

Pollard, S. 1981: *Peaceful Conquest: the Industrialization of Europe 1760–1970*. Oxford: Oxford University Press.

Pondy, L. R. 1969: Effects of size, complexity and ownership on administrative intensity. *Administrative Science Quarterly*, 14, 47–61.

Pounce, R. J. 1981: *Industrial Movement in the United Kingdom 1966–1975*. London: HMSO.

Prais, S. J. 1976: *The Evolution of Giant Firms in Britain*. Cambridge: NIESR.

Pred, A. R. 1965: Industrialization, initial advantage and American metropolitan growth. *Geographical Review*, 158–85.

——1966: *The Spatial Dynamics of US Urban-industrial Growth, 1800–1914: Interpretative and Theoretical Essays*. Cambridge, Mass.: MIT Press.

——1967: *Behaviour and Location: Foundations for a Geographic and Dynamic Location Theory, Part 1*. Lund Studies in Geography, Series B, 27.

——1969: *Behaviour and Location: Foundations for a Geographic and Dynamic Theory, Part 2*. Lund Studies in Geography, Series B, 28.

——1974: *Major Job Providing Organizations and Systems of Cities*. Washington DC: Association of American Geographers. Commission on College Geography resource paper 27.

——1977: *City-Systems in Advanced Economies.* London: Hutchinson.

Randall, J. E. 1983: *Metropolitan Vancouver: Industrial Decentralization and Port Activity on the Lower Fraser River.* Working Party 12, University of Toronto/York University Joint Program in Transportation.

Rawstron, E. M. 1958: Three principles of industrial location. *Institute of British Geographers, Transactions and Papers,* 25, 132–42.

Ray, D. M. 1965: *Market Potential and Economic Shadow.* Chicago: University of Chicago, Department of Geography.

——1971: The Location of United States' manufacturing subsidiaries in Canada. *Economic Geography,* 47, 389–400.

Razin, E. 1988: Ownership structure and linkage patterns of industry in Israel's development towns. *Regional Studies,* 22, 19–31.

Reader, W. J. 1970: *Imperial Chemical Industries: a history. Volume 1: The Forerunners 1870–1926.* London: Oxford University Press.

——1975: *Imperial Chemical Industries: a history. Volume 2: The First Quarter Century, 1926–1952.* London: Oxford University Press.

Rees, J. 1972: The industrial corporation and location decision analysis. *Area,* 4, 199–204.

——1974: Decision making, the growth of the firm and the business environment. In F. E. I. Hamilton (ed.), *Spatial Perspectives in Industrial Organization and Decision Making,* London: Wiley, 189–212.

——1978a: On the spatial spread and oligopolistic behaviour of large rubber companies. *Geoforum,* 9, 319–30.

——1978b: Manufacturing headquarters in a post-industrial urban context. *Economic Geography,* 54, 337–54.

——1979: Technological change and regional shifts in American manufacturing. *Professional Geographer,* 31, 45–54.

——1983: Government policy and industrial location. In J. W. House (ed.) *United States Public Policy: a Geographical View,* Oxford: Clarendon, 213–62.

Rees, J., Hewings, G. J. D. and Stafford, H. A. 1981: *Industrial Location and Regional Systems.* New York: Bergin.

Rees, J. and Weinstein, B. L. 1983: Government policy and industrial location. In J. W. House (ed.), *United States Public Policy: a Geographical View,* Oxford: Clarendon, 213–62.

Regional Studies Association (UK) 1983: *Report of an Inquiry into Regional Problems in the United Kingdom.* Norwich: Geo Books.

Rich, D. C. 1983: The Scottish Development Agency and the industrial regeneration of Scotland. *Geographical Review,* 73, 271–86.

Richards, S. 1981: Industrial activities in the periphery: Hong Kong. In F. E. I. Hamilton and G. J. R. Linge (eds), *Spatial Analysis, Industry and the Industrial Environment. Volume II: International Industrial Systems,* Chichester: Wiley, 465–80.

Robinson, E. A. G. 1931: *The Structure of Competitive Industry.* Welwyn: Nisbet.

Rodgers, A. 1979: *Economic Development in Retrospect: the Italian Model and*

its Significance for Regional Planning in Market-orientated Economies.
Washington DC: Winston.

——1985: The state as entrepreneur: its role in the regional industrial development of the Italian Mezzogiorno. In C. R. Bryant (ed.), *Waterloo Lectures in Geography. Volume 1: Regional Economic Development.* Waterloo: University of Waterloo, Department of Geography.

Roepke, H., Adams, D. and Wiseman, R. 1974: A new approach to the identification of industrial complexes using input–output data. *Journal of Regional Science,* 14, 15–29.

Rosenberg, N. 1972: *Technology and American Economic Growth.* New York: Harper and Row.

Rosenberg, N. 1976: *Perspectives on Technology.* Cambridge: Cambridge University Press.

Rostow, W. W. 1960: *The Stages of Economic Growth.* Cambridge: Cambridge University Press.

——1962: *The Process of Economic Growth,* 2nd edn, New York: Norton.

——1978: *The World Economy: History and Prospect.* London: Macmillan.

Roth, P. W. (ed.) 1984: *Erz und Eisen in der Grünen Mark. Beiträge zum Steirischen Eisenwesen.* Graz: Styria Verlag.

Roux, J. M. 1980: Industrialization and regional disparities. In D. F. Walker (ed.), *The Human Dimension in Industrial Development,* University of Waterloo, Department of Geography, 71–97.

Rowthorn, B. and Wells, J. R. 1987: *Deindustrialisation and Foreign Trade: Britain's Decline in a Global Perspective.* Cambridge: Cambridge University Press.

Royal Commission on the Distribution of the Industrial Population 1940: *Report.* Cmd 6153. HMSO.

Rutt, S. 1986: The Soviet concept of the territorial production complex and regional development. *Town Planning Review,* 57, 425–39.

Sabel, C. F. 1982: *Work and Politics.* Cambridge: Cambridge University Press.

Sachs, I. 1977: *Environment and Development. A new Rationale for Domestic Formulation and International Co-operation Strategies.* Ottawa: Environment Canada and Canadian International Development Agency.

Sandbach, F. R. 1980: *Environment, Ideology and Policy.* Oxford: Blackwell.

Sant, M. E. C. 1975: *Industrial Movement and Regional Development: the British Case.* Oxford: Pergamon.

Sargent, J. 1987: Industrial location in Japan with special reference to the semi conductor industry. *Geographical Journal,* 153, 72–85.

Savey, S. 1983: Organization of production and the new spatial division of labour in France. In F. E. I. Hamilton and G. J. R. Linge (eds), *Spatial Analysis, Industry and the Industrial Environment. Volume III: Regional Economies and Industrial Systems,* Chichester: Wiley, 103–20.

Savoie, D. J. 1986: *Regional Economic Development: Canada's Search for Solutions.* Toronto: University of Toronto Press.

Saxenian, A. 1985: The genesis of Silicon Valley. In P. Hall and A. Markusen (eds), *Silicon Landscapes.* Boston: Allen and Unwin, 20–34.

Schatz, S. P. 1977: *Nigerian Capitalism.* Berkeley: University of California Press.

Schmenner, R. 1980: Choosing new industrial capacity: on site expansion, branching and relocation. *Quarterly Journal of Economics*, 95, 103–19.
Schmenner, R. W. 1982: *Making Business Location Decisions*. Englewood Cliffs, NJ: Prentice–Hall.
Schoenberger, E. 1987: Technological and organizational change in automobile production: spatial implications. *Regional Studies*, 21, 199–214.
——1988a: From Fordism to flexible accumulation: technology, competitive strategies and international location. *Environment and Planning D: Society and Space*: 6, 245–62.
——1988b: Multinational corporations and the new international division of labour. *International Regional Science Review*, 11, 105–20.
——1989: Thinking about flexibility: a response to Gertler. *Transactions, Institute of British Geographers (New Series)*. 14, 98–108.
Schofield, J. A. 1979: Macro-evaluations of the impact of regional policy in Britain. *Urban Studies*, 16, 251–69.
Schofield, R. 1963: *The Lunar Society of Birmingham*. Oxford: Clarendon Press.
Schumacher, E. F. 1974: *Small is Beautiful*. London: Abacus.
Schumpeter, J. A. 1934: *The Theory of Economic Development*. Cambridge, Mass.: Harvard University Press.
Science Council of Canada 1980: *Multinationals and Industrial Strategy: the Role of World Product Mandates*. Ottawa: Supply and Services.
Science Council of Canada 1981: *Hard Times, Hard Choices*. Ottawa.
Scott, A. J. 1981: The spatial structure of metropolitan labour markets and the theory of intra-urban plant location. *Urban Geography*, 2, 1–30.
——1982a: Locational patterns and dynamics of industrial activity in the modern metropolis. *Urban Studies*, 19, 111–42.
——1982b: Production system dynamics and metropolitan development. *Annals, Association of American Geographers*, 72, 185–200.
——1983a: Industrial organization and the logic of intrametropolitan location. I: Theoretical considerations. *Economic Geography*, 59, 233–50.
——1983b: Industrial organization and the logic of intrametropolitan location. II: A case study of the printed circuits industry in the Greater Los Angeles region. *Economic Geography*, 59, 343–67.
——1984: Industrial organization and the logic of intrametropolitan location. III: A case study of the women's dress industry in the Greater Los Angeles region. *Economic Geography*, 60, 3–27.
——1987: The semi-conductor industry in South-East Asia: organization, location and the international division of labour. *Regional Studies*, 21, 143–60.
——1988: *Metropolis: from the Division of Labour to Urban Form*. Berkeley and Los Angeles: University of California Press.
Scott, J. 1979: *Corporations, Classes and Capitalism*. London: Hutchinson.
Scouller, J. 1987: The United Kingdom merger boom in perspective. *National Westminster Bank Quarterly Review*, May, 14–30.
Seers, D. (ed.) 1981: *Dependency Theory: a Critical Reassessment*. London: Frances Pinter.

Seers, D., Schaffer, P. and Kiljunen, M. 1979: *Underdeveloped Europe: Studies in Core–periphery Relations*. Hassocks, Sussex: Harvester Press.

Segal, Quince and Partners 1985: *The Cambridge Phenomenon: the Growth of High-technology Industry in a University Town*. Cambridge.

Sellgren, J. 1989: Assisting local economies: an assessment of emerging patterns of local authority economic development activities. In D. R. Gibbs (ed.), *Government Policy and Industrial Change*, London: Routledge, 232–65.

Semple, R. K. and Smith, W. R. 1981: Metropolitan dominance and foreign ownership in the Canadian urban system. *Canadian Geographer*, 25, 4–26.

Servah–Schreiber, J. J. 1968: *The American Challenge*. New York: Atheneum.

Sewel, J. (ed.) 1979: *The Promise and the Reality: Large Scale Development in Marginal Regions*. Aberdeen: Institute for the Study of Sparsely Populated Areas, Aberdeen University.

Shalit, S. S. and Sankar, U. 1977: The measurement of firm size. *Review of Economics and Statistics*, 59, 290–8.

Shaw, R. N. and Shaw, S. A. 1983: Excess capacity and rationalisation in the West European synthetic fibres industry. *Journal of Industrial Economics*, 32, 149–66.

Sheard, P. 1983: Auto-production systems in Japan: organisational and locational features. *Australian Geographical Studies*, 21, 49–68.

Sillince, J. A. 1987: Regional Policy in Hungary: objectives and achievements. *Transactions, Institute of British Geographers (New Series)*, 12, 451–64.

Simon, H. A. 1957a: *Administrative Behaviour*. New York: Theatre Press.

——1957b: *Models of Man*. New York: Wiley.

——1959: Theories of decision-making in economics and behavioural science. *American Economic Review*, 49, 253–83.

——1960: *The New Science of Management Decision*. New York: Harper and Row.

Sinclair, R. and Walker, D. F. 1982: Industrial development via the multinational corporation: General Motors in Vienna. *Regional Studies*, 16, 433–43.

Singleton, F. (ed.) 1976: *Environmental Misuse in the Soviet Union*. New York: Praeger.

Slater, D. 1975: Underdevelopment and spatial inequality. *Progress in Planning*, 4(2), 97–167.

Smith, D. M. 1966: A theoretical framework for geographical studies of industrial location. *Economic Geography*, 42, 95–113.

——1977: *Human Geography: a Welfare Approach*. London: Edward Arnold.

——1981: *Industrial Location: an Economic Geographical Analysis*, 2nd edn, New York: Wiley.

Smith, W. 1955: The location of industry. *Institute of British Geographers, Transactions*, 21, 1–18.

Souza, A. de and Porter, P. 1974: *The Underdevelopment and Modernization of the Third World*. Washington, Association of American Geographers.

Spitz, P. H. and Weiss, L. H. 1979: Changing locations of the chemical industry. *Chemical Economy and Engineering Review*, 11, 12–16.

Spooner, D. J. 1974: Some qualitative aspects of industrial movement in a problem region in the UK. *Town Planning Review*, 45, 63–83.

Soja, E., Morales, R. and Wolff, G. 1983: Urban restructuring: an analysis of social and spatial change in Los Angeles. *Economic Geography*, 59, 195–230.

South, R. B. 1986: Environmental legislation and the locational process. *Geographical Review*, 76, 20–34.

Stafford, H. A. 1969: An industrial location decision model. *Proceedings, Association of American Geographers*, 1, 141–5.

——1972: The geography of manufacturing. *Progress in Geography*, 4, 183–215.

——1974: The anatomy of the location decision: content analysis of case studies. In F. E. I. Hamilton (ed.), *Spatial Perspectives on Industrial Organization and Decision Making*, London: Wiley, 169–87.

——1977: Environmental regulations and the location of US manufacturing: speculations. *Geoforum*, 8, 243–8.

——1979: *Principles of Industrial Facility Location*. Atlanta, Ga: Conway Publishing.

——1985: Environmental protection and industrial location. *Annals, Association of American Geographers*, 75, 227–40.

——1989: Geographic implications of plant closure legislation in the US. In D. Gibbs (ed.), *Government Policy and Industrial Change*. London: Routledge, 95–116.

Steed, G. 1970: Changing linkages and internal multiplier of an industrial complex. *Canadian Geographer*, 3, 229–42.

——1971: Internal organization, firm integration and locational change: the Northern Ireland linen complex 1954–1964. *Economic Geography*, 47, 371–83.

——1974: The Northern Ireland linen complex, 1960–1970. *Annals, Association of American Geographers*, 64, 397–408.

——1976a: Centrality and locational change: printing, publishing and clothing in Montreal and Toronto. *Economic Geography*, 52, 193–205.

——1976b: Locational factors and dynamics of Montreal's large garment complex. *Tijdschrift voor Economische en Sociale Geografie*, 67, 151–68.

——1976c: Standardization, scale, incubation, and intertia: Montreal and Toronto clothing industries. *Canadian Geographer*, 20, 298–309.

Steiner, M. 1985: Old industrial areas: a theoretical approach. *Urban Studies*, 22, 387–98.

Steiner, M. and Posch, U. 1985: Problems of structural adaptation in old industrial areas: a factor analytical approach. *Environment and Planning A*, 17, 1127–39.

Stephens, J. D. and Holly, B. P. 1981: City system behaviour and corporate influence: the headquarters location of US industrial firms, 1955–1975. *Urban Studies*, 18, 285–300.

Stevens, B. 1961: An application of game theory to a problem in location strategy. *Papers and Proceedings, Regional Science Association*, 7, 143–57.

Stoneman, P. 1978: Merger and technological progressiveness: the case of the British computer industry. *Applied Economics*, 10, 125–40.

Stopford, J. M. and Wells, L. T. 1972: *Managing the Multinational Enterprise: Organisation of the Firm and Ownership of Subsidiaries*. London: Longman.

Storey, D. J. 1982: *Entrepreneurship and the New Firm*. London: Croom Helm.

Storper, M. 1981: Towards a structural theory of industrial location. In J. Rees, G. J. D. Hewings and H. A. Stafford (eds), *Industrial Location and Regional Systems*. New York: Bergin, 17–40.

——1985: Oligopoly and the product cycle: essentialism in economic geography. *Economic Geography*, 61, 260–82.

Storper, M. and Walker, R. 1983: The theory of labour and the theory of location. *International Journal of Urban and Regional Research*, 7, 1–43.

——1989: *The Capitalist Imperative: Territory, Technology and Industrial Growth*. Oxford: Blackwell.

Storper, M., Walker, R. and Widess, E. 1981: Performance regulation and industrial location: a case study. *Environment and Planning A*, 13, 321–38.

Strickland, D. and Aiken, M. 1984: Corporate influence and the German urban system: headquarters locations of German industrial corporations, 1950–1982. *Economic Geography*, 60, 38–54.

Sung Cho, D. and Porter, M. E. 1986: Changing global industry leadership: the case of shipbuilding. In M. E. Porter (ed.), *Competition in Global Industries*, Boston, Mass.: Harvard Business School Press, 539–67.

Susman, P. and Schutz, E. 1983: Monopoly and competitive firm relations and regional development in global capitalism. *Economic Geography*, 59, 161–77.

Taylor, G. D. and Sudnik, P. E. 1984: *Du Pont and the International Chemical Industry*. Boston, Mass.: G. K. Hall.

Taylor, M. 1986: The product cycle model: a critique. *Environment and Planning A*, 18, 751–61.

Taylor, M. J. 1970: Location decisions of small firms. *Area*, 51–4.

——1975: Organizational growth, spatial interaction and location decision making. *Regional Studies*, 9, 313–23.

——1984: *The Geography of Australian Corporate Power*. London: Croom Helm.

Taylor, M. J. and McDermott, P. 1982: *Industrial Organization and Location*. Cambridge: Cambridge University Press.

Taylor, M. J. and Thrift, N. 1982a: *The Geography of Multinationals*. London: Croom Helm.

——1982b: Industrial linkage and the segmented economy. 1: some theoretical proposals. *Environment and Planning A*, 14, 1601–13.

——1982c: Models of corporate development and the multinational corporation. In M. J. Taylor and N. J. Thrift (eds), *The Geography of Multinationals*. London: Croom Helm, 14–32.

——1983a: Business organization segmentation and location. *Regional Studies*, 17, 445–65.

——1983b: The role of finance in the evolution and functioning of industrial systems. In F. E. I. Hamilton and G. J. R. Linge (eds), *Spatial Analysis, Industry and the Industrial Environment. Volume III: Regional Economies and Industrial Systems*, Chichester: Wiley, 359–85.

Teulings, A. W. M. 1984: The internationalization squeeze: double capital movement and job transfer within Philips worldwide. *Environment and Planning A*, 16, 597–614.

Thomas, D. B. 1975: *Capital Accumulation and Technology Transfer: a Comparative Analysis of Nigerian Manufacturing Industries*. New York: Praeger.

Thomas, H. and Logan, C. 1982: *Mondragon: an Economic Analysis*. London: Allen and Unwin.

Thomas, M. D. 1980: Explanatory frameworks for growth and change in multi-regional firms. *Economic Geography*, 56, 1–17.

——1981a: Growth and change in the innovative firm. *Geoforum*, 12, 1–17.

——1981b: Industry perspectives on growth and change in the manufacturing sector. In J. Rees, G. J. D. Hewings and H. A. Stafford (eds), *Industrial Location and Regional Systems*. New York: Bergin, 41–58.

Thornton, C. A. and Koepke, R. L. 1981: Federal legislation, clean air and local industry. *Geographical Review*, 71, 324–39.

Thwaites, A. T. 1978: Technological change, mobile plants and regional development. *Regional Studies*, 12, 445–61.

Tichy, G. 1984: Ein regionales Aktionsprogramm zur endogenen Entwicklung der Obsteiermark. In W. Blaas, G. Rusch and W. Schonback (eds), *Regionalökonomische Analysen für österreich*. Vienna: Wirtschaftverlag Orac, 205–22.

Tiebout, C. M. 1957a: Location theory, empirical evidence and economic evolution. *Papers and Proceedings, Regional Science Association*, 3, 74–86.

——1957b: Regional and interregional input–output models: an appraisal. *Southern Economic Journal*, 24, 240–7.

Todd, D. 1984: Strategies of growth, diversification and rationalization in the evolution of concentration in British shipbuilding. *Regional Studies*, 18, 55–67.

——1985: *The World Shipbuilding Industry*. London: Croom Helm.

Tödtling, F. 1984: Organizational characteristics of plants in core and peripheral regions in Austria. *Regional Studies*, 18, 397–411.

Toffler, A. 1985: *The Adaptive Corporation*. London: Pan.

Tornquist, G. 1970: *Contact Systems and Regional Development*. Lund Studies in Geography Series B, 35. Lund: CWK Gleerup.

——1973: Contact requirements and travel facilities. In A. R. Pred and G. E. Tornquist (eds), *Systems of Cities and Information Flows*. Lund: GWK Gleerup, 83–121.

——1977: The geography of economic activities: some critical viewpoints on theory and application. *Economic Geography*, 53, 153–62.

Townroe, P. M. 1969: Locational choice and the individual firm. *Regional Studies*, 3, 15–24.

——1971: *Industrial Location Decisions*. University of Birmingham Centre for Urban and Regional Studies, occasional paper 15.

——1972: Some behavioural considerations in the industrial location decision. *Regional Studies*, 6, 261–72.

——1976: *Planning Industrial Location*. London: Leonard Hill.

Townsend, A. R. 1983: *The Impact of Recession*. London: Croom Helm.

Tucker, I. B. and Wilder, R. P. 1977: Trends in vertical integration in the US manufacturing sector. *Journal of Industrial Economics*, 26, 81–94.

Tugendhat, C. 1973: *The Multinationals.* Harmondsworth: Penguin.

Udhay-Sekhar, A. 1983: *Industrial Location Policy: the Indian Experience.* Washington, DC: World Bank.

United Kingdom, Business Statistics Office 1988: *Report on the Census of Production 1986: Summary Tables,* London: HMSO.

United Kingdom, HMSO 1978: *A Review of Monopolies and Merger Policy.* Cmnd 7198. London.

United Nations 1988: *Transnational Corporations in World Development: Trends and Prospects.* New York: United Nations.

United Nations Industrial Development Organization 1978: *First World-Wide Study on the Petrochemical Industry: 1975–2000.* Sectoral Studies Section, International Centre for Industrial Studies.

——1983: *Industry in a Changing World.* New York: United Nations.

——1985: *Industry in the 1980s: Structural Change and Interdependence.* New York: United Nations.

——1988a: *Handbook of Industrial Statistics.* Vienna UNIDO.

——1988b: *Industry and Development: Global Report 1988/89.* Vienna: UNIDO.

Utterback, J. M. and Abernathy, W. J. 1975: A dynamic model of process and product innovation. *Omega,* 3, 639–56.

Utton, M. A. 1971: The effect of mergers on concentration, UK manufacturing industry 1954–1965. *Journal of Industrial Economics,* 20, 42–58

——1979: *Diversification and Competition.* Cambridge: National Institute of Economic and Social Research.

Vernon, R. 1960: *Metropolis 1985.* Cambridge Mass: Harvard University Press.

——1966: International investment and international trade in the product cycle. *Quarterly Journal of Economics,* 80, 190–207.

——1978: *Storm Over the Multinationals.* New York: Harvard University Press.

Volgyes, I. (ed.) 1974: *Environmental Deterioration in the Soviet Union and Eastern Europe,* New York: Praeger.

Walker, D. F. 1975: A behavioural approach to industrial location. In L. Collins and D. F. Walker (eds), *Locational Dynamics of Manufacturing Activity,* Chichester: Wiley, 135–58.

——(ed.) 1977: *Industrial Services.* Waterloo: University of Waterloo, Department of Geography.

——1980a: *Canada's Industrial Space-Economy.* London: Bell and Hyman.

——(ed.) 1980b: *The Human Dimension in Industrial Development.* Waterloo: University of Waterloo, Department of Geography.

——(ed.) 1980c: *Planning Industrial Development.* Chichester: Wiley.

——1980d: Political aspects of regional industrial development. In D. F. Walker (ed.), *Planning Industrial Development,* Chichester: Wiley, 129–48.

——1983: Canadian regional development policy. In A. Hecht (ed.), *Regional Development in the Peripheries of Canada and Europe,* Winnipeg: University of Manitoba, Department of Geography, 116–36.

——1984a: Appropriate goals for development strategy. *Environments,* 16, 42–8.

———1984b: Innovation centres and research parks as an element of regional renewal with special reference to Waterloo. In B. M. Barr and N. M. Waters (eds), *Regional Diversification and Structural Change*, Vancouver: Tantalus, 232–42.

———1985: Innovation in regional development. In C. R. Bryant (ed.), *Waterloo Lectures in Geography. Volume 1: Regional Economic Development*, Waterloo: University of Waterloo, Department of Geography, 39–50.

Walker, D. F. and Collins, L. 1975: A perspective. In L. Collins and D. F. Walker (eds), *Locational Dynamics of Manufacturing Industry*, Chichester: Wiley, 1–18.

Walker, R. A. 1985: Technology determination and determinism: industrial growth and location. In M. Castells (ed.), *High Technology, Space and Society*. Berkeley: Sage, 226–64.

Walker, R. and Storper, M. 1981: Capital and industrial location. *Progress in Human Geography*, 5, 473–509.

Walter, I. 1975: A guide to social responsibility of the multinational enterprise. In J. Beckman (ed.), *Social Responsibility and Accountability*. New York: New York University Press.

———1976: *International Economics of Pollution*. London: Macmillan.

Walters, B. J. and Wheeler, J. O. 1984: Localization economies in the American carpet industry. *Geographical Review*, 74, 183–91.

Ward, M. F. 1982: Political economy, industrial location and the European motor car industry in the postwar period. *Regional Studies*, 16, 443–53.

Warren, K. 1973: *The American Steel Industry 1850–1970: a Geographical Interpretation*. Oxford: Clarendon.

———1978: Industrial complexes in the development of Siberia. *Geography*, 63, 167–78.

———1980: *Chemical Foundations: the Alkali Industry in Britain to 1926*. Oxford: Clarendon.

Watkins, M. 1963: A staple theory of economic growth. *Canadian Journal of Economics and Political Science*, 29, 141–58.

Watt, J. A. 1982: Historical aspects of uneven development: the Canadian case. In L. Collins (ed.), *Industrial Decline and Regeneration*. Edinburgh: University of Edinburgh, Dept of Geography and Centre for Canadian Studies, 127–45.

Watts, H. D. 1978: Inter-organisational relations and the location of industry. *Regional Studies*, 12, 215–25.

———1980a: Conflict and collusion in the British sugar industry, 1924 to 1928. *Journal of Historical Geography*, 6, 291–314.

———1980b: *The Large Industrial Enterprise*. London: Croom Helm.

———1981: *The Branch–Plant Economy: a Study of External Control*. London: Longman.

Webber, M. J. 1972: *Impact of Uncertainty on Location*. Cambridge, Mass.: MIT Press.

———1984: *Industrial Location*. Beverly Hills: Sage.

Weber, A. 1929: *Theory of the Location of Industries*, trans. C. J. Friedrich, Chicago: University of Chicago.

Weisskoff, R. and Wolff, E. 1977: Linkages and leakages: industrial tracking in an enclave economy. *Economic Development and Cultural Changes*, 35, 607–28.

Weston, J. F. 1961: *The Role of Mergers in the Growth of Large Firms*. Berkeley: University of California.

Wheeler, J. O. 1981: Effects of geographical scale on location decisions in manufacturing: the Atlanta example. *Economic Geography*, 57, 134–45.

White, L. J. 1981: What has been happening to aggregate concentration in the US? *Journal of Industrial Economics*, 29, 223–30.

White, R. L. and Watts, H. D. 1977: The spatial evolution of an industry: the example of broiler production. *Transactions, Institute of British Geographers*, (New Series), 2, 175–91.

Wilkins, M. 1986: The history of the European multinationals: a new look. *The Journal of European Economic History*, 15, 483–510.

Williams, G. (ed.) 1976: *Nigeria: Economy and Society*. London: Rex Collings.

Williamson, O. E. 1981: The modern corporation: origin, evolution, attributes. *Journal of Economic Literature*, 19, 1537–68.

Wilson, C. 1954: *The History of Unilever*, 2 vols, London: Cassell.

——1968: *Unilever 1945–1965*. London: Cassell.

Wise, M. J. 1949: On the evolution of the jewellery and gun quarters in Birmingham. *Transactions, Institute of British Geographers*, 15, 59–72.

——(ed.) 1950: *Birmingham and its Regional Setting*. Birmingham: British Association.

Wise, M. J. and Johnson, B. L. C. 1950: The changing regional pattern during the eighteenth century. In M. J. Wise (ed.), *Birmingham and Its Regional Setting*, Birmingham: British Association, 161–86.

Wood, P. A. 1969: Industrial location and linkage. *Area*, 32–9.

——1976: *Industrial Britain: the West Midlands*. Newton Abbot: David and Charles.

——1978: Industrial organization, location and planning. *Regional Studies*, 12, 143–52.

——1987: Producer services and economic change: some Canadian evidence. In K. Chapman and G. Humphrys (eds), *Technical Change and Industrial Policy*. Oxford: Blackwell, 51–77.

Woodward, R. S. 1974: The capital bias of DREE incentives. *Canadian Journal of Economics*, 7, 161–73.

Ye Probst, A. 1974: Certain questions on the general theory of the location of industry. In G. J. Demko and R. J. Fuchs (eds), *Geographical Perspectives on the Soviet Union*, Columbia: Ohio University Press, 352–64.

Young, A. 1979: *The Sogo Shosha: Japan's Multinational Trading Companies*. Boulder, Co.: Westview Press.

Yuill, D., Allen, K. and Hall, C. 1980: *Regional Policy in the European Community*. London: Croom Helm.

Zimon, H. A. 1979: Regional inequalities in Poland: 1960–1975. *Economic Geography*, 55, 242–52.

Index